GREEN BUILDINGS PAY

Edited by Brian Edwards

GREEN**BUILDINGS**PAY

Second Edition

Spon Press

London and New York

First published 1998 by Spon Press
11 New Fetter Lane, London EC4P 4EE
Second edition published 2003

Simultaneously published in the USA and Canada
by Spon Press
29 West 35th Street, New York, NY 10001

Spon Press is an imprint of the Taylor and Francis Group

Designed by Stephen Cary
Typeset in Gill Sans by Ninety Seven Plus
Printed and bound in Great Britain by the Alden Press, Oxford

British Library Cataloging in Publication Data
A catalogue record for this book is available from the British
Library.

Library of Congress Cataloging in Publication Data
A catalogue record has been requested.

ISBN 0-415-26271-2

Contents

Contents

The authors

low-energy PowerGen headquarters in Coventry, the Heathrow Visitor Centre, the Royal College of Pathologists in London and the Wessex Water Headquarters Building near Bristol.

Steve Baker is an architect and graduate of the Birmingham and Liverpool University Schools of Architecture. He is a director of Foggo Associates, a multi-disciplinary practice comprising architects, structural engineers, service engineers and quantity surveyors. The practice has a particular expertise in the design of low-energy urban office buildings.

Mel Barlex is a chartered building surveyor, graduate of the University of the South Bank and more recently the University of East London with an MBA. In 1995 he was appointed Head of Property Services for Anglia Polytechnic University where he developed his interest in environmentally conscious building design.

John Beatson trained as a civil engineer at Canterbury University, New Zealand and later as a town planner in the UK. He has held a number of positions in both the public and private sectors in the building and environmental areas. In the 1980s he was Deputy Head of London Scientific Services with responsibility for London's environmental policy. For the last nine years he has worked for Cable and Wireless, where he was project director for a number of construction projects, including the Cable and Wireless College. During that time he also developed Cable and Wireless's first group environmental policy.

Rab Bennetts trained as an architect at Heriot-Watt University. After graduating in 1977 he spent 10 years with Arup Associates, before forming Bennetts Associates in 1987. Bennetts Associates have completed a number of award-winning buildings, prominent among which are the

Richard Brearley is an architect and partner with John Miller & Partners, London. He studied at the University of Nottingham, has lectured widely on low-energy design and his work has featured in many exhibitions and journal articles.

Brian Edwards is Professor of Architecture at ECA, Heriot-Watt University. He trained at schools of architecture in Canterbury, Edinburgh and Glasgow gaining his PhD in 1989, and worked in practice for several years, including a period with RMJM. Author of 15 books and numerous journal articles, he is a member of the RIBA Sustainable Futures Committee.

Graham Francis is an architect and was at Manchester University. He has been a partner of Sheppard Robson for 18 years and was responsible for the recently completed low-energy Helicon Building in London. He is a member of the British Council of Offices Technical Committee advising on office specification. He manages Sheppard Robson Commercial Group.

William Gething is an architect and was educated at Corpus Christi College, Cambridge. He has been a partner with Fielden Clegg Bradley Architects for 18 years and is a member of the RIBA Sustainable Futures Committee. He has a particular interest in environmental issues, IT in construction and the art of building.

Alison Gorf is Senior Lecturer at the University of Huddersfield within the School of Education and Professional Development. She is responsible for work with trainee teachers of basic skills and school learning support assistants, having previously taught basic skills and family literacy and numeracy for a number of years. Her first degree was in environmental and social sciences, and her current research interests include the use of ICT in basic skills teaching and the impact upon continuing professional development of teachers in basic skills.

Lennart Grut is an engineer and was educated at Denmark University. He is a member of the Institute of Danish Engineers and of l'Ingénierie Civile de France. He has been a director at Richard Rogers Partnership for nine years and is responsible for projects in Europe and East Asia. He has a particular interest in sustainable issues.

William McKee is Director General of the British Property Foundation, the trade association which represents the property companies and institutions that form the principal owners and investors in commercial property in the UK. From 1981 to 1992 he was Chief Executive of the London Borough of Merton. Prior to that he was a town planner and transport engineer beginning with the GLC. Later he became Director of Planning and Development, first at the London Borough of Richmond and then at Hammersmith and Fulham.

David Partridge studied architecture at Cambridge University and was a founding partner of Gebler Tooth Partridge, architects. The practice designed office buildings for a number of multi-nationals, including IBM, Digital and (for Argent) United Biscuit's group headquarters. He joined Argent in 1990 where he is responsible for master-planning and building design, and has special interest in energy conscious office design.

David Prichard is a partner with MacCormac Jamieson Prichard and was a founding member of the practice in 1972. Energy issues are a special concern of the practice. He studied at the Bartlett School of Architecture, has undertaken energy research for the Building Research Establishment and has been external examiner for RIBA for 14 years. He was partner-in-charge of numerous housing schemes, urban designs and buildings, including Cable and Wireless College, winner of the RFAC Building of the Year award in 1994.

Alan Rowe is a chartered surveyor. He joined MEPC in 1989 and was seconded to Lansdown Estates Group responsible for new building construction at Milton Park, 100-hectare mixed-use business park near Abingdon in South Oxfordshire. He is currently a development manager working on MEPC's industrial property fund.

Ken Shuttleworth studied at Leicester Polytechnic and received a Diploma in Architecture with distinction in 1977. He joined Foster Associates in 1974 while still a student. After an architectural study tour of USA and Canada he returned to Foster Associates in 1977. He was appointed a director of Foster and Partners in 1984 and worked on HongKong and Shanghai Bank where he was responsible for all aspects of the design. In 1994 he received an Honorary Doctorate from De Montford University.

Peter F. Smith received his architectural education at Cambridge University and obtained his PhD from the University of Manchester. From 1986 to 1990 he was head of the Leeds School of Architecture and is now Emeritus Professor of Leeds Metropolitan University. He is currently Professor of Architecture at Sheffield Hallam University. He is chairman of the RIBA Sustainable Futures Committee and RIBA vice-president for sustainability.

Marilyn Standley is a personnel and facilities manager with a degree in psychology. She is a director of Chesterton Facilities and Property Management. She was Project Director for Addison Wesley Longman. From 1990 to 1994 she has been chairman of the British Institution of Facilities Management.

David Turrent studied architecture at Manchester University and graduated in 1974. He worked in both private practice and local government before setting up ECD in 1980. He is a member of the RIBA Sustainable Futures Committee and regularly contributes articles to the architectural press. He was the architect for the award-winning Slimbridge Visitor Centre.

Peter Yorke is a classics graduate of Cambridge University who has subsequently worked as a buildings administrator. During his 33 years at the University of East Anglia, he worked on buildings with Sir Denys Lasdun, Sir Bernard Feilden, Sir Norman Foster, Rick Mather, and John Miller and his partner Richard Brearley. He became particularly interested in the process of briefing for buildings required to be elegant, economical, energy efficient and user-friendly.

Acknowledgements

I am indebted to two people in particular for helping this publication to see the light of day with depth and critical perspective. Professor Peter Smith, Chairman of the RIBA's Sustainable Futures Committee and Vice President RIBA with responsibility for sustainability, gave unfailing support to the two conferences upon which the book is based and provided encouragement throughout, as well as co-authoring the concluding chapter. William Bordass was also a key figure in pointing me towards unpublished data on some of the case studies, and through his own writing helped to establish a rational framework for assessing green buildings.

Many others provided timely and courteous support, not least Barry Lennox of the RIBA Energy Office, Andrew Field of the Department of the Environment, Dave Hampton of the Building Research Establishment, and Richard Grey at the Centre for Construction Ecology.

My task as editor was made bearable by the professional approach and constructive outlook of the chapter authors. They found time to write, comment on, correct and re-correct the chapters based upon their presentations given at the 'Green Buildings Pay' conferences in London and Manchester in 1996.

I wish also to record my gratitude to my former secretary at the University of Huddersfield, Karen Beaumont, who tirelessly provided support in the belief that green buildings do pay.

Mention should also be made of the financial support from the Department of the Environment, which helped towards the publishing costs and in particular paid for the colour photographs, confirming that green buildings pay in an aesthetic as well as environmental sense.

Finally, I wish to acknowledge the research grant awarded by the University of Huddersfield which enabled the research on schools to be undertaken. In this regard the help of Hampshire and Essex County Councils was invaluable.

Picture Credits

The author and publishers would like to thank the following individuals and orgnizations for permission to reproduce material. We have made every effort to contact and acknowledge copyright holders, but if any errors have been made we would be happy to correct them later at printing.

Photographers
Roger Ball 13.7
Don Coe 2.5
Peter Cook 7.1, 7.2, 7.3, 7.4, 7.5, 7.6, 9.1, 9.3, 9.4, 9.5, 9.8, 20.3
Peter Durant 4.5
Dennis Gilbert 8.1, 9, 12.1, 12.7, 12.10
Richard Glover 5.8
Alison Gorf 14.22, 14.23, 16.9
Peter Greenland 4.3
Ian Lambot 1.4
Andrew Lee 2.1, 2.2
Max Logan 20.1
Joe Low 14.4, 14.9, 14.19, 14.21
Eamonn O'Mohany 10.4, 10.5
Peter Smith 21.6, 21.7
Anthony Weller 19.5, 19.6, 19.7
Ken Yeang 1.5
Nigel Young 1.8, 5.6, 8.3, 8.10, 8.11
All other photographs by Brian Edwards

Individuals and organizations
Allford Hall Monaghan Morris 15.1a
Anglia Polytechnic University/BPRU 18.2, 18.3, 18.4, 18.7
Architects Design Partnership 15.8
Argent Group 6.1, 6.2, 6.3a, 6.3b, 6.4, 6.5
Arup Associates 15.13
Arup Associates/Roland reinardy and Caroline Sohie 15.14
BDP 15.5
Bennetts Associates 9.2, 9.6, 9.7, 21.14
BRECSU 14.27, 14.28, 15.4
BREEM 1.6, 1.13, 1.14
British Steel/Corus 1.8
Building Design Partnership 21.18
Cable and Wireless College 1.5, 20.5, 20.6
Carole Townsend 1.10
David Lloyd Jones 1.11
The Earth Centre 21.9
ECD Architects 18.1, 18.5
Edward Cullinan Architects 14.20, 17.1, 17.2, 17.3, 17.4, 17.7, 17.8, 17.9
Elder & Cannon 15.1b
ETSU 14.10, 15.1c
Feilden Clegg Bradley 12.2, 12.3, 12.4, 12.5, 12.6, 12.8, 12.9, 16.1, 16.2, 16.3
Fitzroy Robinson and Partners 1.1a, 2.4, 5.6, 13.1, 13.2, 13.3, 13.4, 13.8
F.O.B 14.30
Foster and Partners 2.9, 8.2, 8.4, 8.5, 8.6, 8.7, 8.8, 8.9, 21.10
Hampshire County Council 14.3, 14.4, 14.9, 14.12, 14.14, 14.15, 14.16, 14.19, 14.21, 14.24, 14.25, 15.1d, 15.2b, 15.3, 15.6, 15.7, 15.10, 21.16
Jestico & Whiles 14.13
John Miller and Partners 19.1, 19.2, 19.3, 19.4
Kirklees M.C. 14.5, 14.6,
Lansdown Estates 4.3, 4.6
MacCormac Jamieson Prichard 20.2
McEwan Smith Architects 2.3
Nicholas Hare Architects 15.2c
Nottingham University 21.11
Ove Arup & Partners 18.6, 20.4
PCKO 14.11
Percy Thomas Architects 2.10, 2.11, 14.29, 15.9, 15.11, 15.12
Peter Foggo Architects 1.12, 11.1, 11.2, 11.4, 11.5, 11.6
Rhondda Cynon Taff 15.2a
Richard Rogers Partnership 1.9, 2.14, 10.1, 10.2, 10.3, 21.17
RMJM 3.1
Sheppard Robson 1.15, 5.5, 5.9
Short Ford & Partners 2
Studio E Architects 4.4, 21.5

Foreword

Brian Wilson,
Minister for Energy and Industry, DTI

The need for and benefits from environmentally friendly building cannot be doubted. In both use and the construction process itself, buildings harm the environment. The construction process alone in the UK annually creates some 70 million tonnes of waste, 13 million tonnes of which is disposed of unused. Buildings in use comprise nearly 50% of the total CO_2 emissions in the UK. Hence buildings are key to the challenge of reducing waste and minimizing climate change. In the scientific community, global warming is recognized as fact, and governments across the world have come together to address the problem at Kyoto and subsequent summits. Greater energy efficiency and greener buildings are vital if the damage that has been done is not to continue.

Key to this government's approach has been sustainable development. This proposes that a business, whether involved in the construction process or as occupier of a building, can be environmentally friendly while still being economically profitable and socially responsible. The publication of *Building a Better Quality of Life – A Strategy for More Sustainable Construction* in April 2000 was key to the development of this approach for buildings. It set out a framework for action, and the means to monitor and report back on progress. Industry's response has been positive, with action including the work on

post-occupancy studies, increasing application of the principles of sustainable construction (including energy efficiency) and the development of key performance indicators to measure progress. Government also recognizes that, as the construction industry's largest client, it must lead by example. The action plan *Achieving Sustainability in Construction Procurement* (July 2000) laid out a three-year framework for increasing energy efficiency and green procurement practice throughout government departments.

Currently, sectors of the construction industry, ranging from building services to civil engineers, are, with the support of government, developing strategies to tailor the sustainable development principles to their own areas. With the average useful life of buildings being over 50 years, such action is essential if we are to produce today greener, more environmentally friendly and energy-efficient buildings.

I welcome the new edition of the book *Green Buildings Pay*, especially the new case studies and the addition of a section on sustainable schools. The government attaches great importance to the quality of school buildings, believing they can help in achieving through sustainable construction not only greater energy efficiency but better long-term asset value.

PART

ONE

The greening of the property industry

1.1 a, b, c Barclaycard Headquarters, Northampton.
Architects: Fitzroy Robinson and Partners.

How do green buildings pay?

Brian Edwards

ECA, Heriot-Watt University

Most green buildings pay when measured by strictly financial criteria in that the extra construction costs of sustainable design are retrieved through reduced running costs in the first eight to ten years. In some particularly well-designed buildings there may be no additional building cost, as in the Leeds City Park (Chapter 11), or the saving in energy bills may pay for the green measures in less than five years, as in the Queen's Building at Anglia Polytechnic University (Chapter 18). Poor green design is where the additional construction costs are never recovered through reduced heating, lighting or ventilation bills, or increased productivity as a result of higher comfort levels.

To be effective commercially, socially and environmentally, sustainable design needs to give measurable benefits. It is not sufficient, especially in the rigorous field of commercial or educational buildings, to view green design as an act of faith or Utopianism. To persuade private developers and clients in the public sector to risk new approaches and use new sustainable technologies there needs to be maximum benefit and minimum financial exposure.

Direct benefits

The principal benefits of green design for the developers are:
— economies in fuel bills (either for owner or tenant);
— market advantage;
— lower long-term exposure to environmental or health problems;
— greater productivity of workforce.
The risks are:
— will the building perform as predicted?
— are the 'green' costs affordable?
— is the technology reliable?

2

a

b

c

1.2 *Full life-cycle assessment supports green architecture, as here at the Broadgate development, London. Architects: Arup Associates and Skidmore Owings and Merrill.*

1.3 *Student residences heated by solar power at Strathclyde University. Architects: GRM Kennedy and Partners with Kaiser Bautechnik.*

These advantages and disadvantages apply whether the developer is in the private or public sector.

An example of a successful green building is the headquarters of the NMB in Amsterdam constructed in 1990. Lord Rodgers, in his presentation to the conference 'Green Buildings Pay' in 1996, reported that the NMB building saved more than £300,000 a year in energy costs against a conventional office building of similar size. The energy consumption is one-twelfth that of the bank's former building allowing the owner to calculate that the additional cost of plant and equipment was paid for in three months of occupation. In addition, NMB have found that absenteeism is 15% lower than in the old building adding considerably to the bank's performance. Here the bank, built to low-energy and high environmental standards, with plenty of user control over the temperature and humidity of working areas, has proved a success in financial and productivity terms.

The construction of office buildings to attract future tenants is not unlike the building of university accommodation to attract students. In both cases green design is about keeping running costs down, providing a healthy and attractive building, and projecting an image through architecture that has market appeal. Increasingly, office workers and students expect a working environment which is responsive to their needs at a personal level by giving them control over their workspace, while also expressing in the values of the building a concern for wider global problems.

The typical office in the UK consumes 200kWh/m^2 over a typical year. Best practice aims to reduce this to 100kWh/m^2 and several examples in this book achieve even better figures. The Environmental Building recently completed at the Building Research Establishment's (BRE) headquarters near Watford (Chapter 12) is expected to achieve an energy rating of 80kWh/m^2, which is close to the best practice in the USA and Canada where 75kWh/m^2 has been recorded.[1] In these countries greater use of photovoltaics and higher levels of construction achieve by engineering means what in the UK is sought by natural ventilation and more low-technology building methods. However, whether high or low-tech approaches are adopted the target of 100kWh/m^2 is increasingly the bench mark for good design.

The main benefits of green design to a developer are financial: taking a long-term view, the running costs will pay several times over for the greater initial investment. In many cases the distinctive form of a building designed to sustainable principles will set the building apart for neighbours and provide a cachet that attracts tenants. Just as some cars and washing machines are sold as being green (or greener than competitors) so, too, green buildings will

1.4 *Commerzbank Headquarters, Frankfurt. Architects: Foster and Partners.*

1.5 *Editt Tower competition entry by architect Ken Yeang exploits the aesthestic potential of ecological design*

appeal to a section of the property market. To have comprehensive application, green buildings need to show they pay in less direct ways.

Indirect benefits

There are three ways in which sustainable design benefits both the developers and their tenants and has an indirect bearing upon balance sheets. Green buildings:

– are healthier to use;
– have psychological advantage;
– enhance company image.

Healthier to use

The use of more natural sources of light, solar energy for heating or cooling, and more organic materials in construction all add up to a healthier building than that

1.5 *Cable and Wireless College, Coventry, sets an admirable example of attractive green design. Architects: MacCormac Jamieson Prichard.*

represented by the typical air-conditioned office or university building. Healthy buildings which seek to work with climate and use natural materials in construction and finishes tend to suffer from lower levels of sickness and absenteeism. This has obvious advantages in terms of continuity of work and productivity which reflects upon company balance sheets. Taking university accommodation, healthy, low-energy buildings will (as our case studies show) result in contented students, the attraction of good quality academic staff, and improved output all round.

Psychological advantage

People feel 'better' in green buildings. They are not only healthier, but they claim an enhanced sense of wellbeing. The ability to open windows, to activate their own blinds, to pass through well-planted atria or winter gardens, to have trees and planting immediately outside their windows, and to smell the breeze, all lead to a sense of feeling better about work, thereby increasing productivity. In the USA, research has shown that the 'feel good factor' of green design has improved workplace performance sufficient to pay for a typical building's annual energy bills. A 1% reduction in absenteeism pays for the energy costs of a typical commercial building. The 'feel good factor' also leads to greater tolerance of temperature variations. The psychological dimension recognized increasingly by facilities managers has begun to influence building briefs.

Enhance company image

Green design is normally the result of holistic thinking by a team of professionals, including the client, who share similar environmental ideals. To be effective green design needs to consider many factors from the new financial equations implicit in sustainability to the likely reactions of workers and clients. The design team juggles with capital and running costs on the one hand, and balances between energy use, environmental impact and ecology on the other. Only an open, flexible view of design allows this to happen, and the resulting building embodying green principles will inevitably influence the company that uses it. As a consequence the building leads to subtle changes in the culture of the company and the outlook of the workers. Although a

developer or public client may specify a low-energy building, the consequences may be more profound than a mere saving in annual fuel bills.

The Body Shop's green outlook, for instance, influences its products, process and building procurement, and in turn has an impact upon the people who both work for and supply the company, or are sub-contracted by it. The same is true of Cable and Wireless (Chapter 20), which links building procurement to the company's environmental policy, setting an example to others and also saving money. The holistic outlook can spread from a company to its buildings, the building to the company, and the company to the individual, thereby enhancing its image.

Wider global benefits

The term 'green buildings pay' has so far been seen in the context of financial benefits — both direct and indirect — to those who undertake building development. There are several other ways in which sustainable design pays, although the currency here is not so much financial as global. Buildings are a major consumer of fossil fuels and other resources. The Brundtland Commission's definition of sustainability (1987) is development that 'meets the needs of the present without compromising the ability of future generations to meet their needs'. In the UK buildings account for about 50% of all energy use (contributing about the same amount to climate damaging CO_2 production), their construction uses nearly 50% of all raw materials used by industry, they consume 40% of the UK's water, and they are consumer of imported hardwoods — most of which have their origins in distant rainforests.

The philosophy of green buildings is not only a question of designing for low-energy use, but of considering in an integrated way the whole range of environments and ecological impacts involved. In order to consider in a systematic fashion the broader benefits of green design each building should be evaluated against the following perspectives:

- global warming;
- ozone layer depletion;
- biodiversity;
- product miles;
- recycling.

1.6 *Inland Revenue Building, Nottingham, sets a good example of low-energy design. Architects: Michael Hopkins and Partners.*

Global warming

What are the impacts upon global climate instability in terms of CO_2 production? Are the most energy-efficient means being adopted to heat, light and ventilate the building? Are renewable sources of energy being exploited, at least for part of the time? Is waste heat being recovered or lost to the atmosphere?

CO_2 is, of course, involved in both the running and construction of the building. What are the energy costs of construction (the energy needed to make a brick will drive a family car for eight to ten miles), and what is the payback period in energy terms of using high embodied energy materials such as aluminium or steel?

The global warming equation is complex but vital since climate change is likely to be the greatest destabilising force politically and socially of the next century. Buildings that greatly reduce their CO_2 production, use materials such as home-grown softwoods (which beneficially balance the CO_2 equation), and are designed as part of self-sufficient carbon communities where buildings and forests exchange oxygen for CO_2, all point the way forward. These projects act as exemplars influencing practice in Britain and further afield.

Ozone layer depletion

Although the thinning of the ozone layer and global warming share certain similarities, the problems are quite distinct. However, a building which is low-energy in design is likely also to add little to the thinning of the ozone layer. About a half of ozone damage is caused by chloro-fluorocarbons (CFCs) used in connection with air-conditioned, usually high-energy buildings. Designing with natural ventilation avoids ozone damage which has led to 60,000 extra cases of skin cancer a year in the UK alone because of the additional ultra-violet light.

Although the Montreal Protocol (1990) and subsequent European Union directives have begun to phase out the production of CFCs they remain in use in many commercial and educational buildings. Air-conditioning, a requirement for many commercial developments in city-centre locations, tends not to be favoured by building occupiers. A survey by Richard Ellis & Company showed that 89% of tenants preferred non-air-conditioned offices. Its specification by a cautious property industry, however, is still the norm since it allows for all levels of tenant need. Undermining the practice of air-conditioning through alternative approaches to office design, which appeal to user comfort rather than commercial perceptions, will in time phase out the need for

1.7 *Typical office buildings of the 1980s were big users of CFCs as well as fossil fuels.*

CFCs. With hindsight, over-specification of offices in the 1980s was one of the reasons for the collapse of the property market.

Biodiversity

The need to maintain global biodiversity was, like the earlier two points, part of the agreement entered into by the UK and many other world governments at the Rio Summit in 1992. Buildings influence biodiversity in many ways – they are home to species other than man, and the choice of materials used in their construction affects the destruction of endangered global habitats and the creation of others. The specification of hardwoods (many different species are used in commercial buildings) has an impact upon forests at home and abroad. For example, to specify beech helps to conserve domestic and European forests, but to use teak or mahogany threatens more distant rainforests which are not usually managed on sustainable lines.

Biodiversity is also influenced by the choice of more everyday materials such as concrete or brick. The extraction of aggregates, clay, chalk and limestone all alter the face of the land creating gravel pits and quarries that can either be left as wildlife areas or used for landfill sites. In either case, valuable land is lost to agriculture and adds to our growing bank of degraded landscapes (about 12% of the land area of Britain).

Since buildings are colonized by many species other than man they can inadvertently provide shelter for locally endangered species such as bats, or become havens for less desirable colonizers such as cockroaches. Green buildings use organic materials and have a natural process that tends to be more inviting than more sterile building environments. Effective building maintenance is required to ensure that the benign conditions created for man are not unduly exploited by insect colonies, pigeons or roosting starlings. The solar protection screens provided at the edge of many office buildings, for example, provide ready perches for the city's wildlife. The answer increasingly adopted in urban areas is to have an outer glazed protective wall up to two metres forward of the building envelope with solar screens and daylight shelves in the airspace.

Product miles

The environmental footprint of a building can be very extensive. One way to measure this is to use the concept of 'product miles' where the product weight, distance and

1.8 *The cycles of recycling, re-use and refurbishment in the employment of construction materials.*

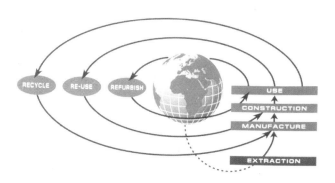

means of transport are considered. Building materials which are imported from other countries involve energy use in transportation, disturbance over long distance if carried by road or air, and leave a trail of pollution across continents. As a general rule it is better to use local products, especially bulky ones, if the environmental impacts are to be minimized.

The environmental impact equation is complex if all the ramifications are followed through. To obtain high-energy performance softwood windows the architect often has to specify suppliers in Sweden, compost toilets are manufactured in Canada, boilers that use waste products (such as domestic or textile refuse) are made in Denmark. Green products may not be available locally, certainly not to the standard demanded of commercial, government or university developers.

Recycling

As the earth becomes more crowded and the standard of living rises, resources will increasingly be in short supply. Though fossil fuels are now abundant they will in time become scarce and expensive – most probably within the lifespan of most buildings now being designed. The same is true of plastics, steel, aluminium and clay products, etc. The long-term answer is to design buildings that:

— incorporate the maximum possible amount of recycled material (either directly or indirectly);
— allow for ready dismantling and reuse.

Several of the case studies in this book incorporate recycled materials and some are designed so that the building itself

can be readily recycled, either through functional change or the re-employment of elements of construction.

Buildings are reservoirs of resource investment which are carried across generations. In most buildings the investment in energy and materials has been made wisely. In others there is the need for upgrading. This is particularly true of those constructed in the 1960s when low specification levels and plentiful supplies of energy led to a decade of leaky, poor performance buildings. Generally buildings are, unlike most consumer goods such as cars, long-term asset resources. The implications are two-fold: first, only rarely should buildings be demolished, but they should be adapted periodically, especially to new energy technologies. Second, buildings should seek to use recycled components, or materials from other industries. An example is the Groundwork Trust headquarters building in Jarrow, near Newcastle, which uses creeper-clad external solar protection made from redundant trawler nets held in place by scrap Ford Transit clutch housings.

Integrating energy, environmental and ecological perspectives

Buildings of the future will increasingly incorporate environmental, ecological and energy factors into the design at a conceptual level. Green design is not a matter of addressing the environmental problems society faces as a bolt-on addition to existing practice, but of evolving design from the starting point of these three perspectives. This, of course, requires a client sympathetic to these ideals, users who understand and value the concepts, and designers and contractors who as a team evolve the design with a green outlook.

Within the triangle formed by Energy, Environment and Ecology, green design can take its precise position depending upon local circumstance.

Where energy costs are the main determining factor, the resultant building will be different from one in which ecology is the prominent force, likewise an urban building will be different from a rural one. However, in each case 'green building will pay' by either saving the client money or by helping to save the planet. In reducing developer and tenant costs through responsible green design, the client is helping to conserve world resources of fossil fuels and in

1.9 *Buildings constructed from components and panels, such as the Kabuki-cho Building, Tokyo, are more readily dismantled than monolithic ones, allowing for potential recycling. Architects: Richard Rogers Partnership.*

1.10 *Central atrium and solar chimney, Groundwork Trust Office, Jarrow, near Newcastle. Architect: Carol Townsend of EarthSense.*

burning less is easing the problems of climate change.

The way to solve the environmental problem is by legislation, education and example. Legislation is important since it gives legitimacy to new directions – the law provides fresh parameters and identifies new frontiers for action. Education is equally crucial: it establishes the climate of opinion through debate and criticism for action. Such criticism is founded on the example of precedent, which properly monitored provides the bench mark for the future. The examples in this book and the perspectives of those in the property industry provide pathways for a more sustainable future. They are not perfect, but they face in the right direction. Taken together environmental laws (and

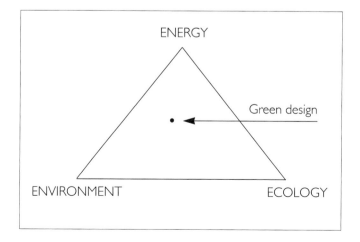

1.11 *Facade design at Marston Book Building,*
Milton Park, Oxfordshire, exploits natural
ventilation and simple solar screening.
Architects: David Lloyd Jones (with RMJM).

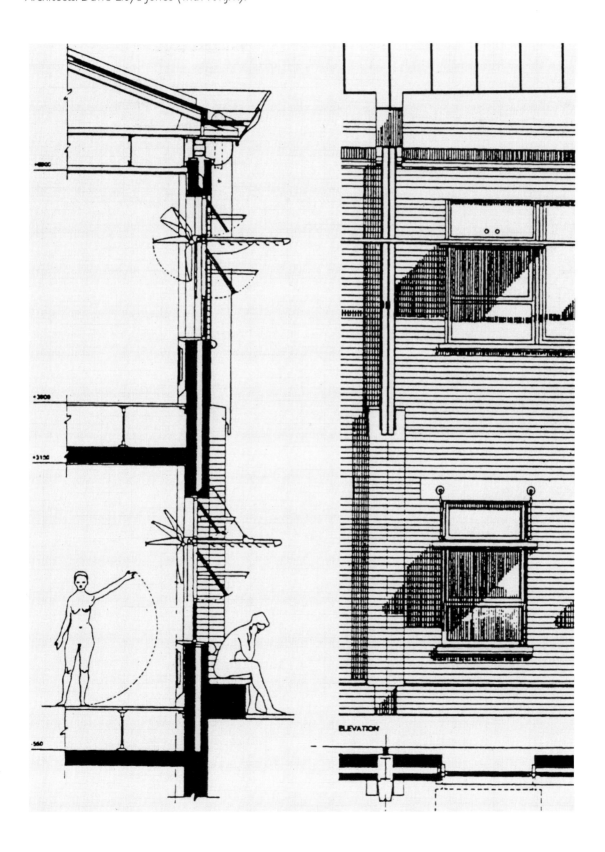

1.12 *Design sketch for*
British Gas offices, Leeds
City Office Park. Architects:
Peter Foggo Associates.

Table 1.1 Annual performance targets for energy-efficient offices

Component load	Narrow-plan building Gas and electric (kWh/m²)	Narrow-plan building All electric (kWh/m²)	Deep-plan building Gas and electric (kWh/m²)	Deep-plan building All electric (kWh/m²)
Lighting	10	10	15	15
Fans and pumps	6	3	8	5
Small power	20	20	20	20
Space heating	40	30	40	30
Domestic hot water supply	7	5	7	5
Total electricity	36	68	43	75
Total gas	47	–	47	–
Carbon dioxide emissions (kg/m²)	34	47	39	52

Source: *A Performance Specification for the Energy Efficient Office of the Future*, Department of the Environment, Energy Efficiency Office, December 1995, p. 6.

here CO_2 taxes may play a positive role in the future), environmental education in the property and construction industry, and the tangible example of built projects will collectively achieve the consensus that green buildings do pay.

Briefing for sustainable design

The role of the brief is crucial if sustainable design is to become commonplace. One reason why so many office and educational buildings perform badly from an environmental point of view is overspecification. Air-conditioning is specified in the brief yet users do not want it. High-technology air-sealed facades are employed where natural ventilation is the better option and deep-plan buildings are designed where shallow plan provides greater flexibility and user comfort. To combat this problem the Energy Efficiency Office at the Department of the Environment (DoE) has issued the following guiding principles for the energy-efficient office:

-   reduce energy loads wherever possible;
-   provide energy input as efficiently as possible;
-   minimize plant operation times – default to 'off' or 'standby';
-   use the simplest solutions that will satisfy the client's requirements and can be managed by the end user.

The principles need to address key areas of performance from the design of lighting (especially the effective use of daylight and controls on artificial lighting), visual comfort, psychological well-being, health and passive control of the working environment.

These guiding principles translate into briefing points, which help in achieving an energy and environmentally friendly office or workplace of the future.[2] Points to consider are:

-   detailed user needs;
-   selection of appropriate technologies;
-   use of innovative (and tested) design ideas;
-   maximum passive environmental control;
-   minimum use of complex HVAC services;
-   energy efficiency considered at all stages;

-   optimization of comfort and health standards;
-   buildability and replaceability;
-   on-site/modular/pre-fab construction opportunities;
-   environmental and ecological impact of building;
-   future flexibility;
-   commissioning appropriate level of specification;
-   training of building occupiers in operation of environmental systems.

Clearly not all building designs need to address each point, but the briefing checklist allows the right mix of parameters to be established. It is also evident that buildings in contaminated or polluted urban areas will have different sustainable characteristics from those on the city edge or greenfield sites. The parameters also point towards the narrow-plan, naturally ventilated and daylit office of the future (perhaps with alternate atria and open light wells). Although the checklist embraces energy, environmental and ecology issues, it is generally true that a building of low-energy consumption (capital and revenue energy costs) is also likely to have reduced impacts elsewhere.

Table 1.2 Sustainability indicators for buildings

-   move from fossil fuel to renewable energy sources
-   efficient use of other resources
-   waste minimization
-   closing cycles
-   life-cycle assessment
-   pollution
-   environmental capacity
-   biodiversity
-   land-use diversity
-   health, safety and security
-   access for all
-   non-car access
-   local sourcing
-   durability
-   flexibility
-   social equity
-   local distinctiveness/richness driven by environmental factors

1.13 *BREEAM logo.*

Environmental quality standards: the example of the Building Research Establishment Environmental Assessment Method (BREEAM)

Once the brief has been prepared the architect and engineer can begin to design the building with green perspectives in mind. It is often advantageous to test the evolving design against bench marks of good practice. One of the best known is BREEAM, developed by the Building Research Establishment (BRE) to provide developers with an independent assessment of the overall environmental credentials of the building. The scheme is comprehensive, tested and monitored by evaluation of buildings in use, and covers a range of building types including offices. Buildings are given a rating on a scale of Fair, Good, Very Good and Excellent. About 25% of all new offices in the UK has been subject to a BREEAM assessment since 1991.

BREEAM is comprehensive, dealing not only with energy performance but issues ranging from global atmospheric pollution to the impact of the building upon the local environment. It also embraces the comfort and health of building users. The main factors measured or assessed are:

- carbon-dioxide emissions with quantified bench marks;
- healthy building features;
- air quality and ventilation;
- minimization of ozone depletion and acid rain;
- recycling and reuse of materials;
- ecology of the site;
- water conservation;
- noise;
- risk of legionnaire's disease;
- hazardous materials;
- lighting.[3]

BREEAM allows a building's likely performance to be predicted, benefiting the designer as well as client. An early assessment allows alternative options to be explored before ideas have hardened. With construction in the UK consuming 366 million tonnes of materials per year,[4] building design has profound implications for environmental management generally.

The environmental quality standard represented by BREEAM encourages the development community to take a stake in environmental matters. The wide parameters of the assessment give weight to legitimate user needs, such as health and comfort. The assessment also provides investors with independent reassurance over any risks involved in new environmental technologies, and it allows government to measure performance against policy objectives. Although energy has been the main thrust of BREEAM to date, new concerns such as water shortage fit well into the matrix of environmental criteria adopted.

BREEAM provides the following benefits for the construction industry:

- developers can improve sales by promoting the high environmental performance of their buildings;
- designers can demonstrate the environmental achievements of their work;
- landlords can audit the property from an environmental point of view;
- managers can reassure employees that the working environment is healthy and of high quality.[5]

These lead to improved productivity, enhanced value, greater profit, and to development which has reduced adverse impact upon the environment. In this sense green building does pay.

1.14 *Stockley Park set a new bench mark for low-energy, high environmental design in the 1980s. Masterplan: Arup Associates.*

The BREEAM audit has recently been extended from the realm of office design to office occupation. The BRE Toolkit allows the environmental impact of office-based businesses to be evaluated. It is no good if the architect creates energy efficient workspace only for the company occupying the office not to use good environmental practices. Toolkit allows the relationship between capital and running costs to be understood, not just with regard to energy but to wider environmental impacts. Designed primarily for facilities or office managers, Toolkit is a self-assessment which helps to improve environmental performance and save money. Like BREEAM it is concerned with direct impacts such as energy, water, paper use and waste management, and indirect ones such as commuting, business travel and internal air quality.[6] There are 17 sections that provide a comprehensive environmental assessment of the office in occupation.

Energy Design Advice Service (EDAS)

Another useful tool in assessing the likely energy performance of a building at the design stage is EDAS, an independent energy auditing scheme sponsored by the Department of Trade and Industry (DTI). The EDAS consultation is concerned primarily with energy performance. In particular it provides a detailed prediction of expected energy loads per

1.15 *Environmental principles for the office of the future.*

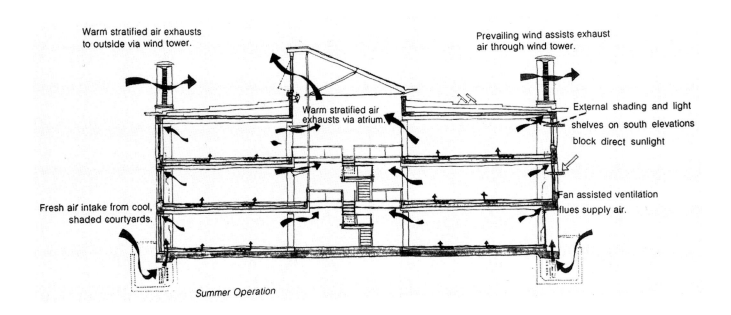

Warm stratified air exhausts to outside via wind tower.

Prevailing wind assists exhaust air through wind tower.

Warm stratified air exhausts via atrium.

External shading and light shelves on south elevations block direct sunlight

Fresh air intake from cool, shaded courtyards.

Fan assisted ventilation flues supply air.

Summer Operation

square metre and likely savings in the volume of carbon dioxide (CO_2) emitted. Also, since EDAS can provide several consultations during the different stages of the design process, it offers a finer level of energy modelling than under BREEAM's broad-brush approach.

The effect of BREEAM and EDAS has begun to change perceptions in the development industry and design professions. Employing energy-conscious design techniques does not have to cost more (though often it does). Modelling environmental and energy impacts at the design stage allows the relationship between capital and running costs to be understood with greater clarity than in the past. Evidence from monitoring the performance of buildings constructed to higher energy standards (the Power-Gen Building, Coventry, Chapter 9, is an example) indicates that good green design is no more expensive than conventional practice. As a new generation of environmentally friendly buildings is constructed, it is increasingly clear that such buildings have the potential to save money by reducing energy costs but without significant increase in capital costs.

Energy labelling

The overwhelming need to use energy more efficiently and to replace fossil fuels by renewables in order to help to stabilize CO_2 emissions[7] has given greater urgency to the role of the advice schemes outlined and to tightening legislative standards. It is clear from the case studies that cost is less of an impediment to progress than ignorance. The UK government in 1996 introduced compulsory energy labelling for new housing under Part L of the Building Regulations and in 1997 engaged in consulting the property industry over a similar scheme for non-domestic buildings.

Energy labelling has two main benefits: it allows tenants and building owners to know in advance what the fuel bills are likely to be; and in drawing attention to energy costs, encourages the generation of low-energy buildings. Energy labelling will raise the general awareness of energy efficiency among designers and developers alike.

Many measures outlined in this book do not add to costs. Good practice such as the correct building orientation and window size, and the use of natural ventilation adds nothing to capital cost yet will save thousands of pounds per year in energy bills, while saving the capital costs of air-conditioning leads to a significant reduction in the volume of CO_2 emitted.

The question posed earlier about whether green buildings do pay has both financial and moral dimensions. There is growing evidence from built projects that in monetary terms alone green buildings do represent a sounder long-term investment than more conventionally designed buildings. But while financial arguments are important, there is also the need to consider the health, comfort and wellbeing of the building occupants and the planet at large.

As sustainability gains greater moral urgency so, too, building development is increasingly responding to many pressing environmental issues rather than just a single one. Returning to the example of the new Groundwork Trust offices at Jarrow, this building incorporates evaporative cooling from a fountain in the triangular atrium; creepers and deciduous trees provide solar shading; solar energy and wind power are both exploited; and underfloor heating uses groundwater and a heat pump. The design by architect Carol Townsend embraces many environmental issues in a holistic fashion. The anticipated energy load is expected to be 75kWh/sq m/year as against the norm for cellular, naturally ventilated offices of 250kWh/sq m/year, and 400-600kWh/sq m/year for air-conditioned offices.[8] Such significant and measurable advantages auger well for a new generation of leaner office buildings.

Summary of principles

The six guiding principles found in the green design are:

– environmental design appropriate to context;
– use of simple, robust techniques rather than unnecessary complexity;
– exploitation of thermal capacity of structure;
– exploitation of natural ventilation as the prime

means of cooling;
– use of easily understood building controls;
– avoidance of over-sized plant with upgradability provided at design stage.[9]

The case studies illustrate these and other principles of green design. The main benefits perceived by developers and users of green buildings are:

– low cost in use (in energy and maintenance terms);
– higher environmental quality of workplace leading to happier, healthier, more productive staff;
– higher occupant control over internal environment;
– lower built-in obsolescence of services;
– enhanced company and building image.[10]

References

1. David Olivier, *Energy Efficiency and Renewables: Recent North American Experience*, 1996, p. viii.
2. *A Performance Specification for the Energy Efficient Office of the Future (Report 30)*, Department of the Environment, Energy Efficiency Best Practice Programme, December 1995, p. 3.
3. Dave Hampton, 'Environmental Issues', *Energy World*, May 1996, p. 9.
4. *BREEAM: An Introduction (leaflet)*, Building Research Establishment, no date.
5. Ibid, this list is an abbreviation.
6. *The Office Toolkit*, leaflet, BRE, 1996.
7. *EDAS Communique*, Issue 5, 1996.
8. *EDAS Case Study N008*, 'Eco Offices', Jarrow, Tyneside, UK.
9. Adapted from Bill Bordass, 'Avoiding office air-conditioning', *The Architects' Journal*, 20 July 1995, pp. 37-39.
10. 'Green Buildings: Benefits and Barriers', *Building Services*, April 1996, pp. 40-41.

2

Brian Edwards

ECA, Heriot-Watt University

2.1 *Enhanced company image and eye-catching architecture often result from commissioning a green building. Strathclyde Police Building, Glasgow. Architects: McEwan Smith.*

The risks and benefits of green design

Since the last edition of this book, many improvements have occurred. The most important of these is the realization amongst property developers that 'green buildings' do in fact pay in terms of the image they create with their customers, and in terms of the enhanced productivity of the workforce within them. These changes in perception have led to a fresh approach to the procurement of buildings by government, to changes in the BREEAM criteria, and to new guidance provided by the property industry to its members'.

The main benefits of investing in environmentally smart buildings, according to the UK's DETR's Best Practice Programme, are:
–   reduced investment risk;
–   improved rental income;
–   increased lettable area;
–   improved building flexibility;
–   lower construction costs;
–   enhanced company image;
–   improved marketability through improved working environment.

Against these benefits, however, are the following risks which concern property developers and which architects and engineers need particularly to consider at the design stage:
–   noise problems;
–   overheating problems;
–   lack of occupant control over working conditions.

In any cost–benefit analysis green buildings need to address both real and perceived benefits as well as real and perceived risks. It is now widely recognized that good environmental design does not necessarily entail cost burdens, nor do green offices, schools or hospitals carry undue risk of overheating

2.2 *Attractive working environment as a consequence of sustainable design practice. Strathclyde Police Building, Glasgow. Architects: McEwan Smith.*

2.3 *Cross section through Strathclyde Police Building showing the central atrium and solar shading (to right). Architects: McEwan Smith.*

2.4 *Cross section through British Energy Office Barnwood, Gloucester. Architects: Fitzroy Robinson.*

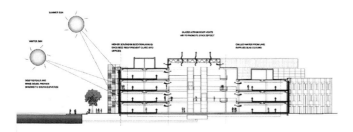

BRITISH ENERGY ENVIRONMENTAL STUDY : SECTION

(in both summer and winter) or of being excessively draughty and noisy. However, the designer of green buildings needs to consider the exposure occupants may have to a working environment which, though largely satisfactory, fails to meet acceptable standards for part of the year. This is why it is imperative that occupants have some control over their own working space by being able to adjust heating controls, open windows or activate blinds.

Here it is important to address the feelings of people who may be under stress by the very nature of their work (for example, at call centres). The building needs to be responsive to both the external climate and the internal mood of office workers. Dealing with stress at work may be partly aided by being able to open a window, to sit in or out of the sun, and to have contact with nature. Over-engineered buildings, no matter how energy efficient, can be counter-productive if occupants are denied power to intervene in the quality of their working space.

So a well-designed green building needs an intelligent system of controls, which can also be overridden by the person who works in that particular space. Buildings necessarily impinge upon questions of office politics and rights, and green offices in particular raise issues of the democratic control of space. There are many trade-offs to be made and, as environmentally smart buildings become more widely accepted by the development industry, these are brought into ever-clearer focus. One touches upon the relationship between energy conservation and noise disturbance at work. The trend in green offices is towards more open working with the growing use of atria and malls inside deep-planned buildings to maximize daylight penetration and promote solar-assisted ventilation. There is also greater intensification of space use, especially in call centres. Steel construction and lightweight partitions have not only brought speed and flexibility but also reduced the acoustic mass of modern buildings, leading to a growing problem of noise in green buildings.

The environmental engineering of green offices requires open volumes which are ideal for the transmission of noise from one part of the building to another. It is noise which often travels diagonally through the glazed malls of modern buildings. Thermal mass where it occurs can help, but solid construction rarely encloses the atrium area or sub-divides the large open-plan offices. Added to this, the need for natural light and cross-ventilation opens the interior to exterior noise (which is also increasing as traffic volumes rise). Interior noise too is growing as a result of the greater use of equipment in modern buildings.

So whereas office workers complain of overheating and excessive variability of temperature in some green buildings (a problem exacerbated by global warming), noise is a significant contributory dimension in worker satisfaction which could limit the wider application of environmental

2.5 *Sketch of atrium in British Energy Office showing the importance of atria to social life in modern offices.*
Credit: Don Coe

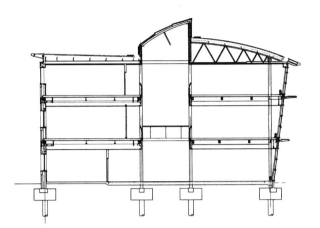

design thinking. Noise is not only a limiting factor in green offices – it has proved a problem with green schools and libraries. The challenge in the next generation of sustainable buildings (those beyond the examples in this book) is to re-engineer our approach to bring energy conservation, noise control and occupant satisfaction into a single virtuous circle. This requires fundamental re-working of the cross-section of building types (rather than re-modelling of plans) with changes in the means of construction, method of control and better understanding of the inter-relationships between thermal and acoustic properties.

Table 2.1 Benefits of green design

Stakeholder	Benefit
Government	– lower health risks; – helps achieve international environmental obligations; – good national or regional image.
Developers	– enhanced business efficiency; – reduced long-term cost; – greater competitiveness through energy conservation; – improved company image.
Design team	– higher profile; – better customer focus; – improved team working between industry players; – greater standardization.
Occupants	– improved health in workplace; – stimulating working environment; – greater attention to stress and comfort; – improved productivity.

Table 2.1 highlights the benefits for those who work in green buildings. These benefits result from good design, clever technology, sound management, and solid understanding by occupants of control systems. Innovative sustainable buildings are, however, rarely a trouble-free venture even for government which invests too little in demonstrating good practice through the buildings it directly controls. It remains a sobering reflection upon the UK construction industry that 20% of all energy used in buildings is wasted by poor design and inadequate management training.[2]

The focus of guidance from government, which is essential if the property industry as a whole is to reform its practices, has moved since the first edition of this book from design and technology solutions to management and procurement ones.[3] Sadly in this change in emphasis key reports such as the Latham Report (1998) and Egan Report (1999) have failed to adequately address the environmental dimension. The need for greater construction efficiency through improved contract procedures, better briefing and greater use of component standardization has arisen independently of the parallel drive towards more sustainable design practices. Recently, however, the two agendas are being joined by initiatives such as M41 which have sought to demonstrate through costed case studies the benefits not only of good design but of innovative sustainable design.

Table 2.2 Key Initiatives Sustainable Solutions from Different Stakeholders

Brief	Design	Construction	Use	Re-use
– Put green issues into brief – Consult with users – Anchor brief into government policy/initiatives on environment	– Put green approach into design at early stage – Consider impact of materials on environment and health – Appoint green consultants	– Waste minimalisation – Use recycled materials – Promote gender and environmental best practice	– Give users control over environment – Create healthy spaces – Allow for change in use of space	– Design for re-use – Robust construction for long life – Allow for access to renewable energy over time
Client	Architect	Builder	User	Future User

2.6 *The relative cost of different green approaches. There is a diminishing return at present in the most costly sustainable technologies.*
2.7 *Key pressures facing the construction industry in the twenty-first century.*

2.8 *This naturally-lit Sainsbury's supermarket in Greenwich was short-listed for the Stirling Prize in 2000.*
2.9 *Swiss Re Headquarters, London shows the integration of green and mainstream architectural practice. Architects: Foster and Partners.*

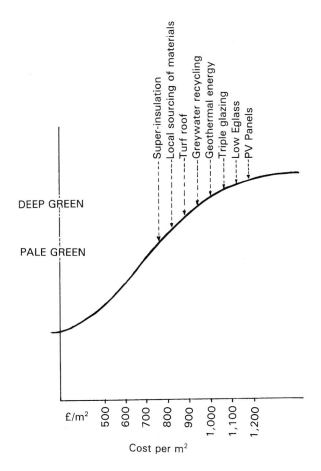

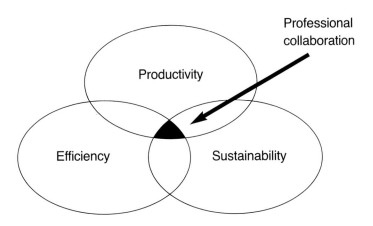

Within this change in emphasis greater attention is being paid to providing evidence that 'green buildings do in fact pay' and that the benefits integrate well with other

2.10 *General section and workplace section of MOD office at Abbeywood, Bristol. Notice the attention to ventilation and daylight penetration. Architects: Percy Thomas.*

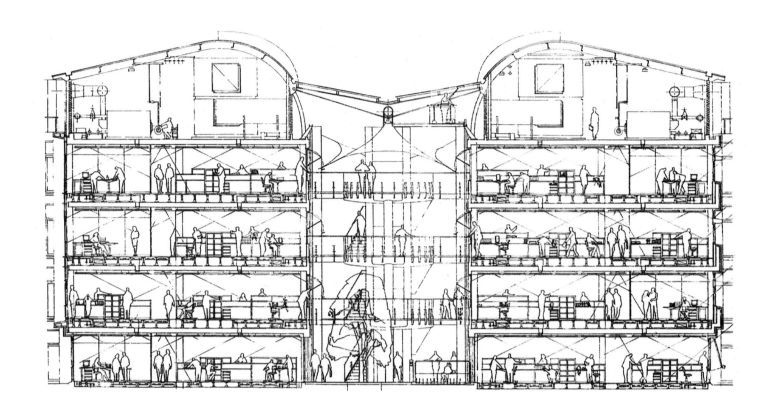

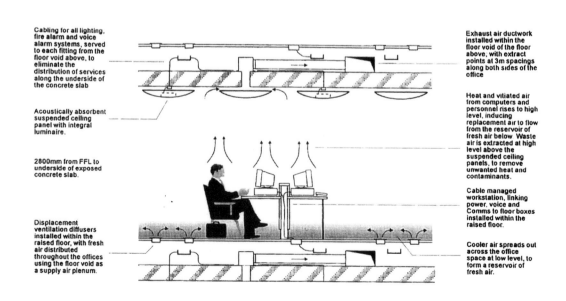

Cabling for all lighting, fire alarm and voice alarm systems, served to each fitting from the floor void above, to eliminate the distribution of services along the underside of the concrete slab

Acoustically absorbent suspended ceiling panel with integral luminaire.

2800mm from FFL to underside of exposed concrete slab.

Displacement ventilation diffusers installed within the raised floor, with fresh air distributed throughout the offices using the floor void as a supply air plenum.

Exhaust air ductwork installed within the floor void of the floor above, with extract points at 3m spacings along both sides of the office

Heat and vitiated air from computers and personnel rises to high level, inducing replacement air to flow from the reservoir of fresh air below Waste air is extracted at high level above the suspended ceiling panels, to remove unwanted heat and contaminants.

Cable managed workstation, linking power, voice and Comms to floor boxes installed within the raised floor.

Cooler air spreads out across the office space at low level, to form a reservoir of fresh air.

2.11 *Plan of MOD office, Abbeywood, Bristol. By using narrow floor plates the building achieves commendable levels of daylight and cross-ventilation. Notice the role of the atrium as both environmental and social spaces. Architects: Percy Thomas.*

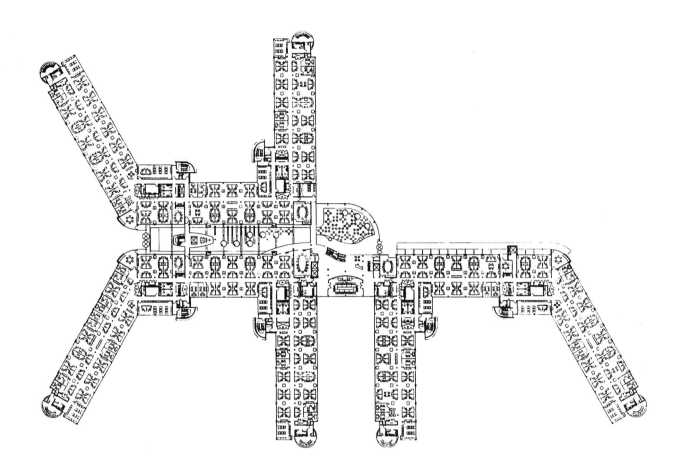

client or government initiatives (greater competitiveness, improved productivity, healthier lifestyles, social cohesion through the ethos of work). This change in approach widens the debate and brings business and management into the realm of sustainable design. What is now being demonstrated through the evaluation of existing green buildings is that there are many formerly invisible benefits of good environmental design and these matter as much to government and building clients as reducing carbon emissions. Such benefits range from improvement in the mental and physical health of those who work in green buildings, to better productivity of workers in green offices and teachers in green schools, more rapid healing of those in well-designed green hospitals, and a better image for companies like Barclaycard which invest in green design.

A key corresponding question flows from this debate. Are the benefits described the result of good green design or simply of good design? Is there a distinction between sustainable design and design, with measurable differences in approach, method and practice which distinguish green from un-green design? The answer is clearly no: green design is simply good design and good design is by definition sustainable design. The RIBA and CABE have long promoted good design through initiatives such as the Stirling Prize and RIBA Design Awards. It is no coincidence that many of the green buildings described in this book have also received RIBA, Civic Trust, Royal Fine Art Commission and other design awards. These buildings have not only helped conserve energy, they have also uplifted the spirit of users, helped improve productivity, played their part in rebuilding communities and added to the richness of our cultural landscape. Green buildings are by necessity also well-designed ones. As such they contribute to the efficient use of resources whilst also bringing about social, economic and cultural regeneration. Green buildings which do not address these wider issues are not genuine examples of sustainable development.[4]

2.12 *Creating an attractive working environment aids retention of staff and overall productivity. Wessex Water Offices, Bath. Architects: Bennetts Associates.*

2.13 *Wessex Water provides a free bus service to its offices near Bath to cut down on car use. Note the bicycle rack on the rear of the bus. Architects: Bennetts Associates.*

References

1. *A Developer's Guide to Environmentally Smart Buildings*, 'Good Practice Guide' 258, BRE, 1999.
2. Paul Ruyssevelt, 'Design for occupant interaction', paper given at the Sustainable Architecture Conference, De Montfort University, Leicester, 3 May 2001.
3. Ibid.
4. Brian Edwards, 'Green schools and wider social benefits', paper given at the Martin Research Centre, Cambridge University, 14 March 2001.

2.14 *Low energy Daimler Chrsler Office, Berlin. Architects: Richard Rogers Partnership.*

3

Green buildings and the UK property industry

William McKee

Former Director General,
British Property Federation

Green office buildings will become commonplace only if they take account of the principles and philosophy of the commercial property industry. Sustainable development is unlikely to materialize if it ignores the economic constraints under which the industry operates. In particular, the decision to provide new commercial buildings is judged against their performance as an asset and their ability to attract tenants thereby generating good rental levels and ultimately, adequate yields.

The property industry has changed substantially since the 1980s. With low inflation, office building returns will depend largely on active management, including a measurable improvement in quality. This is where green buildings may well offer advantages over non-sustainable competitors; there is growing evidence that the healthy, naturally lit and ventilated modern office is seen by occupiers as a genuine improvement.

New tenant needs

The property market in the UK has undergone significant and probably irreversible change over the past five years. Changing business practices have led to downsizing of companies, outsourcing of many tasks, hot-desking (where desks are shared rather than owned), and greater globalization. The result is that tenant companies strive for the minimum building occupational costs conducive to effective operation. Here green buildings can have a perceived edge – they are seen as costing less to run in energy terms while providing healthy workspace where staff are likely to be contented and hence more productive. In this sense providing a wholesome working environment is seen as good business, and the basis of a sound investment by the property industry.

3.1 *Ionica Building, Cambridge. Architects: RH Partnership.*

As the market has undergone these threshold changes, buildings are seen less as a potential asset growth and more as a factor of production. At the same time, real estate has become a boardroom issue and buildings, another company outgoing which should be properly measured and evaluated, not just rental levels. The issues which matter to the company facilities manager are flexibility, health and safety, running costs, effects upon absenteeism, tenant perception, etc. In the 1980s the property industry determined specification levels, size and quality of accommodation, but the emphasis is shifting to the customer. Tenants now influence building design to a far greater degree and it is tenant power which is leading the incorporation of green principles into the commercial property market.

As companies have downsized and decentralized. the demand for different kinds and size of office space has intensified. For example,. the headquarters building has shrunk in size, and to a degree also, in visible ostentation. The demand for large, environmentally sealed office building of 100,000ft^2 (10,000m^2) is reducing and even large government departments in Central London prefer smaller units. Within the shorter business-plan horizons of today's typical office tenants, the accommodation element has to meet stricter standards of performance and flexibility than in the past. Tenants are aware of sick building syndrome, conscious of the hidden costs of poorly designed buildings, and frequently strive to incorporate good environmental practice into their operations (such as the use of recycled paper and low-energy light bulbs). These new tenant needs, particularly whole life costing, are leading to a change in outlook from the property industry. For example with 89% of office occupiers against air-conditioned buildings (according

3.2 *Finsbury Avenue,*
Broadgate. Architects: Arup
Associates.

to a survey carried out by Richard Ellis and Partners in 1992), tenant power is fast altering the commercial property industry.

Consequently as tenant need changes under new company priorities, the low-specification office buildings of the 1960s or the over-specified deep-plan offices of the 1980s, also need to change. Adapting and upgrading the present stock to meet these new tenant needs and fresh environmental standards represents an investment as important as in new office construction. Although much of this upgrading is to meet new business standards demanded by some of the emerging companies of the 1990s, it offers the opportunity to introduce new green measures. Besides green initiatives there are other changes to the structure of the property industry. Location matters more than in the past and a good external environment and access to reliable public transport is seen as increasingly important by government.

Table 3.1 Critical parameters for the green office

Plan depth	13.5-15m (for draught-free cross-ventilation)
Window to core	6-12m
Planning grid	1.5m
Column grid	6m, 7.5m or 9m
Floor to ceiling height	2600-2750mm
Raised floor zone	150mm
Suspended ceiling zone	150mm

Source: *Best Practice in the Specification for Offices*, British Council for Offices, 1997.

Table 3.2 Critical criteria for the green office

— occupational density: 1 person per 14m² net
— integrate active systems of indoor climate control (building services) with passive systems (building fabric)
— orientate building to reduce glare and unwanted solar heat whilst maximizing daylight
— exploit potential of building facade in order to provide solar shading
— exploit atria and malls (glazed streets) for stack effect and cross-ventilation
— use natural ventilation in office areas and air-conditioning in 'hot spots'
— exploit thermal capacity of building fabric for day and night-time cooling
— adopt a greater internal temperature range

Source: *Best Practice in the Specification for Offices*, British Council for Offices, 1997.

The running costs of a green building

The demise of the 'trophy' building has corresponded to the emergence of more homogeneous yardsticks of performance. Offices are more likely these days to be built to standard depths of floorplate (determined by daylight penetration) and more formulaic units of accommodation. A reduction in bespoke specification levels has helped to reduce the cost of providing office space. Compared to a decade ago, the real cost of office occupation has fallen, partly as a result of low-energy costs due to better design. Also, changing relationships between owner and tenant (the result of the demand for more flexible leases) has resulted in contracts where the building owner (not tenant) pays the energy bills. This has focused owners' attention on running costs, adding to the drive to save unnecessary energy consumption and increasing interest by the property industry in low-energy design.

There are, however, serious constraints on the ability of the British property industry to deliver green buildings on a large scale. It is increasingly difficult to meet sustainable design objectives when the economic climate is unfavourable.

There is also a lack of research on the performance of green buildings. The development industry needs hard information on the relative energy efficiency of different types of green offices, as well as the views of tenants and individual office workers.

Although it is now commonly stated that green buildings lead to more productive working, less absenteeism and a greater commitment from the office worker to the company, there is little systematic evidence available to confirm the claim. In America research has shown that green offices lead to at least a 1% improvement in productivity, but information for the UK is not available. Little is known also of the asset performance of green commercial buildings.

As environmental standards rise one should assume that buildings designed in a green fashion will retain their value better than competitors, but as yet the industry has no hard figures to confirm or deny this. Since some low-energy buildings are excessively complex in operation, green design may, in fact, bring about speedier obsolescence and reduced value over time. Certainly for the property industry sustainability needs to lead to a generation of simple, readily understood offices.

Generally speaking, green buildings tend to cost more to construct than conventional offices. The industry would normally expect the extra cost of initiatives such as low-energy design and the use of natural non-toxic materials to be recovered in five to eight years. Beyond that the risks are too high in the uncertain business of property development. There are many green opportunities to be taken in the property industry but sustainable development must be wedded to commercial reality and viability.

There is no doubt that the British property industry (i.e. property companies, institutions and pension funds) is generally supportive of the drive towards environmentally designed buildings, but the difficulties should not be underestimated. The key to more green offices lies not so much in developing the technical side but in adjusting the economic arguments in favour of more sustainable solutions. The technology of green buildings is well understood and the benefits widely acknowledged, but in the current market circumstances where there is an over-supply of commercial floor space it is difficult to see the economic return in adapting present offices in a green fashion. The comparatively low rate of new development is such that genuine improvement lies in tackling the existing stock to make it more energy

3.3 *London's Broadgate development combines green design with good access to public transport. Architects: Arup Associates and Skidmore Owings and Merrill.*

3.4 *Simple solar screening with planting adds to the success of the Broadgate Development. Architects: Arup Associates and Skidmore Owings and Merrill.*

efficient, healthier to use, and more responsive to individual need. Unfortunately green rehabilitation is less well understood than green design. Adapting buildings constructed over the past 30 years from a green perspective is fraught with difficulties. Many have fairly low floor-to-ceiling heights, the structural arrangements offer little flexibility, sites are often polluted or noisy, and deep floor plans are commonplace.

Conclusion

Clients will innovate in green technologies, but only if they are tried and tested. The office building is not the place to test out new design approaches or to experiment with emerging sustainable technologies. The margins in the property industry cannot carry that degree of risk. The property industry should not be seen by government, research councils, designers and engineers as a laboratory for developing and testing new office prototypes. For example, low-energy systems in buildings do not work all the time. With natural approaches (such as stack effect ventilation, solar flueing, even natural lighting) the building needs to provide mechanical back-up. Having two systems

installed can be expensive, adds to operational complexity, and can affect the value of the property even if it saves money in the short term. What the industry requires is added value through good green design; value measured in improved lettability and enhanced asset strength. Certain green approaches have been shown to decrease confidence and undermine property investment. The risks must be kept low by incorporating only simple green technologies and those which have been tried and tested elsewhere.

As mentioned earlier, green approaches to office building will have greater impact upon the perception of investors if they can be shown to offer improvements in returns. From the occupier's point of view, buildings which are environmentally friendly and offer a better place to work, have a market advantage over their rivals', and in the increasingly competitive world of building the health and wellbeing of office staff tends to be more important than relatively small decreases in energy bills. If green offices can deliver measurable benefits to productivity while also achieving say a 40% reduction in energy costs, then the industry will begin to experiment with new office layouts and new sustainable technologies. Without these tangible economic benefits the property industry will not be seduced by the sheer excitement of new green approaches to building engineering.

Table 3.2 Advantages of energy-efficient builds: Positive benefits from specifying energy efficient buildings:

- they need not cost more;
- they have lower running costs;
- they offer a more responsive environment to occupants;
- they justify additional rental value;
- they add to the sale value of the buildings;
- they will be simpler to re-lease in the future;
- Energy efficiency is an enormous contributor to a sustainable resources policy;
- they have a marketing advantage because of their other energy related features;
- the most energy efficient building is one which provides the specified internal environment for the minimum energy cost.

Source: BRECSU, 1997

4

Market advantage through green design

Alan Rowe

Lansdown Estates Group

The property company Lansdown Estates Group (a subsidiary of MEPC) has long had an interest in low-energy design. At Milton Park, a mixed-use business estate of 100 hectares near?Abingdon, Oxfordshire, the company has been constructing green commercial buildings for a variety of occupiers since 1989. Using this experience, Lansdown Estates participated in the Department of Energy's Passive Solar Design research project providing case studies of good practice. In 1994 it also supported the Environmental Code of Practice for Buildings and their Services produced by the Building Services Research and Information Association (BSRIA).

The reason for this interest in green design is a combination of financial expediency, a concern for user comfort, an interest in wider environmental questions, long-term flexibility, and our perception of market advantage.

Financial expediency

The low level of demand for air-conditioned space, when combined with its high cost in relation to rental values in a business park location such as Milton Park (currently around £140/m^2 for new speculative naturally ventilated B1 office space and £70/m^2 for new speculative B8 space), will not usually support sealed mechanically ventilated office buildings. Capital costs, running costs and depreciation costs mean that Lansdown Estates look to eliminate the requirements for air-conditioning where possible. However, we do design our buildings so that they have an upgrade path and can adapt to full or partial air-conditioning should occupiers so require. This seems sensible in a period of transition.

4.1 *Section, New Mill House, 183 Milton Park, Oxfordshire. Architects: RMJM Partnership.*

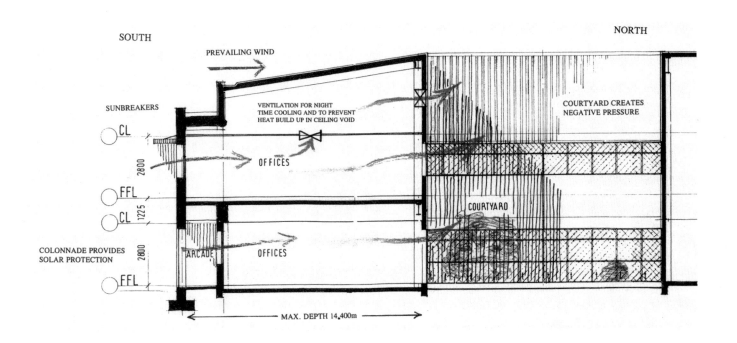

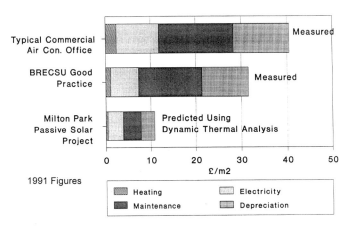

Annual Operating Cost
£/m2 Gross

1991 Figures

4.2 *Comparison of annual operating costs of property at Milton Park, Oxfordshire.*

User comfort

Lansdown Estates devotes significant time to maintaining close contact with existing occupiers at Milton Park through its site-based management team and through independently undertaken post-occupation surveys of particular new buildings. On a more formal basis, we undertake an annual Milton Park census of the views of building occupiers to understand their requirements and establish whether these are best suited initially through existing space, or by constructing new buildings.

Generally, occupiers ask for good natural light (without solar glare) and expect natural ventilation, but the majority do not ask for full air-conditioning. At Milton Park there are only two whole buildings (totalling just under 1200m²) into which comfort cooling has been installed by Lansdown. However, there is a fully air-conditioned building occupied by the computer company Research Machines of some 5100m², but here the air-conditioning was installed by the occupier at their cost. The flexibility incorporated in the design of this building emphasizes that new buildings should provide an upgrade path in the event that mechanical ventilation or air-conditioning is required for specific office areas in the future or for specific clients (where air-conditioning is provided initially it may be prudent to provide a downgrade path).

4.3 *New Mill House, 183 Milton Park, Oxfordshire. Architects: RMJM.*

Concern for the wider environment

Milton Park is situated in the south Oxfordshire country-side, a location which is generally free of significant external noise and pollution. Although the Great Western Railway mainline is on the south side of the park, this causes only intermittent noise. The pleasant setting has encouraged us to develop the estate in as rural a character as commercial conditions allow. Car parks are well screened, buildings designed wherever possible using natural materials (such as brick), and planted open space between the buildings encourages contact between the inside and outside.

Our concern for the husbandry of the environment at Milton Park from green perspectives led us to explore the benefits of sustainability in the design of buildings. We also felt a responsibility to set an example.

Long-term flexibility

Since Lansdown retains ownership of its buildings it has an interest in their success in the long term. Buildings may be used for a wide range of purposes and by many different occupiers during their life. Occupiers frequently move within the park and it is important that there is flexibility in the size, use, quality and distribution of the stock.

We are particularly mindful as major property owners of the implications of the Global 2000 Report in 1980, the Brundtland Report in 1987, and the Rio Earth Summit of 1992. We seek to meet and where possible exceed government legislation, providing a more productive and environmentally friendly workplace for employers and their staff than competitors.

The recent changes to Part L of the Building Regulations and the proposals that were made in 1993 to limit the use of air-conditioning highlight the desirability of explaining the potential benefits of green buildings to occupiers. Our incorporation of simple passive solar design and other energy-saving features is both legislation, and occupier-led. Lansdown believe that increased fuel costs, possible carbon taxes in the future, and widespread concern for the environment will lead to an increased adoption of naturally ventilated buildings for most offices outside city centres.

These factors have encouraged the company to explore low-energy design for nearly a decade. There have been market benefits, but also a sense that developers have a responsibility to innovate in the area of sustainability. The construction of buildings which consume less energy has advantage for occupiers but, when coupled with the provision of buildings that aim to be the most productive premises from which companies of all sizes can operate, the ethos of environmentally friendly design enhances the reputation of the developer and the business park.

Inspired by the example of the NFU Mutual and Avon Group HQ at Stratford-upon-Avon (design by RMJM) Lansdown started in the 1980s to explore mixed-mode concepts of office design in collaboration with the building scientist William Bordass. New companies wishing to locate at Milton Park and Lansdown took the opportunity to explore how offices could be more productive, pleasant and energy efficient. Simple energy conservation had now expanded into a wider concern for environmental conditions and user comfort. Three significant new buildings resulted from this review: New Mill House (183 Milton Park), Marston Book Services (160 Milton Park) and the Business Campus (90-92 Milton Park)

New Mill House, 183 Milton Park, occupied by Research Machines

Research Machines' brief in 1989 was for a 4090m² (44,000ft²) production/warehouse-type building completed as a shell finish with a clear height of 7.5m. The company also required 1020m² (11,000ft²) of fitted open-plan offices, but wanted the whole building to have an unrestricted B1 planning use. Research Machines was particularly keen that the office area should be thermally efficient and effectively address the impact of solar gain without the use of air-conditioning.

Table 4.1 Reasons for adopting sustainable commercial building design by Lansdown Estates

- — long-term financial viability;
- — concern for user needs, and comfort and health in the workplace;
- — interest in wider environmental issues and the need to set a 'green' example;
- — long-term flexibility in the use and provision of buildings, particularly with regard to energy costs and availability of affordable space;
- — perceptions of market advantage through environmentally friendly design.

Under the direction of partner David Lloyd Jones, RMJM produced a flexible design which included a courtyard (21m x 11m) behind the initial offices to enable the office area to be extended northwards to meet changes in operational requirements. The office area incorporated an arcade at ground level with solar shading at first-floor level and conventional fenestration designed to give good opportunities for natural cross-ventilation. The building was one of the first modern office buildings in England to positively address green principles and it is unfortunate that the subsequent computer equipment loadings in the office area proved to be three times the initial designed level with the result that three years after completion Research Machines installed air-conditioning. Without air-conditioning, the building completed in April 1991 cost £490/m² and has subsequently been adapted to provide a mezzanine level of offices in the former production area.

160 Milton Park, occupied by Marston Book Services

In July 1994 Marston Book Services came to us with a requirement for a new 5000m² (54,000ft²) warehouse with 930m² (10,000ft²) of ancillary offices. Lansdown had progressed its design thinking and David Lloyd Jones (now in practice as Studio E Architects) further developed the concept of modern non-air-conditioned commercial buildings specifically for Marston.[1]

4.4 *Section, Marston Book Services Building, 160 Milton Park. Architects: David Lloyd Jones with RMJM.*

4.5 *Marston Book Services Building, 160 Milton Park. Architects: David Lloyd Jones with RMJM.*

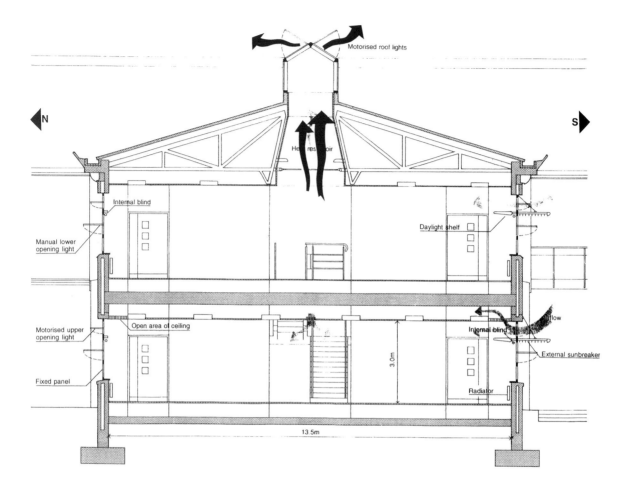

The offices are arranged on two floors and incorporate various innovative features of sustainable design, including combined light shelves and solar screens, low-energy lighting and the positive use of thermal mass. The principle innovations at the Marston Book Services building are:

— An 'Interactive Window System' (developed with and now marketed by Colt International) to address the requirements for controlling the solar gain at the building edge, providing efficient natural ventilation, and also acoustic control. This is the first building in the UK into which this intelligent window system has been incorporated. The extra cost compared with ordinary windows was about £30,000.

— The ground-floor office ceiling incorporates egg crate tiles to enable advantage to be taken of the thermal capacity of the concrete planks which form the first floor slab. The extra cost was about £1000. By exposing the concrete in this way it can effectively moderate peaks and troughs in temperature.

— The first-floor office uses a substantial central light well to enhance the amount of natural light while enabling summer temperature levels to be moderated by stack effect ventilation. The extra over cost compared with a plain roof ridge was about £27,000.

These three relatively straightforward features are complemented by energy saving solutions in the mechanical and electrical services, including low-energy lighting with movement detectors, anti-stratification fans in the warehouse, and radiator heating circuits compensated for external temperature.

4.6 *The Business Campus,*
90-92 Milton Park.
Architect: Nicholas Hare.

The green features were discussed and developed with Marston at the design stage and they positively welcomed the opportunity to enjoy a more natural working environment. Marston's directors and staff were subsequently briefed to help them to gain maximum advantage from the building's design features. An independent post-occupation evaluation has been undertaken by Building Use Studies, a London-based company specializing in monitoring the performance of buildings and feeding the results back to designers and their clients.

The building was completed on programme on 29 September 1995 at a cost of about £440/m² including fees.

The Business Campus, 90–92 Milton Park

The Business Campus consists of three buildings designed to suit a range of business uses, including office, production, laboratory, and research and development. They each incorporate green features and gave Lansdown the opportunity to explore the potential of recycling. The site was formerly occupied by three ordnance buildings which were demolished and provided a large amount of crushed concrete for fill and aggregate. This simple measure saved about £50,000 and greatly reduced the need for polluting lorry movements through Milton Park and adjoining areas.

The new buildings are each two storey, the smallest being 1700m² and the other two (which have atria) some 3100m² each. The larger buildings have a width of 12m either side of a 12m wide light well making an overall width of 36m. For users an acceptable working environment is achieved with openable windows on the external facades, producing cross ventilation through the space to the central light well where a high-level fan-assisted extract duct is located. However, other uses, particularly with partitioning around the perimeter of the light well, may require additional means of introducing fresh air to the deep-plan areas, particularly of the ground floor. A simple cost-effective ground cooling method was designed by Nicholas Hare Architects and the M&E consultants Hoare Lea & Partners. A ventilation system which made the most of the embodied energy of the ground below the building was developed. It is estimated that the ground temperature at the level of the pipes under the floor slab is generally constant at around 14-16°C. When the external air temperature varies by more than 5°C either side of this then either useful heating or cooling is expected to take place.

The system developed by Hoare Lee will rely upon fresh air taken in at the roof plant room level and ducted down risers to be passed through standard Hepsleeve ceramic pipe ducts some 750mm below the slab. The cooled fresh air is then introduced via floor channels into the ground floor. The system also serves the deep-plan sections of the first-floor area, when air is introduced into the raised floor void with the aid of a small fan and heater battery.

The principle of ground cooling with ceramic pipes has been successfully employed by Von Scholten in the Lessor office project at Gydevang on the outskirts of Copenhagen and similar installations have been used for offices and residential projects in Germany where very little heating is required in winter.

The initial cost of the underground pipework for this system is about £60,000 and this has to be considered in relation to future savings in energy consumption and the likely costs of air-conditioning plant in a more conventional building.

Conclusion

Lansdown is convinced that the green measures it has taken account for the fact that Milton Park enjoys a higher than average letting rate, currently 90%. The company believes that success in the future will be centred on:

— providing value for money for occupiers through green measures;
— maintaining accessibility by both public and private transport, and taking advantage of nearby rail links;
— reducing fossil fuel energy costs by working with natural forces and renewable sources of energy;
— making provision for young companies by providing flexible environmentally friendly workspace;
— providing flexible and responsive space by exploiting environmental and low-energy design.

Reference

1. Articles on the building can be seen in CIBSE Journal, December 1995, and Architecture Today, January 1996.

The relevance of green buildings to the procurement and marketability of offices

Graham Francis

Sheppard Robson

My position as a member of the Technical Affairs Committee of the British Council for Offices (BCO) and as a partner at the London office of architects Sheppard Robson provides a good base from which to explore the relationship between green design and the marketability of offices. There is an obvious correlation between procurement policy, the level of specification, sustainability, cost and marketing. From a practical point of view, all green office development needs to be viable within market constraints; offer value for money especially where new and relatively untried technologies are being employed; and provide genuine reduction in running costs.

Property development is a hard-headed business, particularly now when so much surplus office space exists. However, few developers construct green offices simply because of a hunch that there is money to be made from sustainability. Most property companies invest in green buildings for both long-term financial and ethical reasons; they feel that sustainable development and positive environmental management carry moral connotations with which they empathize. When, in terms of global warming, the ecological footprint of London is the size of the UK, we cannot continue with over-specified, poor energy performance offices.

Definition of the green office

It is important to define what we mean by the term green offices. The typical green office today has some or all of the following features:

— natural cross ventilation or mixed mode;
— natural daylight;
— sophisticated shading devices for solar control;
— good light distribution to the building core;

5.2 *Facade detail, Helicon Building, London. Architects: Sheppard Robson.*

ulate orientation for energy purposes and there is often overshading, which reduces the effectiveness of windows for interior light. Solar shading in urban areas tends also to provide perches for pigeons and starlings, which then soil the building facade reducing the effectiveness of windows and spoiling the appearance of the building. At Sheppard Robson's Helicon office building in the City of London, built in 1995 for Manchester Assurance, the latter problem was overcome by placing the solar blinds within a triple-glazed facade – the outer pane also provides further sound and thermal insulation and allows us to exploit the thermal flue effect at the building perimeter

Highly glazed facades can be an attractive letting feature on offices as long as they do not lead to over-heating, or become shabby through poor maintenance. Generally speaking, clear glass buildings allow improved contact with the outside and thereby enhance the office workers' sense of environmental wellbeing. Managers are increasingly recognizing the benefits of the naturally lit office to worker productivity and the psychological advantage of greater contact with the exterior environment.

The green investor

The green office requires a client willing to invest in new environmental technologies, happy to agree standards and environmental objectives above the regulatory minimum, able to take a long-term view of building investment, and willing to design for flexibility. In modern offices up to 90% of staff move location or adapt their workstation to new information technology each year. Sustainable design solutions need to integrate with facilities or building management – the eco-system of the office and the eco-system of the building must correlate.

For the developer the sustainable office carries certain risks. In practical terms, for example, the green office requires:

- more time for design;
- the need to bring together appropriately skilled professionals;
- the need to visit green buildings and become familiar with research reports;
- the preparedness to take risks in developing new office prototypes;

- passive (i.e. user) controls;
- thermal capacity dampening of structure;
- stack effect ventilation incorporating atria;
- displacement air-chilled ceilings;
- upgradable base specification.

Needless to say, the typical green office (and many examples can be found in this book) encounters problems in urban sites where, for other sustainable reasons, the property industry is increasingly required to focus its attentions. City areas have poor air quality which undermines natural cross ventilation. The excessive noise and vandalism, and crime or bomb threats invalidate openable windows. Few urban sites provide the freedom to manip-

5.3 *Broadgate Development, London, succeeds in creating good contact with the outside even in a city centre. Architects: Skidmore Owings and Merrill.*

5.4 *Judge Institute, Cambridge, demonstrates an unusual approach to green design in the education sector. Architect: John Outram.*

— a proper understanding of the relationship between capital and running costs (in financial, energy and environmental terms).

There are complex financial balances to be struck such as the consanguinity between facade costs and building servicing costs, or between Building Management System (BMS) costs and lighting costs. Normally (but not always) energy-saving technologies cost more in terms of capital costs than orthodox solutions, but they also save money in a predictable fashion. Understanding the balance of benefits is part of good green design.

Design implications

As a designer, I recognize there are problems which parallel those of the green client. While the architecture profession may wish to develop new approaches to sustainable development within the office or education sector there are constraints such as:

— time required for design in relation to client programme and fee;
— the risks and costs of innovation (especially against competitive fee scales);
— the need to develop and test prototypes;
— contractor/sub-contractor relationships and understanding;

– problems with certain contract forms (such as design and build);
– the need for feedback and monitoring to inform new projects;
– lack of coherent government incentives.

Both the design professions and BCO recognize the role of a softer green specification in bringing about a new generation of affordable, environmentally friendly office buildings. In 1994 the BCO introduced a new value-for-money standard office specification following a conference in Bristol. It sought to reduce costs and bring about a revival of the speculative office market based upon a new value-for-money bench mark of quality The office building was no longer to be invariably air-conditioned with over-specified facilities, but naturally-lit and ventilated, solar protected, and lower cost (both running and capital). As companies down sized in the 1990s there was overwhelming evidence that differently configured, more flexible and cheaper offices were needed. Energy efficiency fitted remarkably comfortably into the new paradigm and before long the sustainable office had taken on a virtue none of us had anticipated a decade ago.

In terms of CO_2 emissions the rural footprint needed to deal with city energy use is in area terms in relationship of 1 to 25. Many in the property industry are beginning to take positive environmental action by insisting upon incorporating energy saving measures. In my experience, they are driven as much by the need to conserve the planet as the imperative to save money. Buildings are resources of materials and energy that pass through generations of owners and occupiers – and hence a long-term view of environmental problems is increasingly prevalent.

The urban site

There are many examples today of sustainable office buildings constructed on greenfield sites, but still relatively few in urban areas. The city-centre office building poses particular problems and it is rarely possible to adopt ecological principles to the same degree. The urban site is often polluted, contaminated, overlooked and dangerous. Natural ventilation is replaced by the mixed mode system where cleaned (but not necessarily clean) air is pushed around using an atrium to aid circulation.

The Helicon Building, with floorplates 2175m^2 in area, uses this system. It is highly glazed to allow for maximum use of daylight (lighting can be indirectly responsible for up to 60% of energy costs in a typical city office). Solar screens that double as light shelves prevent excessive heat build-up and deflect daylight at relatively even distribution into the centre of the building. A similar project in George Street, Croydon, integrates mechanical and engineering services with the structure using thermal mass to cool internal air temperatures, and a similar system of thermal flues to create a third glazing layer to form an insulating jacket around the building. This extra perimeter skin is used in summer to draw the heat out of the building by stack-effect and in winter to protect it from the cold.

When in 1994 the BCO introduced its new lower specification for urban offices it was to redefine the level of specification appropriate to the needs of most office occupiers incorporating the ability to upgrade the performance of the building if required, during its life. The idea was a kind of 'long-life, loose-fit, low-energy' specification which offered flexibility for localized or more compre-hensive performance enhancement at a later stage. In theory it is possible to move from the BCO basic specification to full air-conditioning without great disruption. By using high floor-to-ceiling heights, sensible floor-plates (13.5-18m deep), a high percentage of external glazing, and largely open plans, the new office of the 1990s offered cost benefit advantages over its counterparts of the 1980s while also being less environmentally damaging.

Compiling the brief

A key to green office design lies in agreeing the brief and pro-ducing a clear statement of project objectives by the client and full design team. There are a few guiding principles, but often each project has to develop its own characteristics from local conditions. For example, Rab Bennetts' office building for John Menzies near Edinburgh placed the spaces that had special environmental needs at one side of the building away from the main office areas. Here they could exploit passive principles more readily and provide the specific ambience needed by the client. In effect, the building adopted a pragmatic approach to natural ventilation: different parts of the building are dealt with environmentally in different ways.

5.5 *Base specification for green office. Architects: Sheppard Robson.*

5.6 *Environmental principles of green office design. Architects: Fitzroy Robinson & Partners.*

Floor to floor section: the base specification

Key design points

- Opening windows, natural ventilation.

- Interstitial blinds, solar control.

- Exposed concrete soffit, night cooling.

- Uplighter as element of furniture, not fitting.

- 350 raised floor, cable management

- Radiator heating.

5.5

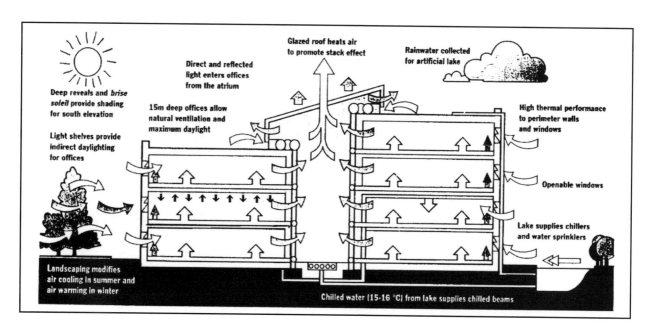

5.6

*5.7 Section, Helicon
Building, London. Architects:
Sheppard Robson.*

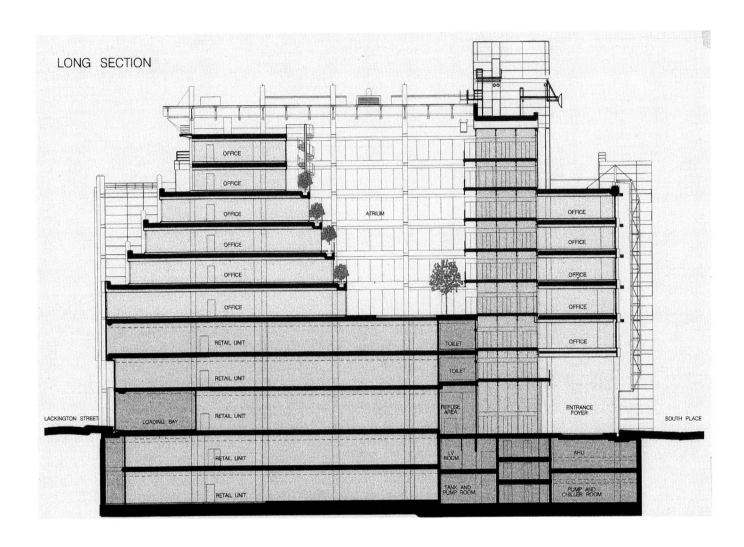

With a specific client in mind, either as developer or tenant, it is easier to compile the brief from a green perspective. Most clients require measurable benefits from sustainable design, not merely environmental platitudes. Such measures do not have to be solely financial, many developers recognize the health, comfort and productivity advantages of a more natural building. In addition, some also value the contribution the building makes to the reduction of global problems – but only in so far as these benefits can be measured and used in the promotion of the development or company image.

Sustainable design involves greater risk (financial and professional) than conventional approaches. It requires more attention to detail, but the benefits of a successful green building outweigh the dangers. Working with some local authorities a green developer may be more likely to obtain planning consent and relaxations under building regulations. Green buildings are more likely to comply with longer-term changes to environmental legislation thus retaining their value. With the current focus upon brownfield rather than greenfield sites, a developer reusing a contaminated inner site for sustainable development may well attract grants as well as concessions over land use or building height. For the architect, too, a green building design will keep the practice at the leading edge of change, which may attract further work and exposure in the professional journals.

We are at an interesting stage in the development of green architecture. There are many prototypes around, but

5.8 *Helicon Building, London: note how each facade varies according to orientation. Architects: Sheppard Robson.*

when monitored they frequently do not behave as predicted. Sheppard Robson's Helicon Building (designed with services engineers Ove Arup and Partners) incorporates the flexibility of layout and design that allows modification if the performance is not what we expect. Our client has taken a risk, especially on the facade, which as an element of construction cost about 25% more than the norm for office buildings in Central London. The justification is a combination of energy conservation and sound insulation as the site is an island surrounded by heavy traffic. On cost grounds, Helicon shows some remarkable economies. Energy running costs are about £50/m² per year which is significantly less than that of conventional office buildings. In a sense Sheppard Robson turned the site

problems to sustainable advantage. The building is an example of mixed-use development with a four-storey Marks and Spencer shop, bank and lettable offices within a single building envelope.

A learning experience

Each green building is a learning experience for the developer, contractor and professional team. It is important that there is continuity between projects so that the lessons learned in one can be applied at the next. This requires leadership and commitment from the client, and knowledgeable and skilled professional advisers. Such understanding is rarely possible with certain contract forms since

5.9 *Helicon Building, London: section through triple-glazed facade. Architects: Sheppard Robson.*

5.10 *Atrium, Helicon, Building London. Architects: Sheppard Robson.*

Table 5.1 Marketing advantages of green office buildings

– user satisfaction;
– benefits to health and comfort;
– company image;
– commercial advantage of environmental ethics;
– value for money in long term.

Table 5.2 Marketing disadvantages of green office buildings

– lack of consistent performance standards and feedback;
– lack of exemplar projects;
– complexity of comfort and control;
– limitations on cellular space;
– PC screen reflectance problems (with high daylight levels).

Table 5.3 Helicon Building, City of London: green principles

– mixed-use commercial development with large shop, bank and office;
– atrium to assist natural ventilation;
– triple glazing with ventilated cavity integral solar shading and glare control;
– clear floor-to-ceiling glazing to maximize daylight penetration;
– solar controlled blinds which cannot be overridden;
– displacement air-conditioning which uses water-filled panels at ceiling level for cooling rather than VAV system. The system costs 15% more, but it should be 16% cheaper to run;
– balcony planted atrium to enhance psychological wellbeing.

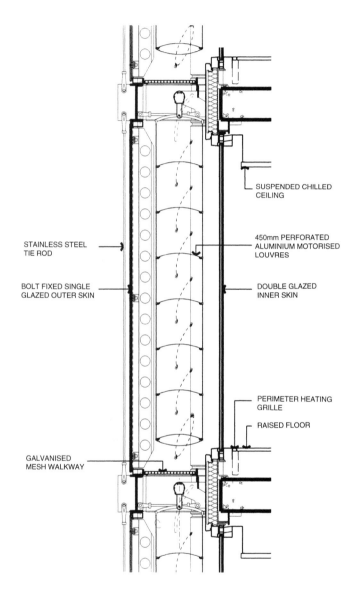

STAINLESS STEEL TIE ROD

BOLT FIXED SINGLE GLAZED OUTER SKIN

GALVANISED MESH WALKWAY

SUSPENDED CHILLED CEILING

450mm PERFORATED ALUMINIUM MOTORISED LOUVRES

DOUBLE GLAZED INNER SKIN

PERIMETER HEATING GRILLE

RAISED FLOOR

the fee scales and quality of construction often do not allow for innovation. Government procurement policy, rather than discouraging green building as it does at present, could set an example to the private sector

The 1992 survey of office buildings and user needs by Richard Ellis and Partners (Chapter 2) opened up the prospect of marketing green buildings as leading to greater consumer satisfaction and less absenteeism. The firm's research suggests that the costs saved by a company occupying a green building more than pay for the extra investment in sustainable design.

In the speculative office market it is particularly important that tenants understand the green intentions behind the building. The building manager has a key role to

play in maintaining continuity between developer aspirations from a sustainable perspective and tenancy use of the building. This relates to controls and to wider philosophical issues. Green buildings need to be respected and appreciated for the values they represent by successive tenants. Active building management and the adoption of BRE's Toolkit for office operation encourage synergy between design and occupation. Where mutual understanding exists there is more likely to be the presence of a 'forgiveness factor' which allows tenants to accept wider variations in temperature than is the norm.

Conclusion

Green offices in cities have quite different characteristics from their counterparts in the countryside. Urban sites place obvious limitations on the use of natural ventilation, yet with modern technology it is possible to supplement passive solar principles with the more sophisticated solutions used by us at the Helicon Building and by Rogers' office at Daimler Chrysler in Berlin (Chapter 10). Many examples of green offices currently under construction (such as BRE's demonstration building near Watford, Chapter 12) are not appropriate for the urban situation. Offices in city centres, where generally speaking the market wants them, will cost more if constructed to green principles than those on business parks. The cost equation for green offices is not universally applicable – the extra cost gearing in cities will only be justified if there are tangible benefits to comfort, health, productivity and the psychological state of the office employee.

6

David Partridge
Argent Group

Achieving institutional levels of office design through sustainable approaches

Argent has an investment portfolio of offices worth £276m with property let mainly on long leases. The company owns and lets institutional property, much of it to companies of national or international standing such as British Telecom and Lloyds Bank. Our property programme is designed to have wide appeal across the property market. The issue of market appeal is the main justification for our approach to green design: we see the creation of sustainable, healthy buildings as providing a sound long-term investment with advantages over those of our competitors. This is not only true of Argent, but also of companies that have formed development partnerships with us, such as Citibank, Hypobank and the British Telecom Pension Scheme. Green design is about taking the long-term view – of opting for quality without over-specification. As owners of property, the Argent Group believe that performance flexibility linked to the sensible use of renewable energy (in daylight and passive cooling) provides greater robustness over the life of the building than the conventional view of the air-conditioned office.

Market appeal

Argent has reached the conclusion that while in the short term (up to ten years) green buildings often do not pay, in the longer term they do. Bridging these two time frames has proved difficult. An unknown occupier has unknown performance criteria and to appeal to the market our buildings need to offer the standard specification enjoyed by more conventional offices (i.e. air-conditioned). Argent's buildings are therefore flexible, high-performance and provide an air-conditioning path for different levels of occupancy. It is relatively easy to design green office buildings

for known occupiers, such as RMJM's Scottish Office Building in Leith, Hopkins's Inland Revenue Building in Nottingham, and Foster's Mistral Building in the Thames Valley Park, but quite another story when you are building for the speculative market.

The problem for the property industry is that the standard, naturally ventilated or mixed mode atrium surrounded by a bank of relatively narrow office space does impose restrictions on office layout. The level of ventilation and the stack effect depends upon the effective use and management of the building. Tenants require as a matter of course a level of performance that tends to undermine the use of green office concepts. With energy costs relatively low (amounting normally to less than 1% of typical company outgoings) there is little incentive for the developer or tenant to opt for the green solution.

The Argent solution to speculative green design

Where competitors employ deep-planned, sealed office buildings with partial or full air-conditioning, Argent has developed high-performance offices for the institutional client which use:

6.2 *Section, One Brindley Place, Birmingham. Architects: Anthony Peake Associates.*

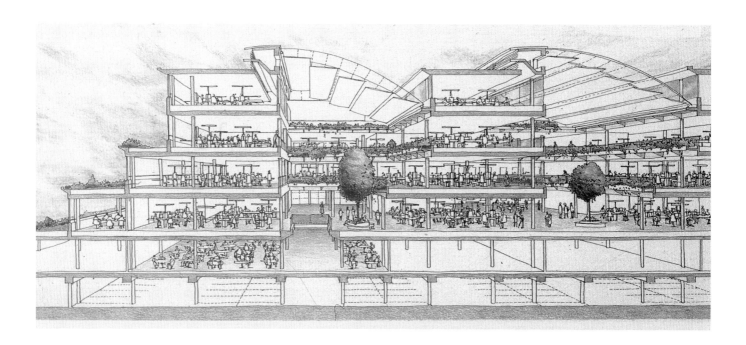

- solar passive or mixed mode cooling;
- heavy masonry walls to moderate internal temperatures;
- openable windows with light shelves, solar screens and low F coatings;
- central atria with narrow floor plate perimeter offices;
- lighting controls which allow dimming from 500 to 350 lux, and non-occupancy switch off;
- high structural floor heights (normally 4m).

Of course, not all these features are found in every building developed by Argent, but the company has a policy of environmental development linked to best practice guidelines. Each building learns from the experience of the one before: our developments at Brindley Place, on former derelict land in central Birmingham, have pushed at the frontiers of green office specification in an urban context; at the Thames Valley Business Park, near Reading, we have explored aspects of sustainable design more appropriate in greenfield settings.

Argent started exploring green speculative office development in 1990 in a project called Solaris in Basingstoke. The company looked at every possible avenue for green buildings; it produced impressive building sections with little arrows showing naturally ventilated air dutifully progressing around and graphs showing thermal lags between inside and outside temperature and how nighttime cooling used the thermal mass of the structure. For a brief period this project held the highest BREEAM rating ever awarded, though it was never actually constructed.

In 1991 the company became involved in a study group with the Department of Energy to explore passive solar design. We submitted one of our existing buildings, Temperway House, a fine example of 1970s architecture, to see whether one could actually convert it to green design principles. It had shallow plans (it was only about 12m wide) and working with the Short Ford Partnership we looked at ways of trying to cross-ventilate using thermal chimneys on the busy side so that there would be no necessity to actually open windows. Ideas were explored about using the thermal mass, stripping the building to expose the structure and cross-ventilating, but our tenant was unconvinced of the benefits and the project did not proceed.

The experience led us to the view that green offices potentially had benefits for both developer and tenant, especially when questions of energy use were widened to embrace other environmental issues. Today we are convinced that the comfort and health of office workers is best achieved through sustainable design principles, and this

6.3 a, b *Five Brindley Place, Birmingham: top, perspective by Jock Bevan to design by Siddell Gibson; bottom, plan. Architects: Siddell Gibson.*

a

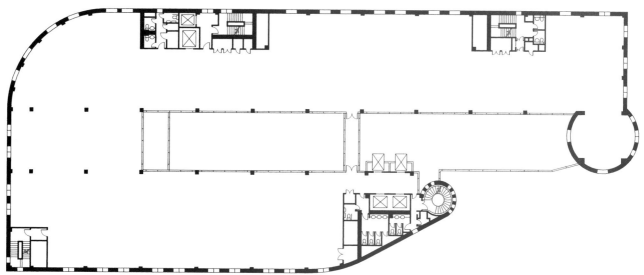

b

6.4 *Solaris House, Basingstoke (project).*
Architect David Partridge
of Argent Development Corporation.

is reflected increasingly in tenant needs. From starting with energy as a prime factor in shaping the design of offices, Argent has now moved to a wider environmental and ecological agenda.

Since Argent is a developer and owner of property the company has an interest in design and long-term asset strength as investments. Although Argent has constructed green offices (and is currently developing designs for several

others) it remains thwarted by the conventional institutional specification with its emphasis upon the sealed envelope, mechanical ventilation systems and artificial lighting. Many green clients, moreover, tend to commission their own buildings (British Gas, Chapter 8) rather than searching for office space within the speculative market. Whether this is through lack of availability of green offices or choice is a debate in which the industry needs to engage.

Conclusion

The circle of specification, product and demand is a vicious cycle of closed perceptions. The circle can be broken as Argent is doing by offering buildings that do everything required of the traditional specification, but at no extra cost to the tenant. For the developer green buildings do not at present pay – energy costs are low and the relationships between environmental wellbeing and productivity in the workplace not yet fully appreciated.

Although green office buildings do cost more initially, the question for companies like Argent is whether they may be worth more in five or ten years time. The issue of enhanced value in the medium to long term, as environmental problems increase and resources become more scarce, is what drives Argent towards sustainable design.

Table 6.1 Comparative performance criteria for green and speculative offices

	A 'green' office building	A typical speculative office
Floor loadings	3.5kN/m²	4kN/m²
Lighting levels	350 lux	500 lux
Occupancy density	1 person per 14m²	1 person per 10m²
Small power loading	10-15W/m²	20-25W/m²
A/C upgrade to cope with additional cooling requirements	Some specialist areas	Additional 15W/m² over 30% floor area
Design temperature	Up to 26°C	21°C± 1.5°C
Predicted number of working hours in excess of design temperature	10-20 hours	None
Floor depths	12-15m	Any
Ability to cellularize	10-15%	100%
Sub-divisibility of tenancies	Limited	Easier

6.5 *Thames Valley Park, Reading, development proposal by the Argent Development Corporation. The holistic nature of green development is evident in this model. Architects: Siddell Gibson.*

Table 6.2 Green speculative offices under construction in 1996 by Argent Development Corporation

Location	Cost	Architect	Green features
Birmingham			
Three Brindley Place	£12.5m	Porphyrios Associates	– doughnut-shaped floorplates (13.5m wide) – openable windows set in thick masonry walls
Four Brindley Place	£16.2m	Stanton Williams	– linear atrium – varied foorplates and size of accommodation to encourage mixed tenure – shaded glazing set in masonry walls – openable windows
Five Brindley Place	£14.5m	Siddell Gibson	– up-low ventilation system serving air at 18°C – 13m floorplate – openable windows
Reading			
Thames Valley Park	£14.2m	Siddell Gibson	– orientation for solar protection – heavy masonry wall on south side, lightweight wall on north side – openable windows

7

Marilyn Standley

Addison Wesley Longman,
now with Chetterton Group

7.1 *Addison Wesley Longman Building, Harlow, Essex. Architects: Conran Roche (now CD Partnership).*

Balancing human, energy and building costs

Rather than describe a building in detail, my chapter recounts the commissioning of a green office building from the perspective of a client. From 1991 to 1995 I was the project director on behalf of the Addison Wesley Longman Group for the new headquarters building at Harlow in Essex. Their previous building designed in the 1960s by Sir Frederick Gibberd was air-conditioned, inefficient and poorly regarded by staff. As a major publishing house, the group had specific needs for a combination of open-plan and cellular space, but above all the company needed modern, healthy office accommodation that fostered greater communication and creativity in staff.

Developing a people-centred brief

My task as project director was to help to evolve the brief, to liaise with the design team and contractor, and to create a building which satisfied Addison Wesley Longman's needs while also providing a sound investment for the company. For while the group required a new headquarters building, publishing is a volatile business and we had to be sure that the building could be let to a quite different company. In the event, soon after completion a third of the building was, in fact, rented by the supermarket group Tesco, and subsequently sold in total in the investment market with Addison Wesley Longman and Tesco remaining as tenants.

The brief evolved from two perspectives: the needs and preferences of the existing staff and the perceptions of the property market in terms of sub-let tenancy requirements. Whereas most green buildings are for specific clients with distinctive needs, such as the PowerGen (Chapter 9) or Ionica Building, we structured the brief to allow for multi-occupancy. It was this factor which led to

the division of each floor into six distinctive office areas divided by three atria on a linear configuration. The need for flexibility was vindicated when during the construction of the building the parent company Pearson restructured the business resulting in a surplus of 4000m² of office space (about 20% of total).

My role as project director for the new building took advantage of my background in facilities management. Addison Wesley Longman was keen that the new head-quarters, expected then to cost about £21m, should reflect the needs of occupiers, i.e. the existing staff. In this regard the building is facilities management driven, but also shaped by user preference and market constraints. It is the combination of the three elements which made the brief for the Addison Wesley Longman Building different and which led to the construction of an office which is a departure from the norm.

Why build a green building?

As a publishing company there is little direct advantage in being 'green' from an image point of view (unlike The Body Shop or PowerGen), but there are many advantages in being green from the point of view of building running costs and staff productivity. The company has a higher than average usage of IT which has implications for heating and ventilation,

and which in turn helped to shape environmental thinking.

We had a site in mind not far from the existing building in central Harlow. It was not ideal but workable: a railway line to the north and busy road to the south determined the alignment on a north/south axis whereby the building had views eastwards over a nearby park.

The building was to be a marriage between site needs and people needs – but people came first. We undertook surveys and interviews with existing staff and quickly evolved the bones of the brief from the point of view of the people who make the business work. The brief sought a sensible balance between energy costs (which are usually fairly low) and people costs (which are normally fairly high). From the outset we tried to generate a brief which created the right working environment for people. That meant natural ventilation with windows that could be opened by the office staff themselves, plenty of daylight, views to the outside world, and a human scale for the workplace. Staff specifically expressed a wish to avoid air-conditioning and deep, characterless office areas.

It was clear from contact with staff representatives through our briefing teams that we needed to avoid the overspecification common to many other modern office buildings. We were fortunate in our choice of site: although environmental conditions were not ideal, they were not so poor that we had to seal the outside world from the inside.

7.2 *Staff dining room,*
Addison Wesley Longman
Building, Harlow.
Architects: Conran Roche.

7.3 *Contact with the outside is*
an important aspect of the
Addison Wesley Longman
Building, Harlow.
Architects: Conran Roche.

In fact, the vast majority of staff expressed a preference for opening windows, views and contact with nature.

The brief was not long and dealt rather more with principles than with detail. Its main elements were for a building which was:

— responsive to different management needs;
— flexible, especially with regard to IT use;
— encouraging to teamwork;
— easy to maintain; cheap to run;
— low-energy in design;
— environmentally friendly;
— a pleasure to be in.

Environmental factors

The brief led to a functional analysis tempered by environmental factors, not merely the priorities of space planning. With human and environmental considerations to the fore and a site that gave access to cycleways, a park and a railway station, the framework existed for a new type of office for the company which had much in common with the 1990s generation of office buildings described elsewhere in this book.

With the Latham Report emerging at about the same time, which called for closer links between design professionals and the construction industry, we were keen to appoint the design team and contractor early on to encourage an integrated team approach. We appointed the CD Partnership (formerly Conran Roche), because of their design style, flexibility and experience of working within new towns (Harlow was one of the first generation of post-war new towns). The CD Partnership helped to develop the feasibility study and was subsequently appointed to act as architect for the building and its fit-out. Other key consultants were EC Harris Project Management, and services engineers Cundall Johnston and Partners. ECD Architects carried out the BREEAM assessment and the design achieved 20 credits out of a possible total of 21.

With innovative buildings a non-adversarial team approach is important The brief was subsequently developed by user groups that crossed functional and hierarchical boundaries. Several sub-briefs were prepared for specific aspects of the building or for special problems such as IT integration, workspace environment, corporate areas and site services. Each analysis of need was undertaken via the same framework:

— consultation;
— project board;
— project manager; user groups;
— professional team.

The importance of user groups

The inclusion of user groups in the functional analysis ensured that environmental and staff workplace needs were taken into account. Green architecture is a symptom of enlightened patronage and by giving prominence to staff needs, the green dimension arose naturally. It also meant

7.4 *Human scale and good diffused lighting characterize the office environment in the Addison Wesley Longman Building, Harlow. Architects: Conran Roche.*

that users of the building had a stake not only in its evolution but in its operation. Stake-holding is important especially when the 'forgiveness factor' comes into play if the building fails to perform exactly as predicted.

Typically in a company such as Addison Wesley Longman's 75% of its total costs are in staff salaries. Anything the business can do to make staff more productive and to reduce absenteeism through illness pays

dividends. Staff costs far exceed energy building costs so user contentment is more important to the employer than good environmental design. However, what this building shows is that by involving staff in the generation of the brief the framework for design evolves from the joint perspectives of good management practice and low-energy design. For a healthy and satisfying workplace is invariably one which is energy efficient and productive.

7.5 *One of three atria providing solar-assisted ventilation at the Addison Wesley Longman Building, Harlow. Architects: Conran Roche.*

Drawing up the design plan

Staff expressed a preference for a human-scaled workplace and this suited our energy strategy. Rather than create one large, single entity building, the Addison Wesley Longman office consists of six work areas per floor (some open plan, others cellular), each divided by vertical circulation areas or atria. There are three atria to each floor arranged in linear form to separate the 13.5m deep office areas. Both atria and floorplates are similar in width with the two 90m long offices divided into three units by solidly expressed core and stair towers. Perceptually the plan allows each 13.5m x 30m unit of office accommodation to be read as a self-contained part, each with its own energy controls at the command of users. As the building is five and, in the centre, six storeys high, the subdivision of the office areas into fairly small units adds significantly to the arrangement whereby there are in total 72 separate heating and ventilation zones. The advantage is that fine tuning can occur to suit user or tenant needs, and that the areas requiring special environments, such as the restaurant and print room, can have their own energy strategy.

In a building of 16,000m² there is sense in breaking down the scale. This not only gives staff a feeling of belonging to a defined area of territory but the smallness of the parts creates a greater sense of teamwork and engenders collaboration in the way our previous amorphous office never did. The three atria serve a distinct function – they are social and meeting spaces, their openness generates interaction between teams (so important in publishing where creativity is particularly valued), and the central atrium acts as an entrance space. In these senses we ensured that the environmental strategy for the building reflected closely the management strategy.

Controlling light and ventilation

The building is arranged with shared facilities on the ground floor (café, print room) and top floor (restaurant, boardroom, meeting rooms). Both top and bottom floor have views over terraces or gardens to the wider landscape. By separating these two most heat intensive floors the linking atria effectively build up enough stack effect to naturally ventilate the office areas. The use of high-level manually

opened windows, tall ceilings, exposed *in-situ* concrete structure, external solar screens and internal blinds effectively minimize summer heat gain. In winter when office windows are not likely to be opened, heat is provided by perimeter radiators and ventilation via ducts in the 300mm raised floor.[1] Energy saving is also achieved with the use of a lighting control system which switches uplighters off when daylight is sufficient or when offices are unoccupied.

As with many office buildings, the external control of sunlight supplements daylight penetration through reflective louvres. Daylight is maximized by the use of exceptionally large windows and white-painted concrete structure. The sunlight shades are part of an integrated facade system developed by Schüco which consists of five main parts:

7.6 *Ground floor café, Addison Wesley Longman Building, Harlow. Architects: Conran Roche.*

- top section of clear, double-glazed, inward-opening windows with etched glass to reduce glare;
- external aluminium curved louvres of varying depth to suit angle of incidence;
- middle section of clear double-glazed outward-opening windows;
- lower section of fixed double-glazed windows;
- bottom section of polyester powder-coated insulated aluminium panel with integral 100mm foil-backed insulation.[2]

By setting the glazing deep within the structural frame high sun shading is provided for the top window panel, while the external louvres protect the two lower windows. The arrangement is energy efficient and gives control of ventilation to users without obstructing views.

Unusually for such buildings, the atria are not roof but mainly wall-glazed. Light enters the three atria spaces predominantly via walls of glass, which project through the roof of the building. Energy modelling at the design stage confirmed that good light penetration and natural ventilation could be achieved without roof-top glazing. The central atrium has a solid roof and the north and south atria have circular rooflights punched through the concrete. Perimeter wall glazing of the atria avoids the problem of solar shading the rooftop (Daimler Chrysler, Chapter 10) and allows daylight to wash down the interior walls without glare.

Conclusion

Built at a cost of £21m the Addison Wesley Longman Building is 5% more economical than the norm (the final cost was £1073/m² in 1995) though with higher external envelope costs.[3] Additional costs associated with thermal massing were approximately £13/m² and roof planting about £8/m². However, the use of exposed concrete rather than suspended ceilings resulted in a saving of £20/m² and energy running costs are about 35% that of comparable air-conditioned offices.

The Addison Wesley Longman Building is a user-led reaction against the anonymous, deep-plan office of the 1980s. We set out to achieve a healthy, responsive, low-energy new headquarters building that was easy to understand and not over-elaborate in operation. With

Table 7.1 Addison Wesley Longman Building, Harlow: main green features

- 80% of staff expressed preference for opening windows;
- large office divided by atria into small working areas;
- elaborate facades with integral solar screens and large opening windows;
- high ceilings and exposed concrete structure (columns and ceilings) for thermal capacity;
- three atria of different form for energy reasons;
- design evolved in close collaboration with users;
- building divided into 72 heating and ventilation zones, most under individual control;
- semi-urban rather than rural site within walking distance of railway station;
- lighting control system related to daylight quality and room occupancy.

between 15% and 30% of the office space on any one floor as cellular accommodation at any one time we also had to ensure that there was flexibility in terms of energy operation.

We did not set out originally to produce a 'green building': the environmental dimension grew as we consulted with staff and looked seriously at the health, maintenance and energy costs of a typical air-conditioned office block. When we asked staff initially to list the eight features they most desired in the new building; 80% opted for opening windows. It was this decision, which, more than any other, shaped the design and which with post occupancy surveys has led the users to express pleasure in working in the building. Pleasure, job satisfaction and productivity go together and justify the energy strategy in more than fiscal terms alone.

References

1. Details can be seen in *The Architects' Journal*, 30 May 1996, p. 28.
2. Ibid, p. 32.
3. *The Architects' Journal*, 30 May 1996, contains a full cost breakdown.
4. Ibid, p. 30.

TWO

Case Studies of best practice

8

Mistral Building, Reading

Ken Shuttleworth

Foster and Partners

The practice of Foster and Partners has been designing low-energy office buildings for several years, especially in Germany and France where green thinking is more advanced than in the UK. Commerzbank in Frankfurt is an example. To explain the background to Foster and Partners' offices for British Gas in the Thames Valley Park, near Reading, Berkshire, due for completion in 1997, it is worth looking first at the Commerzbank Building and other developments in Europe.

Commerzbank, Frankfurt, and other European projects

Constructed in 1997, Commerzbank is the first high-rise, naturally ventilated building in the world. The bank is triangular in plan, two sides are offices and the third a garden enclosed within an atrium rising through 60 storeys – the height of the building. The differential temperature between inside and outside air pressure provides cross ventilation for the offices.

The atrium is a key element of the design. The four-storey high gardens corkscrew around its edge deflecting air movement in response to different wind direction. Every ninth floor the atrium is sealed to stop the build up of an excessive stack effect throughout the full height of the building. The combination of radiant cooling, opening windows and an environmentally efficient plan form allows the tower to achieve remarkable energy performance.

The Frankfurt office building owes the direction of its innovation to a school the Foster office designed at Fréjus in the South of France. Known as Lycée Albert Camus it, too, was naturally ventilated with fresh air taken between a double skin roof constructed of two layers of concrete

8.2 *Micro-electronic Centre, Duisburg. Architects: Foster and Partners.*

and lightweight steel. The thermal capacity of the concrete roof moderated the temperature to the point where, with solar shading on the south side, the school remained cool even in summer. The trick is to keep the air moving by establishing thermal currents both within the building itself and through the structure of walls and roof.

Another French design by the practice, an office for EDF (the national electricity grid company in France), exploits internal chimneys to draw air in from the perimeter. By placing the chimneys in the centre of the building and employing extensive external shading, constructed in this case of locally grown timber, the air goes between the layers of the external cladding pulling in fresh cool air from outside. As with the school, the orientation of the building in relation to wind, sun and shading was crucial.

Zero energy bill at Duisburg

A group of business park buildings constructed between 1992 and 1994 by Foster and Partners at Duisburg in Germany explored the potential of co-generation where gas is burned to make electricity and provide winter space heating. Based on combined heat and power (CHP) principles, about half the electricity produced powers the building, the remainder is sold at a profit to the national grid. In conjunction with the use of absorption chillers, which convert sunlight into coolth, radiant cooling in the ceiling, trickle ventilation and a triple-glazed external skin

that takes away the heat as it hits the glass wall to the top of the building, the Duisburg buildings have proved to have a zero energy bill.

The Mistral Building for British Gas

At Reading, Foster and Partners' task was to design an energy efficient office for British Gas on a site bounded to the south by a railway line and noisy access road. The attractive views were to the north over a park and the River Thames. We located the Mistral Building, as it became known, to the northern edge of the site where the environment was better, aware that it would expose the south elevation to potentially difficult problems of solar gain and internal glare.

The design was evolved to mitigate these problems without resorting to the high environmental costs associated with totally sealed offices, which was the solution adopted by most other architects at the Thames Valley Park. It seemed natural to us to develop a design in a parkland setting that brought the external environment to the centre of the building through the use of naturally ventilated, shallow-plan built forms. The strategy was to have four fingers of buildings 16.5m wide penetrating into the park with curved ends against the river. This allowed us to locate the plant rooms on the south side providing useful solar protection. Part of the environmental strategy developed with building services engineers Roger Preston and Partners also involved placing the buildings and lake in close proximity in order to use the chilling effect of air passing over water.

As the scheme for British Gas evolved, the four fingers of accommodation were pushed out as peninsulas towards the lake with the water also brought partly inside the building. Car parking was placed on the south side where it was hidden from inside the building by the plant rooms, with toilets and staircases placed as solid stone walls on that elevation. The largely solid south elevation contrasts with the mainly transparent north where clear glazed walls provide good views over the parkland. The finger concept brings the perception of the external environment and its physical benefits into the heart of the building. Dividing the building into fingers and cores allows for phased construction: two fingers and a linking atrium have recently been constructed so we can monitor energy performance before completing the whole project.

8.3 *Mistral Building. Reading. Architects: Foster and Partners.*

8.4 *Site plan, Mistral Building, Reading. Architects: Foster and Partners.*

8.5 *Cross section through atrium, Mistral Building, Reading. Architects: Foster and Partners.*

8.6 *Ground floor plan of phase one, Mistral Building, Reading. Architects: Foster and Partners.*

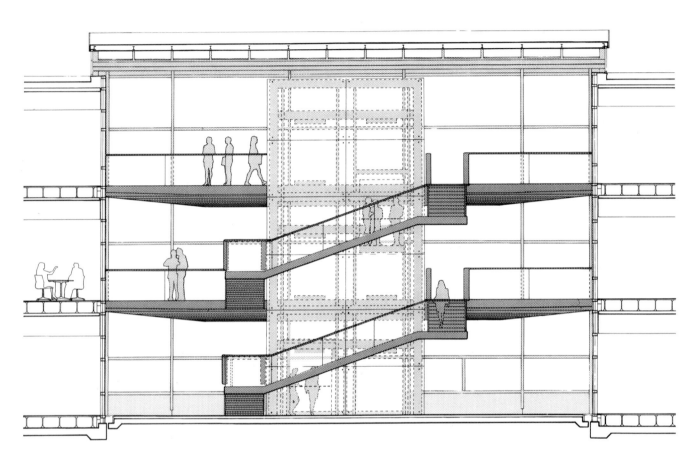

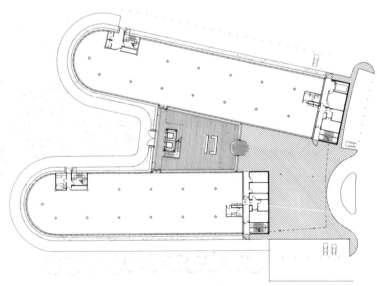

8.7 *Long section through atrium, Mistral Building, Reading. Architects: Foster and Partners.*

8.8 *Cross section, Mistral Building, Reading. Architects: Foster and Partners.*

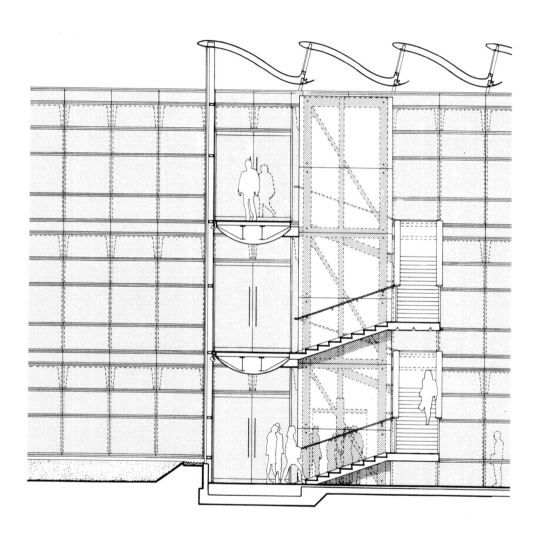

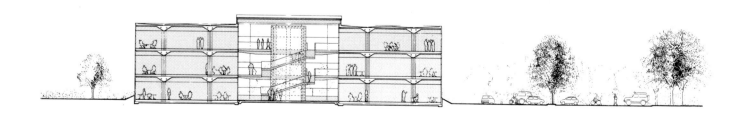

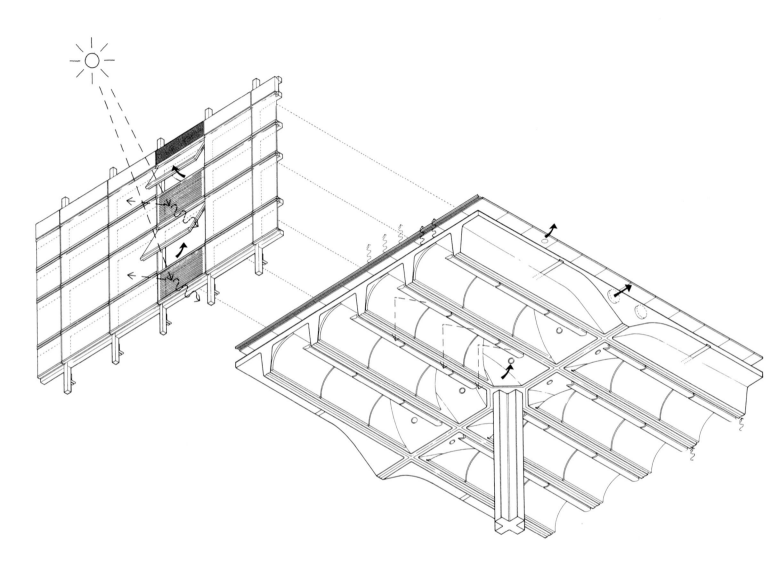

Ventilation

As with all green buildings, the cross section is as important as the plan – arguably more so. The 16.5m deep offices obtain their ventilation via opening windows which exploit the differential air pressures set up by the atrium and inside/outside conditions. Windows are designed so that flaps open at night to cool the structure. By using an exposed concrete ribbed floor structure the offices exploit cooling, particularly at the edge of the building where the ribs extend as cantilevers outside the glazing line. The high thermal mass of the concrete frames and the deliberate policy of leaving the structure exposed to the internal and external air, provide an effective low-energy means of moderating internal temperatures. In extreme weather conditions, however, a mixed mode system operates.

The cantilevered structural edge extends 4.5m beyond the column line. The columns themselves are buried within the thickness of the partitions some way back from the glazing line, providing a column-free space in the centre and at the perimeter of the building. The concrete ribs on a 1.5m grid are expressed on the building facades providing architectural interest by day and night.

Cladding, glazing and lighting

The strategy of expressing the concrete ribs in order to exploit the high thermal mass of the building for radiant cooling influenced our thinking with regard to cladding. Since the building facades face in all directions our starting point was the design of the building envelope, which reflected the different performance needs of east, west, north and (to a lesser extent) south facades. We deliberately avoided using the same cladding design all the way around the building, developing virtually clear elevations on the north and east sides, and more solid panels on the west facades where the low afternoon sun posed difficulties. As noted, the plant rooms, lifts and services are generally placed on the south elevation providing the necessary solar protection.

We tested the glazing thoroughly before installation. Computer modelling and the construction of trial panels allowed the performance to be evaluated from thermal, acoustic, wind and pressure points of view. With innovative buildings it is better to test ideas on a rig rather than the building site. The glazing uses a different combination of clear, fritted and insulated panels according to orientation. The glazing, too, has different areas which can be opened according to aspect, and is designed so that air can circulate through the window itself, rather than from outside to inside.

The coffered floor slabs combine lighting in the form of uplighters which run around the inside of each coffer and reflect on a baffle. Lighting and structure are, as in most of our buildings, closely integrated. By being close to the concrete structure, the heat of the lights is absorbed rather than dissipated into the working environment.

Choosing natural materials

The Mistral Building achieved an excellent BREEAM rating. By providing measures such as bicycle sheds, water conservation measures, timber from sustainable sources and, of course, low-energy design, the building is among the top three or four in the country. However, while being green it is not devoid of

Table 8.1 Mistral Building, Reading: main green features

- building partly constructed below ground level;
- orientation for solar protection;
- distribution of service zones and circulation to south side for solar shade;
- high thermal capacity combined with transparency on north and east elevations;
- exposed concrete ribs for radiant cooling;
- fairly narrow plan depth (16.5m) combined with partial atria;
- timber from sustainable sources (beech and iroko);
- elevations which vary in transparency and insulation according to orientation;
- facade venting through cavity;
- openable windows;
- partial stack-effect ventilation;
- use of exterior lake for cooling.

architectural interest or bravado: on the contrary, the energy-saving measures give the building a distinctive aesthetic quality. The atrium in particular with its timber bridges and the staircase wrapping around a timber-clad lift shaft has a soft green feel which alludes to the parkland environment outside. The external wall goes all the way around the building, but also through the atrium where it does not change (as walls do in most atria) but remains the same thereby helping to explain the function of the atrium as a climate modifier.

The use of timber poses problems for architects today. Since hardwood forests are the world's major reservoirs of biodiversity and contribute significantly to the conversion of CO_2 into oxygen (and hence moderate global warming) the specification of hardwoods is fraught with difficulty. Foster and Partners consulted with BREEAM over the best species to use and chose Iroko from guaranteed sustainable sources. Timber is widely used as a finish: it is employed as flooring, as cladding on the bridges that criss-cross the atrium, and as an external canopy. Timber used in combination with natural stone on the perimeter walls and the practice's more usual high-tech finishes creates an atmosphere which is soft yet efficient. As an energy-efficient building, we endeavoured to use natural finishes to complement the natural ventilation and radiant cooling strategy.

8.10 *Use of sustainable
hardwood, Mistral Building,
Reading. Architects: Foster
and Partners.*

8.11 *Exterior view of entrance canopy, Mistral Building, Reading. Architects: Foster and Partners.*

We also used nature as a green metaphor. The choice of materials (greenish stone and green finished metal framing) creates a building which is green in both concept and appearance. This, added to the generous reinforcement of tree planting in the park, sets the building apart from its neighbours. Since the Mistral Building is partly buried in the ground (up to sill level) for energy saving purposes, the appearance is one of the ground plane of grass and shrubs entering directly into the building. When the ground-floor windows are opened, the view out over the blades of grass symbolically unites the building with the landscape.

Conclusion

British Gas commissioned us to design an energy-efficient office building, initially for their own occupation, but subsequently as a building that could be let to others. Our thinking in the design of the building moved outwards from energy performance to embracing wider environmental and ecological considerations under the influence of BREEAM. The site demanded a sustainable approach from master-planning to the specification of materials.

It is difficult to say at this early stage whether the building pays in the full range of benefits and impacts involved. Certainly the energy bills will be only about 20% of those of a more conventionally designed office building. Although construction costs were slightly higher than the norm for speculative offices, the building represents for British Gas a symbol of its commitment as a major energy producer to environmental issues. At present energy cost levels, I would estimate that the pay back period is 12 to 15 years, though I like to think that the approach to the design from an environmental perspective adds value to the building, which would be reflected in any subsequent sale.

9

9.1 *Office interior, PowerGen Building, Coventry.*
Architects: Bennetts Associates.

PowerGen Building, Coventry

Rab Bennetts

Bennetts Associates

PowerGen is one of the three major electricity generating companies in England formed by privatization of the industry in 1990. The company appointed Bennetts Associates as architects in 1991 to design an initial scheme for its new headquarters in Birmingham because of the practice's 'analytical approach and experience with natural ventilation'.[1] After studying several possible sites, that at Coventry was chosen in 1992. The brief was for a low-energy building which optimized daylight and user control of the internal environment. PowerGen's brief did not stipulate natural ventilation, but left the design team to make proposals. However, they did not like air-conditioning and wanted to have opening windows.

The decision to construct a new building rather than rent existing floorspace was in order to pursue long-term operational efficiency linked to energy conservation. The building had to be able to accommodate around 600 staff under one roof, but without a hint of corporate extravagance. A single headquarters building held the prospect of operational integration and greater energy efficiency than had the building been split as earlier into separate units. The brief also required high levels of internal comfort without relying upon conventional control from a central plant room.

Evolution of the design strategy

The focus of design effort was upon the workplace and its environmental conditions rather than overt corporate or architectural image.[2] However, in evolving a design strategy the importance of building or room shape, colour, daylight, views, circulation routes and meeting places emerged with greater force than in a conventional office building.[3] The

9.2 *Typical floor plan,*
PowerGen Building,
Coventry. Architects:
Bennetts Associates.

Key

1	Office	4	Computer facilities
2	Atrium	5	Restaurant
3	Service Tower	6	Servery
		7	Kitchen

analysis of client need showed that PowerGen's operations were best met by narrow width floorplates of six structural bays served by a circulation route on the long side. The design selected was to use four such floorplates divided by a long central atrium stacked vertically into a three-storey building.

The orientation of the building helped to reduce solar gain and control glare from low sun angles. The PowerGen Building is on an east/west axis exposing one long elevation to the north and the other to the south. This orientation restricts the problem of glare and afternoon solar gain to east and west-facing glazed elevations. In restricting the area of glass on east and west facades by positioning the staff restaurant, conference area, plant rooms and air-conditioned communication rooms against the gables, the awkward low-angle sun was cost-effectively masked. Simple solar shading was required on the south elevation, however, but the relative expense was lower than with full air-conditioning.

No office building of this size can be totally free of mechanical ventilation. We sought at PowerGen to restrict air-conditioned areas to a minimum and to place such accommodation at opposite ends of the building where it could act as a buffer. In addition, the photocopiers and printers were located in air-conditioned business centres in line with the stair cores in the atrium, where they could act as a point of social contact. We also provided separate areas for computer suites, which needed mechanical ventilation, rather than design all the offices to such high standards.

Besides careful attention to the positioning of accommodation relative to orientation and ventilation load, we sought to maximize daylight penetration by restricting the

floorplates to 12m in depth. As daylight maximization without sunlight on the workplane is crucial to low-energy design we evolved a building section that optimized daylight opportunities from both the exterior and interior via the atrium. The two mainly open-plan office areas are divided by a linear atrium, which bisects the building on its long axis. The floorplates are identical on each of the three floors with only the configuration of the accommodation in the gables varying.

Maximizing the use of daylight

The basic arrangement eases shading requirements for the facades and optimizes the availability of diffuse sky-light.[4] This enters the building from the atrium where rooftop solar shading filters out direct sunlight except in specific areas where background brightness was desirable. Angled ceiling soffits in the atrium and glazed balustrading to the office areas allow a gentle glare-free transition from the bright and airy atrium to the working spaces. Daylight enters the office areas mainly from the north and south elevations and here lighting levels are evenly distributed throughout the building section. As with the light graduation from atrium to office areas, contrasts in the visual field at the perimeter are dealt with via a combination of external screening and daylight shelves.

The building footprint and cross section are designed to maximize daylight and to exploit natural ventilation through the stack effect, or via cross ventilation. These two priorities shaped many subsequent decisions, including the design of the windows. The windows extend from just above desk

9.3 *South elevation,*
PowerGen Building,
Coventry. Architects:
Bennetts Associates.

height to ceiling with a flush joint between the window head and structural soffit. The detail avoids glare and provides a better spread of daylight across the ceiling than with traditional window design. The windows are clear-glazed, double-paned, using low-E units, with upper panels of tinted glass to reduce sun transmission on the south elevation.[5] Each vertical panel of glazing is divided into three vertical units, the lower two being operated manually by users and the upper section linked to the Building Management System (BMS) for night-time chilling of the structure. This allows the users to choose a high or low level air-stream, according to external conditions. Glazing represents less than 50% of the total facade area.

Ventilation solutions

Both the open aspect of the site and the freedom to exploit orientation afforded advantages which the design of the building and its window systems exploit. The surrounding area provides a relatively quiet and clean environment, which we have sought to bring indoors via the atrium and large opening windows. Computer simulation confirmed that a combination of a long thin building with a three-storey sandwiched atrium would provide the natural ventilation and high quality environment required of the brief.

It was clear in the modelling of the building that with the exception of still days, cross-ventilation with such a shallow floorplate would be the dominant factor in moving air around the building rather than the stack effect. Only on windless days is the stack effect a major contributor to natural

ventilation in a building of these dimensions. Detailed research into local weather conditions indicated that very hot days were never still and that still days were generally experienced at modest temperatures. In consequence, the design team concluded that the convention of designing for a hot, still day was not applicable in this case.

Thermal mass is used to moderate internal temperatures. The concrete structure of round columns and coffered ceiling is left exposed in office areas in order to modify the interior climate. Night-time ventilation exploits the heavyweight *in-situ* construction to provide passive cooling during hot summer days. This has proved to be of critical importance in use.

The architectural benefits of coffered ceilings

Leaving the concrete structure exposed allowed us to take advantage of the architectural framework as the main ingredient of the tectonic experience. With no need to provide suspended ceilings except in a few dedicated areas of air-conditioning, the coffered ceilings and fair-faced concrete columns assume an important environmental and aesthetic role. As with much green design, the architectural benefits are an important by-product of sustainability.

The detailed design of the coffered ceiling is the result of many factors – structural, environmental, acoustic and visual. The raking of the structural coffers to the outer edge provides good daylight penetration; the elliptical profile avoids acoustic focusing; the optimum visual depth is sufficient to provide a clear span across the floorplate; and the suspended

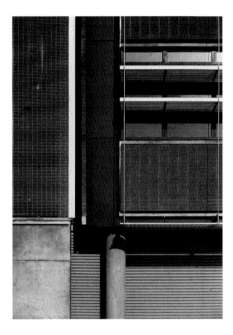

Factors that determined the building's configuration

There is a delicate balance struck at the PowerGen Building between five inter-related factors:

– office floorplate to atrium width dimension;
– daylight penetration and solar gain;
– orientation of building;
– fabric heat loss;
– local environmental conditions.

These factors determined not only the size and shape of the building, but the floor to ceiling heights, the distribution of types of accommodation, and the choice and method of construction. Concrete was used for the structure because of its benefit over steel in terms of night-time cooling. *In situ* concrete, with a painted, high-quality finish, was cheaper and easier to detail than pre-cast concrete. Externally the building uses panels of brickwork for the same reason. The thickness of the concrete floor slab and its surface area is crucial to the use of thermal capacity for radiant cooling. Research suggests that the optimum thickness is between 150mm and 190mm with the first 50-70mm being the most effective on a daily thermal cycle.[8] Post-occupancy analysis suggests that the coffered profile provides 2-3°C more cooling effect than a flat slab construction.

PowerGen forms a marriage between the functional needs of the company and its commitment to good environmental practice. PowerGen knew when we were appointed in 1992 that it had a particular type of desk configuration in mind. In effect, the company had an idea of the environmental and operational characteristics of the working environment. In fact, the function and organisation of the office space was dominant and hence the design evolved from the inside out. Our task was to develop a typical floorplate for 40-45 people (the maximum team size) and to test this against performance criteria – energy use, lighting, acoustic, circulation, flexibility, etc. We modelled the area using computers and made a physical mock-up which was assessed using light meters. This confirmed the environmental assumptions and the space syntax qualities of the building. Having perfected the floorplate diagram it was a short step to placing the heavily serviced accommodation at one end and the special hot spot accommodation (copiers, fax machines, etc.) by the cores in the atrium.

lighting boom uses the structural soffit to diffuse artificial light in an even fashion.[6] Ducts when they are needed are positioned in the 450mm raised floors thereby avoiding compromise with the multifarious function of the ceiling.

Acoustic elements

There can be a conflict between thermal and acoustic design in offices with exposed structures. The exploitation of the thermal coefficient of exposed concrete construction readily leads to a noisy indoor environment. The answer at the PowerGen Building is to provide areas of sound-absorbent covering placed as wings on either side of the light fittings hung beneath the coffered ceiling. The acoustic material made from perforated metal filled with sound-absorbing mats soaks up sound on both the upper and lower surfaces, and therefore absorbs direct noise from the office workstations and indirect noise reflected off the concrete coffers.[7] With open-plan offices that use structural elements to moderate temperatures, it is important to integrate architectural, thermal, acoustic and lighting issues. Besides the combined light and acoustic fittings, we designed the shape of the coffers to absorb noise, the profile being elliptical not radial in cross-section.

9.6 *Exposed concrete structure helps to stabilise temperatures, PowerGen Building, Coventry. Architects: Bennetts Associates.*

9.7 *Section through external wall of south elevation, PowerGen Building, Coventry. Architects: Bennetts Associates.*

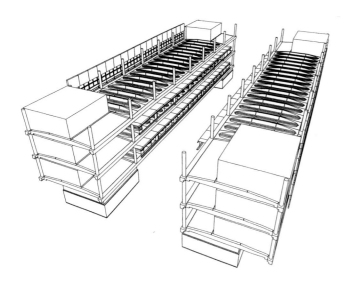

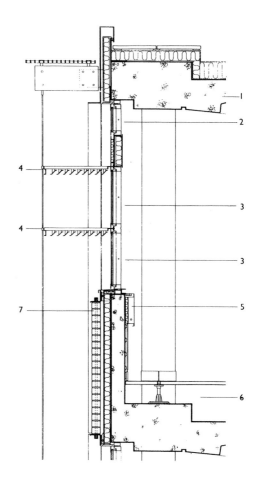

Key: 1. In-situ *concrete floor slab.* **2.** *Opening window on BMS for night-time cooling.* **3.** *Clear double-glazed windows with low-E units.* **4.** *Combined solar shading and daylight shelves.* **5.** *Combined heater sill.* **6.** *Raised floor* **7.** *Brickwork panel.*

The company and design team (which included Ernest Griffiths & Sons as building services engineers[9]) were not just looking directly for a low-energy solution, but a building which offered environmentally something more than the standard office interior with its flat suspended ceilings and architecturally neutral spaces. The decision to expose the structure, to use narrow floorplates within a linear building, and to develop the long coffered ceiling profile led to an office building that looked rather like a solid warehouse structure from the 19th century. We rather like the way the PowerGen Building alludes to the industrial revolution in its imagery — after all it is merely a factory processing information.

The column-free interior of the offices makes for elegant spaces where the structural soffit and integral lighting and acoustic fittings are dominant. Today 95% of the staff at PowerGen work in offices which have natural ventilation, access to openable windows, and views out to the sky and internally to the atrium.

Although the design evolved through three distinct stages, the shape and pattern of the floorplate remained the same. What did change was the relationship between the circulation areas and the floorplate, and the grouping of the floorplates relative to the atrium. By placing the cafeteria areas, computer suites and meeting rooms at the perimeter of the offices, we effectively screened the floorplates at the vulnerable east and west ends, and provided greater architectural modelling of the facades. A consequence of the design strategy is the greater exterior length than in an air-conditioned office, and the greater cost of the facade elements (because of solar screening and expensive glazing design). However, as an architect it seems better to invest in the architecture that people see rather than in the hidden services (as with air-conditioned buildings), which are of little aesthetic benefit and a short economic life.

Conclusion

PowerGen cost no more than a conventional office building, yet it uses only 40% of the energy load of air-conditioned floor space. With its opening windows and sense of the outside penetrating to the interior, the building is a model

9.8 *The energy planning of the PowerGen Building, Coventry, is clearly visible at night. Architects: Bennetts Associates.*

Table 9.1 PowerGen Building, Coventry: main green features

- 12m office floor plates;
- linear building with sandwich atrium;
- double-glazed top-opening windows with solar screening;
- arrangement of non-standard accommodation to provide solar screening buffer zones;
- deep coffered slab for radiant cooling;
- integral light fittings with sound absorbent wings;
- roof-vented atrium;
- integral window-head and ceiling for smooth daylight penetration;
- orientation of building to reduce low-angle sun penetration;
- heat-emitting office equipment placed in concentrated areas, with local A/C.

of the healthy natural office of the future. Like many green designs today it owes a debt to Arup Associates' pioneering work, especially the Wiggins Teape Building in Basingstoke, and in its turn we have refined the PowerGen model at the John Menzies Building near Edinburgh.[10] Each building is a logical development of the former: each confirms that by taking a holistic view of architectural design, green buildings do in fact pay. The building was constructed at the modest cost in 1994 of £700/m² (about £900/m² fully fitted out), which is viable in terms of market rents and cheaper than an equivalent air-conditioned office.

References

1. *The Architects' Journal*, 2 March 1995, p. 44. This issue contains a detailed case study of the PowerGen Building.
2. Ibid.
3. Ibid.
4. Adam Jackaway and David Green, 'PowerGen in the light of day', *The Architects' Journal*, 14 March 1996, p. 46.
5. Ibid.
6. *The Architects' Journal*, 2 March 1995, p. 46.
7. Iain Clarke, 'Sounding out the soffit', *Architects' Journal*, 7 March 1996, p. 44.
8. Alistair Blyth, 'Using the building fabric to balance energy demand', *Concrete Quarterly*, Spring 1996, p. 13.
9. Detailed case study of PowerGen services design, *CIBSE Journal*, March 1995.
10 Case study of John Menzies Building with article by Rab Bennetts on evolution since PowerGen. *The Architects' Journal*, 30 November 1995.

10

Daimler Chrysler Building, Berlin

Lennart Grut

Richard Rogers Partnership

In 1993 Daimler Benz AG (now Daimler Chrysler) appointed Richard Rogers Partnership to design three buildings – two office blocks and a residential block – which form part of the masterplan of the Potsdamer Platz development in Berlin designed by the Renzo Piano Building Workshop with Christoph Kohlbecker. The main entrance to the buildings faces onto Linkstrassen Park and the basic form of each building is based on a typical Berlin block with a centralized courtyard. District heating and district cooling as well as the main electric supply is supplied by BEWAG by means of CHP plant and absorption chillers.

This chapter concentrates on one of the Daimler Chrysler office blocks known as B6. The key objective was to design three buildings that would form a new European standard for the integration of low-energy design into architecture suitable for dense urban environments. Each building aims to optimize the use of passive solar energy, natural ventilation and natural light to create a comfortable and energy-efficient working environment.

Environmental strategy

The strategies adopted in the design of the office block are as follows:

— opening up the courtyard to optimize daylight penetration, improve passive solar gain in winter and enhance views to the park;

— using an atrium to act as a thermal buffer, induce natural ventilation through the atrium and the building, and create a well-tempered entrance hall;

— using a high-performance building envelope to minimize conflicts between solar gain and daylight to 'fine-tune' the facades in response to solar exposure, and

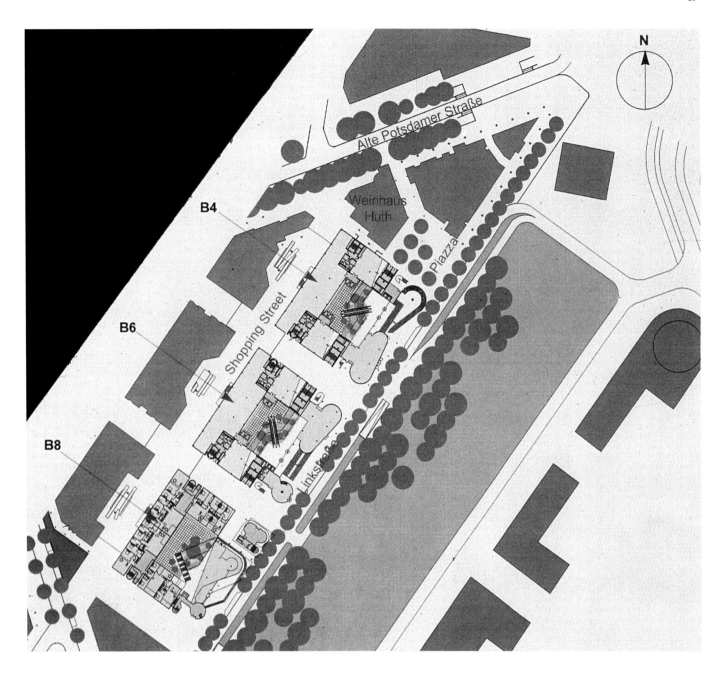

develop a modular facade system which can be modified according to external conditions and user requirements;

— naturally ventilating the building throughout the year by using optimized window configuration and night-time free cooling.

Predicting the results

A well-designed daylit and naturally ventilated office building in Berlin will normally have an annual primary energy consumption of approximately 140 kWh/m^2. In comparison, an air-conditioned, standard office building with conventional services design and control could consume between two to five times more energy. Our target was to reduce the annual primary energy consumption of each office building to approximately 80 kWh/m^2. Initial analysis indicated that each office block would consume approximately 35% of artificial lighting and 30% of heating and cooling energy normally used by a typical naturally ventilated office block in Germany.

Here follows a summary of the analysis undertaken by ourselves and building services engineers Schmidt Reuter and Partners of Hamburg in order to achieve the environmental objectives:

10.2 *Diagrammatic sections and plans showing relationship between daylight factor and built form, Daimler Chrysler Building, Berlin. Architects: Richard Rogers Partnership.*

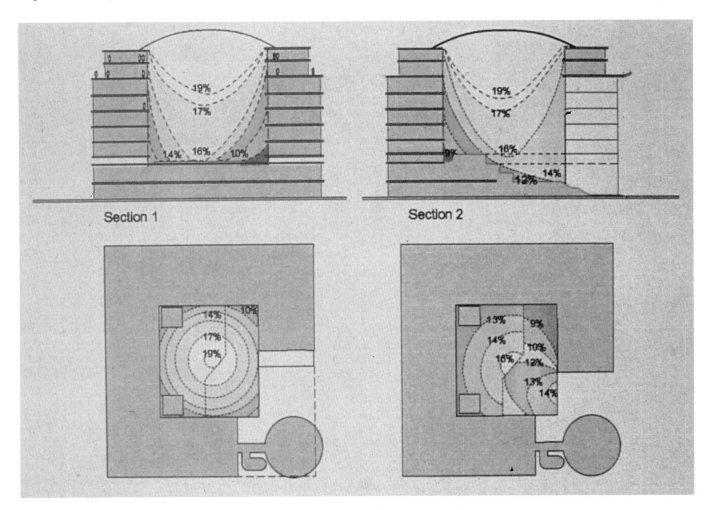

- The building form was examined.
- The building envelope was analysed.
- The internal environment, including natural ventilation and daylight, was also examined.

Computer modelling techniques and physical models were used in the design process to integrate architectural form, functional requirements and environmental performance. Tools used included:

- ESP+Suite, ARIA Suite, Dynamic Thermal Modelling (DTM)
- Computational Fluid Dynamics (CFD), TAS Suite, CARasol, Heliodon and Artificial Sky.

Natural ventilation using a plenum

The initial concept

The benefits of a well-designed atrium are widely acknowledged. At the Daimler Chrysler Building the atrium creates a sheltered buffer space of approximately 600m², which can be used all year round and reduces the heating demand of the facing offices. Potential overheating can be minimized by providing shading and sufficient ventilation.

The initial concept for the atrium was to use natural ventilation based upon a low-level opening at the front of the south-east atrium facade for air intake and high-level outlets at the top of the atrium driven by natural buoyancy. Shading devices were placed immediately below the atrium roof to reduce solar gain. However, DTM and CFD indicated that there would be an uneven air flow through the atrium resulting in poor ventilation into the adjacent offices.

The interim concept

The design was modified to introduce a plenum between the floor of levels 1 and 2. Air inlets of approximately 60m² were found to be the correct size. The inlets were distributed evenly along three sides of the building. This allowed air to flow smoothly into the atrium, and is reflected by the evenly distributed temperature profiles up the atrium. No air intake was made from the shopping mall side due to the risk of air contamination. The plenum also minimizes the risk of cold down draughts along the internal atrium facades. The hottest zone is located above the shading away from the occupied areas. However, the proximity of the horizontal shading devices to the office levels 7 and 8 helped in terms of radiation exchange to the spaces.

The final concept

CFD analysis indicated that for a typical fifth-floor office the average standing head height temperature was in the region of 0.5°C above that when atrium roof shading was used. Therefore the ventilation criteria could be met with an increased performance for the atrium-facing office facades. As a consequence of removing the atrium roof shading it was necessary to improve the thermal performance of the atrium roof glazing to minimize overheating in the atrium in summer. The specified type of glass, Ipasol Natura, has a particularly favourable ratio between solar gain (34%) and daylight transmission (68%), and is double glazed to reduce condensation.

Further thermal analysis indicated that a heated single-glazed atrium entrance facade and double-glazed office facades would reduce condensation to an acceptable level. On the south-east entrance facade the use of an electrically heated laminated glass panel would avoid condensation. The atrium would be maintained at a minimum of 12°C with heating provided by fan coil units located within the plenum.

Atrium roof shading versus office shading

Four main aims led to the final concept of applying shading to the outside of the atrium-facing offices rather than to the atrium roof:

- to reduce visual cluster and obstruction at the top of the atrium;
- to optimize unobstructed sky views and daylighting to the atrium-facing offices, particularly at low levels;
- to improve accessibility and reduce both maintenance and the costs of the shading system;
- to provide occupants with the control of the shading systems.

The thermal modelling indicated that the optimum position of air outlets would be to distribute the openings evenly along the perimeter of the roof. The total outlet area approximately equalled the total inlet area of 60m². This allowed an even air flow outside the atrium-facing office facades. An additional opening of 3.3m² at the apex of the atrium roof relieved the hot air pockets and prevented them from spreading downwards. An additional 30² of openings at the top of the roof were used for smoke extract.

Solar gains on facades

The facades of the building have been designed on a modular basis to meet summer-time over-heating criteria and optional comfort cooling criteria. Solar gains analysis, taking into account external obstructions, was carried out for all four facades. Thermal analysis was conducted to calculate the number of hours during the occupancy period when the internal temperature was likely to exceed 28°C. The additional target for the chilled ceiling load for optional cooling in the future was set at 66W/m². The building is subdivided into different zones according to the internal office layout and the exercise was repeated with varying facade elements until the design criteria were met.

The outcome of the studies indicated that from an environmental perspective, both the external shading strategy and the integrated performance glass facade can satisfy the thermal performance criteria. The advantage of the latter system is the relatively simple maintenance and detailing, reduction in ventilation obstruction and the cluster of the facades. On balance, the integrated performance glass facade was the more favourable option. Depending on the orientation of the facade, various elements such as clear glass, performance glass, mid-pane blinds, internal blinds and opaque panels can be incorporated into the system.

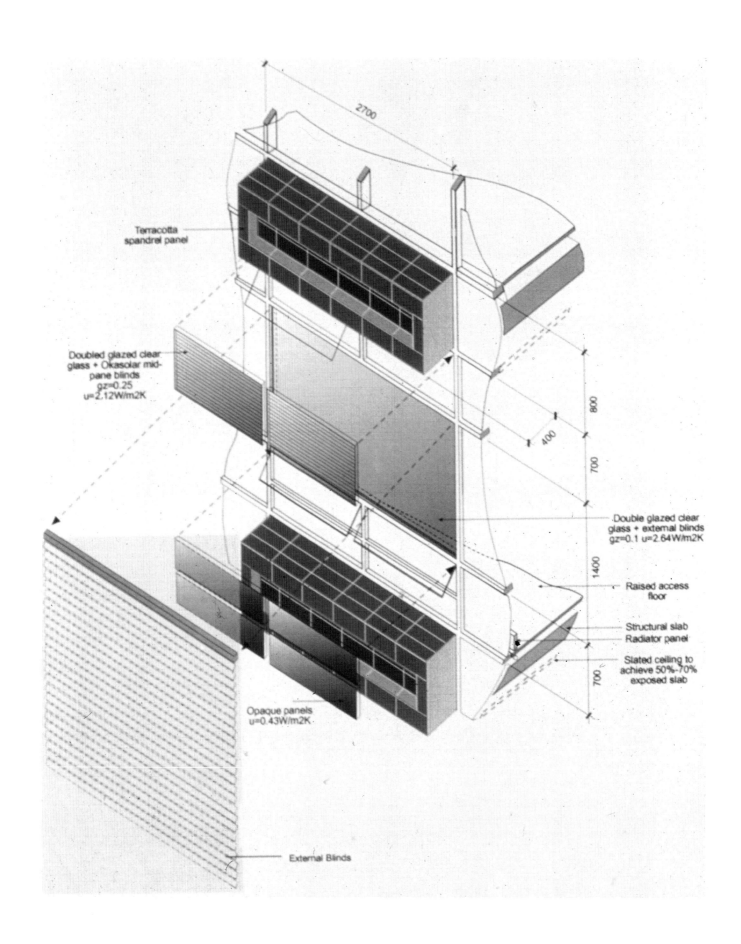

Terracotta
spandrel panel

Doubled glazed clear
glass + Okasolar mid-
pane blinds
gz=0.25
u=2.12W/m2K

2700

800

400

700

Double glazed clear
glass + external blinds
gz=0.1 u=2.64W/m2K

1400

Raised access
floor

Structural slab

Radiator panel

Slated ceiling to
achieve 50%-70%
exposed slab

700

Opaque panels
u=0.43W/m2K

External Blinds

10.3 *Facade detail, Daimler Chrysler Building, Berlin. Architects: Richard Rogers Partnership.*

10.4 *View of south-east facade of Daimler Chrysler Building, Berlin. Architects: Richard Rogers Partnership.*

A similar strategy was adopted for the atrium-facing office facades. Here, vertical external blinds are used on the upper levels where solar gain is problematic. The use of external blinds is reduced towards the lower levels while the amount of clear glass panels increases to admit more daylight.

South-east facade

This facade has conflicting criteria to reconcile, including views out over the park versus excessive solar gain and almost perpendicular incident angles due to unobstructed low-angle sun in the morning. Fins and overhangs would not be effective here. An initial thermal analysis indicated that the optimum device for this facade would be automatically controlled external retractable blinds. Overheating would be kept below 40 hours per annum. This, however, was rejected on grounds of the obscured view out, poor aesthetics and maintenance.

Further analysis examined the option of using a combination of opaque panels, mid-pane blinds, performance glass and internal blinds. The final proposal utilized performance glass with mid-pane blinds in the top and bottom panels and performance glass and internal blinds in the middle panel.

Typical facades

For the other three facades, a step-by-step analysis was used to examine the effect of opaque/translucent panels, external shading and performance glass. The three steps were:

- reducing the glazing area by using opaque and translucent glass where required: this lessened the number of hours exceeding 28°C, but was still unacceptable in many areas particularly on the upper two levels and the southern corners;
- adding vertical and horizontal external shading, daylight-controlled artificial lighting and exposed slab for night-time free cooling, which resulted in figures dropping by approximately 75%;
- replacing the external shading with performance glass; the number of hours exceeding 28°C reduced slightly, and in most cases the target could be met, apart from some areas on the top two floors where external retractable blinds will be used.

Natural ventilation in offices

In order to maintain thermal comfort in the office spaces, a more comprehensive study of the criteria as set out for the facade was undertaken. A detailed dynamic air-flow analysis was carried out for a typical externally aspected office module. This examined the viability of utilizing natural ventilation in an occupied office with still outside wind conditions for a summer scenario, using various window opening configurations. The analysis also assessed the overall natural ventilation efficiency All studies were based on motorized top-openable windows and manually-openable bottom windows.

In general, the half-bay top-openable windows are motorized and can be manually over-ridden by the occupant during the normal occupancy period. Outside this period the top windows are controlled by a Building Energy Management System. Bottom-openable windows are located on every bay.

Slatted ceiling panels expose the slab for night-time free cooling. Motorized internal blinds are located at every half bay for street-facing offices only. Atrium-facing offices have internal blinds only where external vertical blinds are not needed. Artificial lighting is controlled by a photo-electric dimming system.

Heating to the offices is provided by radiators located at the street-side perimeter There is provision for the

*10.5 View into atrium, Daimler Chrysler Building, Berlin.
Architects: Richard Rogers Partnership.*

installation of chilled ceilings and mechanical ventilation. The air-handling units, which incorporate heating and cooling coils, can be connected to riser branch valves and heat output meters if required by the future tenants.

Daylighting

The atrium

Initial analysis using CARasol confirmed that by opening up the courtyard natural lighting levels within the atrium increased. To further reinforce the concept, the opening width of the south-east atrium facade increased with height. Further analysis demonstrated that in the summer the atrium received sunlight in the morning and early afternoon, and in the winter, in the morning only.

The daylight levels within the atrium suggested that planting would be most successful towards the front entrance and centre of the space. At entrance level, daylight level is sufficiently high (approximately 10-16%DF). The ratio of minimum to maximum levels is no more than 60%, with the darkest corner furthest away from the entrance. Direct glare from sunlight is limited to the morning hours only. On the whole, the daylight quality will enhance the atrium environment creating a comfortable space for the occupants.

The offices

Initial analysis established that the office depth and urban setting would be compatible with a good use of daylight. The basic daylight targets are as follows:

- to achieve 3% daylight factor (DF) 2m from the facade;
- to minimize daylight levels dropping below 2%;
- the front half of the room should be of an illuminance no greater than 5:1 compared to the back.

Modelling further suggested that external shading would reduce DF significantly and therefore external shading would have to be retractable. As facades become more obstructed high-level glazing plays an important role and hence the top panels at lower levels are primarily of clear glass or performance glass.

Conclusion

The building form was developed according to a set of environmental criteria such as daylight usage, passive solar

Table 10.1 Daimler Chrysler Building, Berlin: main green features

---

- built form to optimize daylight, natural ventilation, solar control and views;
- ventilating facade complemented by night-time free cooling;
- use of atrium as thermal buffer and to induce natural ventilation assisted by air plenum;
- modular facade developed for solar shading with offices positioned to protect atrium from low sun;
- window configuration to maximize natural ventilation with minimum draught and good user comfort;
- facade costs 20% higher than usual (facade costs are 9% of total building cost) but help to reduce running costs by 60%; annual energy consumption predicted as 75kWh/m²;
- embodied energy and CO_2 emission 30% less than typical office building.

---

gain and natural ventilation, as well as aesthetic criteria. The design team believes that it has progressed the traditional atrium design by introducing a purpose-made air plenum zone with simple air inlets. This resulted in a near-external quality atrium with fully controllable and efficient natural ventilation.

Although the design first concentrated on the control of solar gain in summer in order to satisfy the thermal comfort criteria, components were subsequently selected to optimize the effective use of natural ventilation and daylight. Analysis of the final design indicates that annual energy consumed by the use of artificial lighting will be cut to approximately 35%, heating and cooling down to 30%, and thus CO_2 emission down to 35% when compared with a typical fully naturally ventilated office building in Berlin.

Furthermore, the embodied energy and CO_2 emission is approximately 30% less than that for a typical office building although the life cycle embodied energy is relatively high due to the choice of materials. The annual total energy consumption is approximately 75kWh/m², which is a quarter of that consumed by a typical office building. The building confirms that innovative approaches to design are essential if green buildings are to perform effectively at a personal, local and global level.

11

Leeds City Office Park

Steve Baker

Peter Foggo Associates

This office building project constructed in 1995 for British Gas Properties is, in addition to its low-energy strategy, of particular significance for three reasons. First, the building was and, at the time of writing, remains the only speculative commercial office building of this nature. Second, the building is constructed on a previously contaminated site close to Leeds city centre. Third, the mixed mode strategy for the building is a particular response to the urban location of the site and, for example, does not rely upon the opening of external windows to maintain comfort conditions within the office space.

Designed by Peter Foggo Associates, architects, engineers and quantity surveyors, the building is the first of several detached pavilions planned for the site. The brief from British Gas in 1992 was to provide 20,000m^2, subsequently increased to 50,000m^2, of B 1 quality office space available to let at market rents, plus parking for cars, all set within a landscape framework that reflected sustainable principles and dealt effectively with the land contamination.

The key elements

The linear progression of ideas from earlier buildings by Peter Foggo Associates and Arup Associates (where many members of the practice had worked together as a team for more than 25 years) to this one contains consistent elements applied en route to other projects, notably Gateway House in Basingstoke constructed in 1982. These elements are:

- building elevations that respond to climatic demands according to aspect;
- mixed mode ventilation to promote energy efficiency;
- adaptable office space;
- minimizing fossil fuel use while maximizing the use of renewables;

11.1 *Daylight curve at window with and without sunscreen, Leeds City Office Park. Architects: Peter Foggo Associates.*

11.2 *Site plan, Leeds City Office Park. Architects: Peter Foggo Associates.*

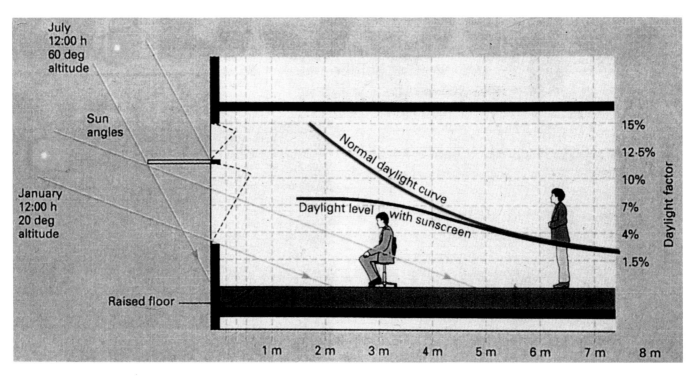

11.1

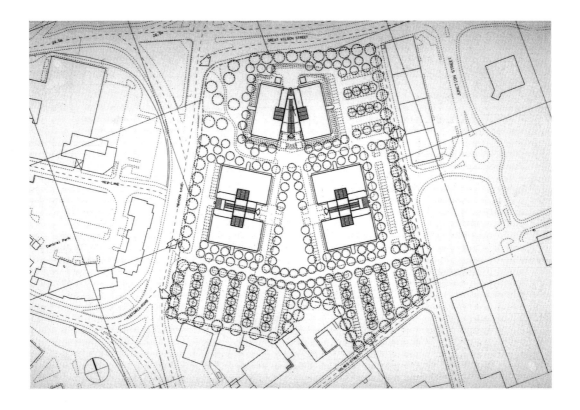

11.2

11.3 *Detail of south facade,
Leeds City Office Park. Architects:
Peter Foggo Associates.*

— structural design influenced by thermal capacity needs;
— architectonic expression of energy strategy.

Maximizing natural daylight

With the Leeds project we were keen to address artificial and natural lighting as imaginatively as possible. Since artificial lighting is the main element of bought-in energy consumption, the maximizing of daylight penetration became an early priority. With daylighting, however one problem is the differential levels between the edge and centre of the building with the tendency for lights to be left on even when working levels by daylight are adequate. When direct daylight and sunlight is allowed to enter offices at the edge of the building uncontrolled, the perception of

gloom elsewhere leads to lights being put on unnecessarily.

The answer at Leeds was to use solar shades at the perimeter of the building designed in such a way that they act as light shelves which, to a certain extent, deflect daylight back into the centre of the offices and, more importantly, reduce light levels at the perimeter. We designed the lighting shelves so that they doubled as maintenance walkways on the building facades. The use of steel and aluminium screens which combine solar shading, daylight shelves and access walkways, provides tectonic articulation of the mainly glazed facades.

Light, too, influenced the section of the building. The atrium was angled and stepped to optimize daylight penetration with materials selected for their light reflectivity The atrium structure was kept as lightweight as possible to provide little obstruction to daylight penetration. The structure here, mainly painted steel and bleached timber, contrasts with the heavyweight concrete structure employed for thermal capacity reasons in the office wings.

In the plan the two angled wings were splayed to maximize solar gain in the naturally ventilated atrium. The effect is to open the heart of the building onto the sunny landscape park to the south and to close the building where traffic noise is greatest. The three-storey office wings and the atrium have different structural solutions, which serve different energy strategies. In the offices the concrete is left exposed as a troughed soffit for night-time radiant cooling and as an internal climate modifier during the day. In the atrium the stair towers project forward to enhance the experience of moving through the building with views of the parkland. A lightweight bridge at the front of the atrium joins together the two wings and provides secondary solar screening.

The atrium is larger than one would expect in a building of this scale. It has two main functions: energy conservation and as a social gathering space. On the latter point it serves as an area for informal business gatherings, to house small exhibitions and to provide the social focus an office building needs. The trees and dappled sunlight provide the office staff with an attractive, sheltered area to eat and drink. While the atrium serves an important function in terms of sustainable design, it is perhaps the equivalent of a small city square for the people employed in the building.

The three equal floors of office space providing 6900m² gross area are bisected by a core of staircases, wcs and main service risers. It encroaches into the 15m office floorplate where least conflict with daylight and cross-

11.4 *Long and cross section,*
Leeds City Office Park. Architects:
Peter Foggo Associates.

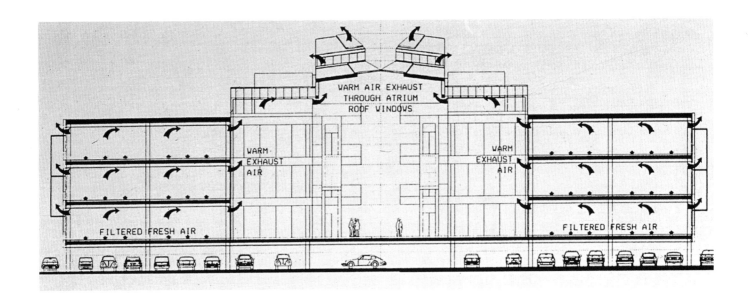

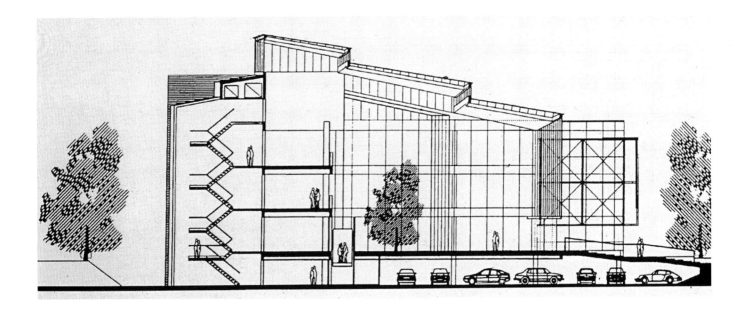

ventilation occurs. A combination of shallow floorplates, angled wings, well-positioned cores and a large roof-glazed atrium provides a minimum daylight factor of 1-2%.[1]

The building's form and elevations reflect directly the energy strategy. The stepped and rising atrium section in particular enhances the natural stack effect of solar cooling within the atrium, providing up to ten air changes an hour in the summer.[2] The high level positioning of the plant room also responds to energy needs by allowing the return ducts of the

displacement air system most effectively to vent the adjacent offices while drawing in clean air at high level. The solid to glass proportion of the atrium roof responds also to the balance between daylighting and internal comfort levels.

Central to the energy strategy is the use of heavy concrete structure left exposed as columns and troughed soffits in the office wings in order to provide radiant cooling. For economy the primary beams do not span the full depth, but are supported at their midpoint on large

11.5 *Section through typical office with workstation, Leeds City Office Park. Architects: Peter Foggo Associates.*

11.6 *Ground floor plan, Leeds City Office Park. Architects: Peter Foggo Associates.*

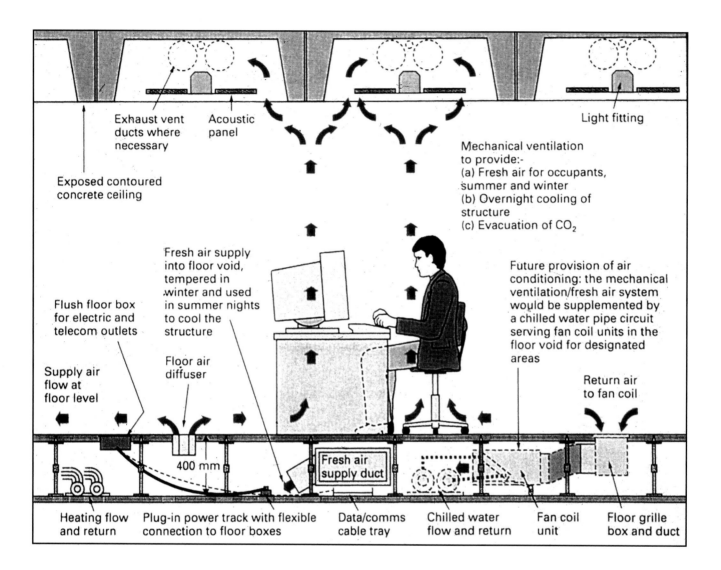

Exhaust vent ducts where necessary

Acoustic panel

Light fitting

Exposed contoured concrete ceiling

Mechanical ventilation to provide:-
(a) Fresh air for occupants, summer and winter
(b) Overnight cooling of structure
(c) Evacuation of CO_2

Fresh air supply into floor void, tempered in winter and used in summer nights to cool the structure

Flush floor box for electric and telecom outlets

Future provision of air conditioning: the mechanical ventilation/fresh air system would be supplemented by a chilled water pipe circuit serving fan coil units in the floor void for designated areas

Supply air flow at floor level

Floor air diffuser

Return air to fan coil

400 mm

Fresh air supply duct

Heating flow and return

Plug-in power track with flexible connection to floor boxes

Data/comms cable tray

Chilled water flow and return

Fan coil unit

Floor grille box and duct

round *in-situ* columns placed 7.5m from the facade. The exposed structure acts directly as a climate modifier while articulating the office areas into working bays. The exposed pre-cast ribs of the troughed soffit provide greater surface area than conventional beam and slab ceilings and hence maximize the radiant cooling effect of the structure.

Green solutions and cost restraints

The aim of creating a healthy, natural and attractive building within commercial office market cost constraints (both capital and running costs) led inevitably to specific solutions. Balances had to be struck between mixed-mode ventilation and air-

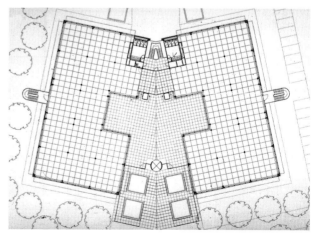

11.7 *Upper area of atrium, Leeds City Office Park. Architects: Peter Foggo Associates.*

11.8 *Open windows between atrium and office areas, Leeds City Office Park. Architects: Peter Foggo Associates.*

conditioning, between sealed and opening windows, between daylight gain and heat loss, and between high insulation levels and radiant cooling. British Gas Properties was keen that air-conditioning should not be ruled out and the design allows for subsequent upgrading if needed by tenants. However, the aim was one of encouraging green design within and, to a certain extent, beyond the limits of market preconceptions.

With openable windows arranged as three pairs per structural bay, a heat exchanger to pre-heat the incoming fresh air in winter, and large openings in the atrium roof to create a chimney for summer-time cooling, the building combines energy conservation with the provision of healthy working conditions. The building has a night vent system which blows air through the offices increasing the daytime air-change rate from 2.2 to 5.0 per hour.[3] Linked to a Building Management System (BMS) the arrangement ensures that the atrium roof windows are open when the night vent system is operating and that the fresh-air fans do not operate until the following afternoon in order to conserve cooling. Sophisticated modelling of the building by Halcrow Gilbert indicates that even in hot weather internal temperatures only exceed 25°C for a few hours a year.[4]

Predictions indicate that energy consumption will be about 30% of a comparable air-conditioned office building. In 1993 the design was awarded a BREEAM rating of excellent and received the highest score ever given at the time for office design. It will be monitored under the European Union's Thermie Programme (part of the Energy

11.9 *Detail of facade, Leeds
City Office Park. Architects: Peter
Foggo Associates.*

11.9 *Detail of facade, Leeds City Office Park. Architects: Peter Foggo Associates.*

Table 11.1 Savings in capital and running costs

Leeds City Office Park	Standard air-conditioned office
– shallow floorplate – opening windows – exposed concrete structure – displacement ventilation system – lighting control system linked to BMS – supplementary night-time ventilation – large wedge-shaped atrium – solar shading/daylight shelves	– deep floorplate – mechanical cooling – sealed envelope – large plant spaces
95% cost	100% cost

Savings in running cost

30%	100%

Comfort 2000 project involving eight other European buildings). Detailed monitoring suggests that solar energy provides 48% of the heat gains (68% in the cellular offices) making total gains of $75kW/m^2$. To ensure conditions remain acceptable in the offices, internal blinds under occupier control are needed on certain windows.[5] These would prevent excess solar gain and glare especially where direct sunlight enters offices via the atrium.

Conclusion

What is most significant is that the 70% saving in fuel bills has been achieved in a building slightly cheaper in capital cost terms than the norm for full air-conditioned offices.[6] The window element – an all-glass, structurally glazed cladding system developed specifically for the building – cost 20% more than conventional cladding. However, the raised floor needed to house the fan coils for the recirculated air did not add greatly to the building cost. The additional facade and structural costs were offset by savings in building plant needed for air-conditioning. The lean and healthy Leeds City Office Park shows that low-energy design can be both cost effective and architecturally distinguished.

Table 11.2 Leeds City Office Park: main green features

- large stepped atrium to enhance stack effect ventilation;
- differential thermal capacity between offices and atrium to support energy conservation;
- use of natural materials;
- holistic approach to building design and landscape design;
- shallow floorplate and facade glazing to optimize daylight use;
- integral solar screens, daylight shelves and maintenance walkways on glazed facades;
- use of timber finishes from sustainable forest sources;
- reuse of contaminated inner-city site;
- service areas placed as acoustic screens towards busy perimeter roads;
- simple to operate and understand building management system.

11.10 *Entrance, Leeds City Office Park. Architects: Peter Foggo Associates.*

We approached the development from a holistic point of view. The design combines energy, environmental and ecological thinking both in the building and landscape elements. The close planting of trees to the facades, for instance, provides summertime solar screening as well as improving the air quality entering the building. Shade and natural scents from tree blossom outside complements the heavily planted atrium inside. Similarly, the lake formed as part of the landscape park is designed for wildlife as well as amenity. Reeds and grass areas help to create a natural habitat where formerly there was contaminated industrial land.

References

1. *The Architects' Journal*, 12 October 1995, p. 37.
2. Ibid, p. 39.
3. Ibid, p.40.
4. Building Services: *The CIBSE Journal*, November 1995, p.45.
5. Ibid.
6. Ibid, p. 24.

12

The Environmental Building: The Building Research Establishment, Watford

William Gething

Feilden Clegg Bradley Architects

The Building Research Establishment (BRE) has long been a champion of energy-efficient design and has in the past put theory to the test in its own buildings. The Low Energy Office, built in 1982 by the then Property Services Agency showed what was possible at that time to reduce energy consumption to a level that set an extremely challenging target which remains creditable today: 120kWh/m²/ annum.

More recently these concerns have focused in the Energy Efficient Office of the Future (EOF) Project, a partnership between BRE and industry to 'identify new technologies and refinements in existing practice required to meet energy and environmental targets that will be in place in the early part of the next century, while satisfying the demands of owners and occupants'.

Demonstrating the potential of low-energy design

In 1995, the EOF Group produced a draft brief for office buildings, now published under the Best Practice Programme, which it sought to be tested in a series of real projects in a number of different types of location with a view to demonstrating the potential of low-energy environmental design to developers and building specifiers as an alternative to deep-plan, artificially-lit, air-conditioned building types.

At the time BRE was in the process of consolidating its estates by moving the Fire Research Station from Borehamwood to temporary accommodation at Garston pending the redevelopment of workshops at the centre of the site. This was seen as a prime opportunity to test the low-energy brief at Garston in what equated to a fairly typical business park setting with the further benefit of ongoing research and monitoring potential on the doorstep.

The Environmental Building, The Building Research Establishment, Watford

12.2 *South elevation,*
The Environmental Building,
BRE, Garston. Architects:
Feilden Clegg Bradley.

12.3 *Ground floor plan,*
The Environmental Building,
BRE, Garston. Architects:
Feilden Clegg Bradley.

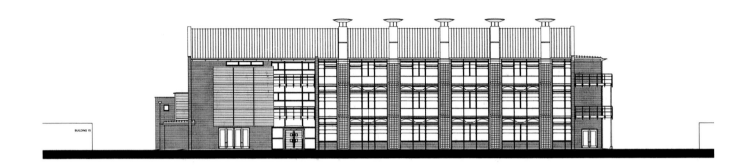

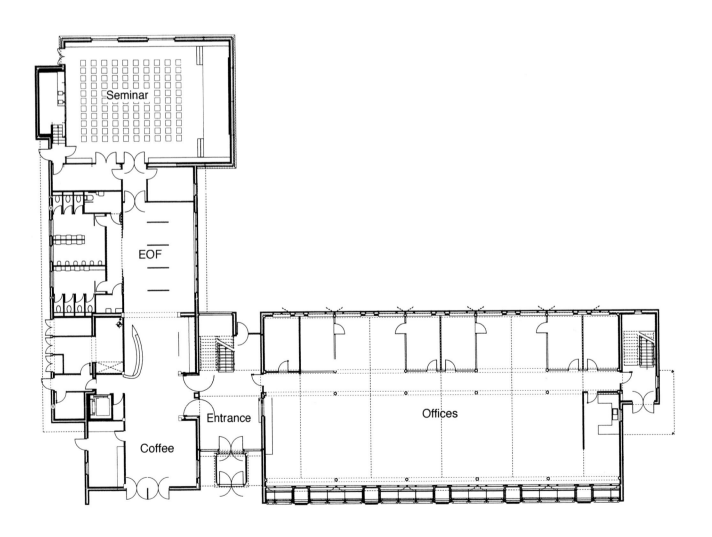

BRE appointed BWA Project Services to manage The Environmental Building project and set up a selection process that resulted in the appointment of a design team lead by Feilden Clegg Bradley Architects with Max Fordham and Partners as environmental consultants and Buro Happold as structural engineers. The building that has resulted is a genuinely collaborative effort – all consultants were involved from the earliest stages and were joined by the main contractor John Sisk and Sons, during the production information stage, adding their construction expertise as part of a two-stage appointment using the NEC form of contract.

The brief

Intentionally open ended, the brief simply called for low-energy office space for 100 people that would be flexible and functional, and capable of providing both open plan and cellular spaces. This was to be coupled with high-quality seminar facilities to complement existing provision on campus. The Environmental Building was to be of a high architectural standard and was required to integrate an environmentally friendly approach with energy performance substantially better than existing designs (80kWh/m²/ annum). It was required to obtain an 'Excellent' BREEAM rating and to avoid the use of air-conditioning.

The site of the original workshop buildings, which had been partially destroyed by fire, was at the core of the campus, close to seminar, lecture and meeting spaces in the original Mansion building, the Library Building and the previous Low Energy Office, and near to the campus social facilities. To the south was a car park, which was included in the site. A variety of building positions and configurations were explored. The final layout is an L-shaped building with a three-storey wing fronting a landscaped, car-free area to the south with a new parking area for 70 cars to the north.

The quiet pedestrian area formed provides a usable landscaped setting for both the new building and the other nearby 'public' buildings, and reduces noise and pollution on the predominantly windward side of the new building. The building itself is simply arranged with offices on three floors facing north/south separated from a stack of seminar spaces to the west by a glazed stair and entrance space. On the ground floor, a single-storey wing extends to the north to house a seminar space for 100 people, and exhibition and reception areas.

Ventilation

The relatively shallow office plan (13.5m) with fairly highly glazed facades exploits natural daylight and is well suited to cross ventilation through BMS (Building Management System) controlled windows at high level with manually openable windows at lower level. Occupants will be able to override automatic control of all aspects of their environment – a most important issue for any building, and one which a naturally ventilated building should be able to address more effectively than a sealed box. Cross ventilation is a natural choice for open-plan arrangements, but a degree of ingenuity is required to deal satisfactorily with cellular offices that normally interrupt a simple cross building air path. The approach taken here was to split the plan asymmetrically into a 4.5m deep zone on the north side of the building, better suited to cellular offices with single-sided ventilation, a circulation zone 1.8m wide, and a 7.5m deep zone on the south side best suited to open-plan workspace.

The wave floor

The southern zone was too deep for the given comfort criteria to be met by single-sided ventilation. To maintain cross ventilation of this area while avoiding acoustic problems between offices, a wave-form floor slab design was developed to incorporate ventilation routes that pass over the ceilings of cellular spaces. The high points of the wave have corresponding high level windows and daylight can thus penetrate deep into the plan. At the low points, large ducts are formed within the overall floor depth by bridging across the tops of the wave with precast concrete planks. Fire separation between storeys is at plank level so the ducts form part of the lower floor.

The wave-form floor structure is interrupted by the circulation zone which has a thin slab at the level of the planks over the floor ducts. This forms a crossover zone for air from the occupied spaces to pass into the ducts in the floor structure. The high level windows are at the same level as the floor zone and are arranged to coincide with the undulations in the slab to ventilate the ducts in the low points and the occupied spaces at the high points. The combination allows a number of possible air paths to suit a variety of planning arrangements and wind conditions. Air can pass, say, through the open-plan area, into the corridor

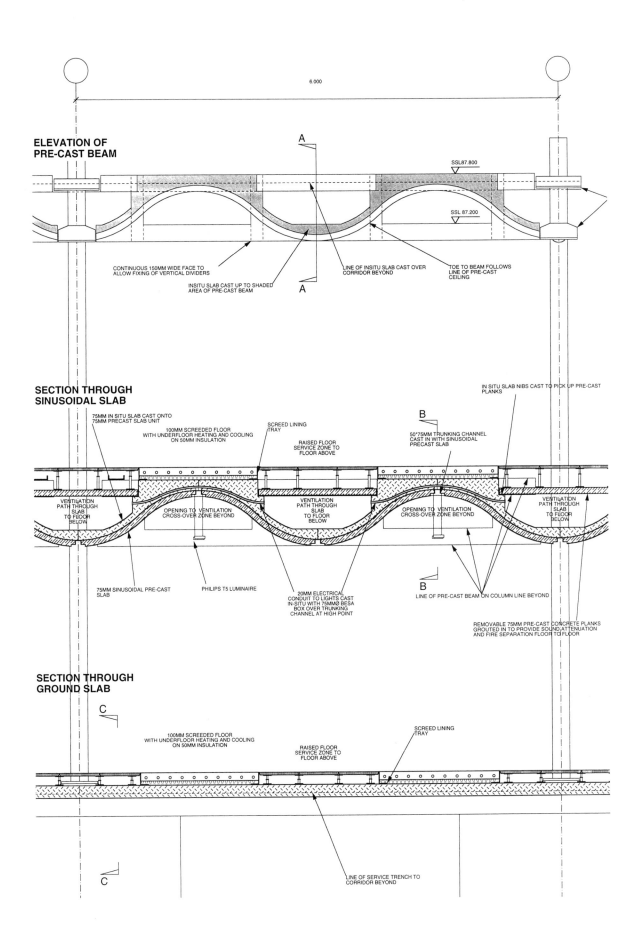

6.000

ELEVATION OF PRE-CAST BEAM

A

SSL87.800

SSL 87.200

CONTINUOUS 150MM WIDE FACE TO
ALLOW FIXING OF VERTICAL DIVIDERS

LINE OF INSITU SLAB CAST OVER
CORRIDOR BEYOND

TOE TO BEAM FOLLOWS
LINE OF PRE-CAST
CEILING

INSITU SLAB CAST UP TO SHADED
AREA OF PRE-CAST BEAM

A

SECTION THROUGH
SINUSOIDAL SLAB

IN SITU SLAB NIBS CAST TO PICK UP PRE-CAST
PLANKS

75MM IN SITU SLAB CAST ONTO
75MM PRECAST SLAB UNIT

100MM SCREEDED FLOOR
WITH UNDERFLOOR HEATING AND COOLING
ON 50MM INSULATION

SCREED LINING
TRAY

RAISED FLOOR
SERVICE ZONE TO
FLOOR ABOVE

B

50*75MM TRUNKING CHANNEL
CAST IN WITH SINUSOIDAL
PRECAST SLAB

VENTILATION
PATH THROUGH
SLAB
TO FLOOR
BELOW

OPENING TO VENTILATION
CROSS-OVER ZONE BEYOND

VENTILATION
PATH THROUGH
SLAB
TO FLOOR
BELOW

OPENING TO VENTILATION
CROSS-OVER ZONE BEYOND

VENTILATION
PATH THROUGH
SLAB
TO FLOOR
BELOW

75MM SINUSOIDAL PRE-CAST
SLAB

PHILIPS T5 LUMINAIRE

20MM ELECTRICAL
CONDUIT TO LIGHTS CAST
IN-SITU WITH 75MMØ BESA
BOX OVER TRUNKING
CHANNEL AT HIGH POINT

B

LINE OF PRE-CAST BEAM ON COLUMN LINE BEYOND

REMOVABLE 75MM PRE-CAST CONCRETE PLANKS
GROUTED IN TO PROVIDE SOUND ATTENUATION
AND FIRE SEPARATION FLOOR TO FLOOR

SECTION THROUGH
GROUND SLAB

C

100MM SCREEDED FLOOR
WITH UNDERFLOOR HEATING AND COOLING
ON 50MM INSULATION

RAISED FLOOR
SERVICE ZONE TO
FLOOR ABOVE

SCREED LINING
TRAY

C

LINE OF SERVICE TRENCH TO
CORRIDOR BEYOND

106

Top: Mistral Building, Reading.
Architects: Foster and Partners.

Bottom: EDF Headquarters, Bordeaux.
Architects: Foster and Partners.

Below, both views: Millennium Village Primary School.
Architect: Edward Cullinan and Partners

Below: Elizabeth Fry Building, University of East Anglia.
Architects: John Miller and Partners

Right : Greater London Authority Building.
Architects: Norman Foster and Partners,London.

12.4 *Detail of wave floor, The Environmental Building, BRE, Garston. Architects: Feilden Clegg Bradley.*

12.5 *Section through ventilation stack, The Environmental Building, BRE, Garston. Architects: Feilden Clegg Bradley.*

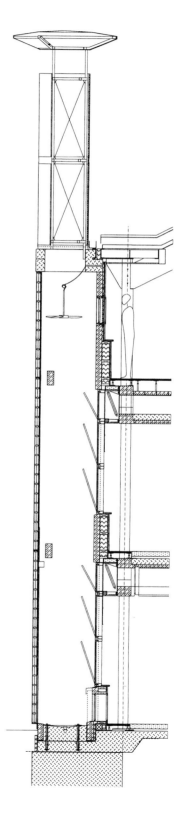

zone and then into the ducts in the floor structure over a cellular office. Similarly, night-time cooling can be provided by opening high level windows on both sides of the building to allow air to pass directly through the floor ducts and/or across the office spaces or a combination of the two.

The wave form increases the spanning capacity of the slab, provides a beautiful ceiling to the office areas, and also increases the exposed surface of concrete and, therefore, available thermal mass for cooling. This is effectively further increased as, thanks to the ducts within the structure, both sides of the slab and the inner faces of the ducts are available to help to reduce peak temperatures. The floor spans between integral lattice beams at column lines, which allow partitions to be positioned against flat soffits.

While the design team was confident that the EOF brief could be met without the need for additional cooling, the opportunity was taken to test a further step of elaboration of the floor structure. The floors are divided into 1.5m strips of raised access floor, for flexible servicing, alternating with screeded areas which incorporate pipework that can be used for heating in winter (in combination with radiators for quick response) and cooling in summer. The cooling source is a new 70m deep bore hole into the chalk below BRE supplying water at approximately 12°C which is passed through a heat exchanger and returned to a second bore hole 20m deep. It is anticipated that this will reduce peak temperatures in the offices by about 2°C and the source is also used for the main seminar space where cooling in addition to ventilation was needed to meet comfort criteria.

Ventilation stacks

A building that uses cross ventilation as its principal ventilation strategy requires alternative measures to deal with hot, still summer conditions. The approach taken here was to incorporate ventilation stacks on the south facade of the building connected to the lower two floors. The stacks are positioned to draw air through the ducts in the floor structure, but there is also a gap between the south facade and the wave form slab that allows the stacks to drain off hot air from adjacent high points in the office spaces.

Stack performance has been investigated by Cambridge Environmental Research using a Salt Bath model. This indicates that, under hot, still conditions, air will enter the build-

12.6 *Section through glazed facade showing Colt International motorized glass louvres, The Environmental Building, Garston. Architects: Feilden Clegg Bradley.*

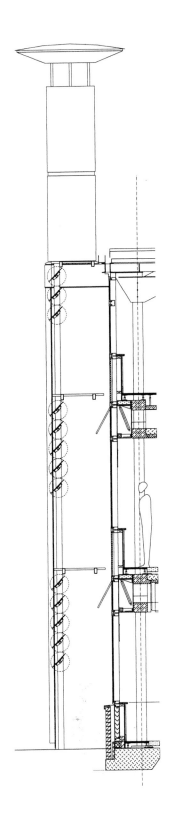

ing through high level windows into the cool slab ducts and drop into the centre of the plan, pass through the office spaces and exhaust via the stacks. To maximize their usefulness, the tops of the stacks are positioned clear of ridge and eaves eddy zones. They contain low resistance propeller fans (80W each) mounted at top-floor level. This gives them a predictable minimum performance if required and also means that they can be used for other ventilation scenarios such as to pull air through the floor ducts and across the office spaces on still nights.

The stacks are glazed using etched glass blocks, offering the opportunity for BRE to investigate whether there is a useful solar contribution to the stack effect here. The interior vents into the stacks are bottom-hung windows, also glazed with etched glass, allowing daylight to be admitted through the stacks themselves to contribute to the natural lighting of the office area. The stacks also fulfil a variety of functions in addition to ventilating the lower two floors in hot, still conditions:

–   they provide shading against low-angle oblique sun from east and west;
–   they provide a support structure for horizontal grilles at each floor level, which double as shading devices and as maintenance/cleaning access to windows and their motors;
–   they provide a support structure for active external shading systems described below.

The top floor of the building differs from the lower levels to exploit the possibilities of daylighting and ventilation through the roof. As there was no requirement for the ceiling at this level to be constructed from non-combustible materials, a timber roof structure was adopted. The section is stepped along the line of the circulation zone with the south-facing roof rising to provide clerestorey light and cross ventilation over the northern cellular office zone. The stacks are not tall enough to provide additional useful ventilation to this level in still conditions, but the loftier section here generates its own stack effect. The roof is constructed using 75mm thick softwood structural decking spanning between purlins, which in turn bear on principals supported on steel columns. The combination of the thick decking with 200mm of mineral fibre insulation above is predicted to give adequate performance in terms of thermal mass and insulation.

Lighting and energy demand

Substantially glazed facades in combination with high ceilings and a relatively shallow plan depth mean that the need for artificial lighting and the consequent electrical load will be significantly reduced as compared with a conventional office building. However, as a corollary, the need to control glare and solar gain becomes correspondingly more important. In The Environmental Building these factors are controlled by using BMS-controlled external motorized glass louvres manufactured by Colt International, one of the EOF participating companies, used here for the first time in this country. These are 400mm wide, set about 1.2m from the facade and with the lowest blade on each floor at 1700mm above floor level. They are extremely slim when rotated to their horizontal position (10mm) but, being wide, are set well apart so that a reasonable view can be maintained when they are not required for shading. It is also possible to rotate the blades beyond the horizontal to a position where they can act as adjustable light shelves to reflect direct sunlight onto the ceiling deep into the office. Unlike fixed horizontal light shelves, they will have a minimal impact on the diffuse light from an overcast sky entering the building.

Initially the intention had been to use fritted glass for the louvres to control solar gain while still allowing a good view out even when the blades were fully closed. Glare was to be dealt with separately by internal blinds. However, following input from BRE's daylighting research department and experimental work by the University of Westminster as part of a European Union Thermie grant, it was decided to try to deal with both aspects as far as possible by using 'fully fritted', i.e. translucent external glass louvres. The louvres are controlled by the BMS, but occupiers can override the automatic setting as they wish. The BMS will eventually reset them to an optimum position to avoid the common situation in which glare is controlled primarily by internal blinds, which, once drawn, tend to be left down and artificial lighting used more than necessary.

Control of daylight is mirrored in the careful regulation of artificial lighting (and thus a significant part of the building's electrical load) using the new high-efficiency T5 fluorescent lamps by Philips Electrical, another EOF Group member, linked to presence and light sensors, but with occupier override using infrared controllers. They provide general lighting at around 300 lux, which is supplemented by task lighting where and when required, and have an uplighting component to wash the wave-form ceiling to provide a balanced visual environment. Each of the lamps is separately addressable by the BMS to allow different light output levels to be assigned across the floor plan and thus take maximum advantage of daylight.

Electrical loads are further reduced by the incorporation of a bank of 50m^2 of thin film amorphous silicon photovoltaic cells on the south facade with a peak output of 3kW. The sloping south-facing roof of the building is designed to provide a surface for a further PV installation.

Recycling

While energy efficiency aspects of the project formed a major focus, the environmental aspects of the materials used to construct the building, and particularly the use of recycled materials, were also considered in some detail. The redundant buildings on the site were cleared with a view to maximum recycling. This was monitored by BRE which has estimated that 95% by weight was recycled, for example:

- brick and concrete was crushed on site and used as hardcore;
- roofing timber was sold to a company making pine furniture from recycled material;
- electrical fittings were given to local schools.

Reuse of bricks from the workshops on the site was considered, but these had been laid in cement mortar and were not reclaimable. Even if this had been practicable, the process would have only yielded a small proportion of the total quantity required. A potential local source of bricks for the entire external skin was identified as work started on site (a nearby hospital awaiting demolition), however, at the last minute there was a hold up with the start of that project and second-hand bricks were sourced from a reclaimed building materials company near Cambridge. The process served to highlight both the possibilities of using large quantities of recycled brick and the drawbacks (cost, guarantee of supply and brick size, etc.).

12.7 *Translucent glass louvres in operation, The Environmental Building, BRE, Garston. Architects: Feilden Clegg Bradley.*

12.8 *Elevation and part section of one bay of south facade, The Environmental Building, BRE, Garston. Architects: Feilden Clegg Bradley.*

In The Environmental Building lime mortar was used for the internal cross walls of the entrance area (which do not take wind loading) to enable the bricks to be reclaimed once again. Valuable lessons were learnt for future projects on the structural consequences of using lime mortar.

Crushed concrete from a demolished concrete panel system building in London was used as concrete aggregate for the foundations, ground slab and much of the *in-situ* superstructure – another first in the UK. Again lessons were learnt on aspects of mix design, structural design liability, procurement (identifying potential sources, testing and stockpiling crushed material) and costs associated with using recycled aggregates.

Internally in the reception and exhibition areas, wood-block flooring was reused from County Hall in London, a concurrent John Sisk building contract. Gyproc screeds, based on gypsum from power station waste, were used throughout the building.

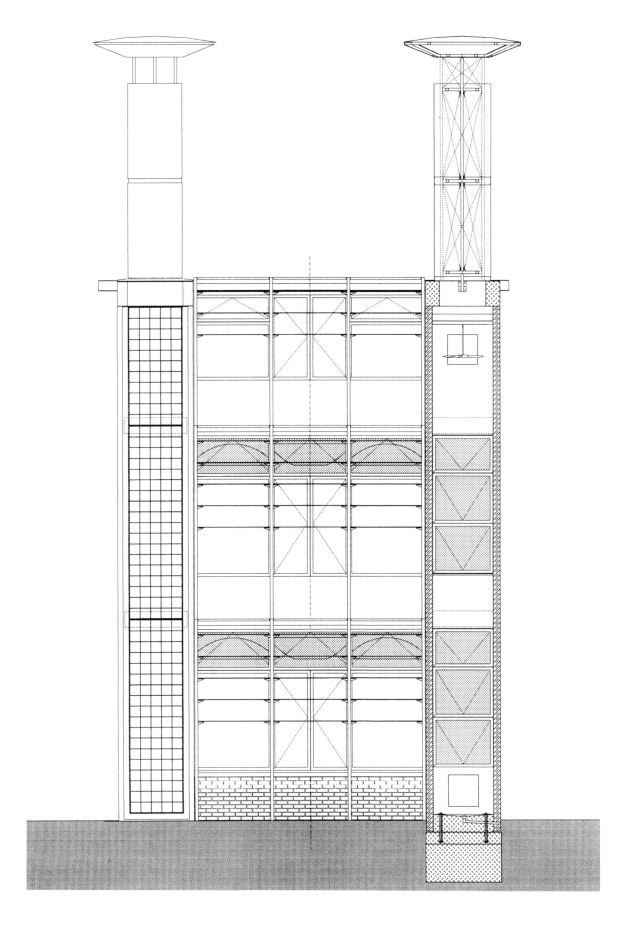

12.9 *Section through office area showing integration of structure, ventilation and lighting, The Environmental Building, BRE, Garston. Architects: Feilden Clegg Bradley.*

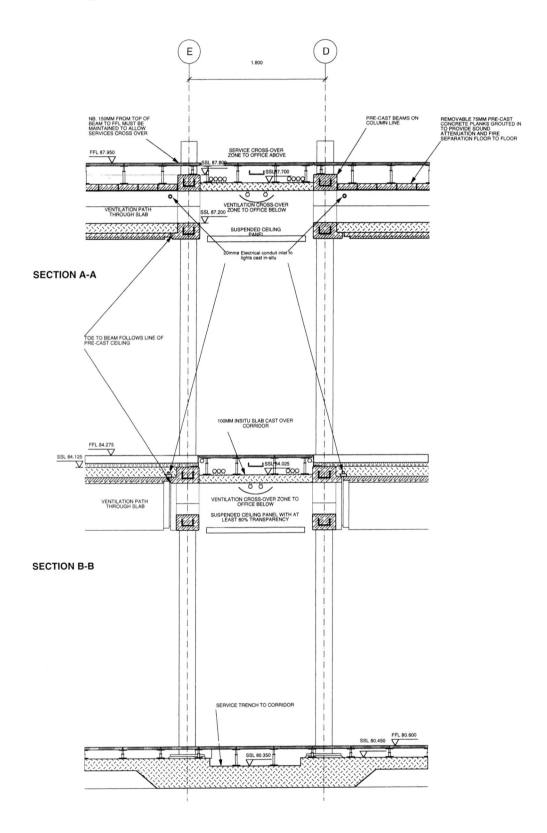

E   1.800   D

NB. 150MM FROM TOP OF BEAM TO FFL MUST BE MAINTAINED TO ALLOW SERVICES CROSS OVER

FFL 87.950

SSL 87.800

SSL 87.700

SERVICE CROSS-OVER ZONE TO OFFICE ABOVE

PRE-CAST BEAMS ON COLUMN LINE

REMOVABLE 75MM PRE-CAST CONCRETE PLANKS GROUTED IN TO PROVIDE SOUND ATTENUATION AND FIRE SEPARATION FLOOR TO FLOOR

VENTILATION PATH THROUGH SLAB

SSL 87.200

VENTILATION CROSS-OVER ZONE TO OFFICE BELOW

SUSPENDED CEILING PANEL

20mmø Electrical conduit inlet to lights cast in-situ

SECTION A-A

TOE TO BEAM FOLLOWS LINE OF PRE-CAST CEILING

100MM INSITU SLAB CAST OVER CORRIDOR

FFL 84.275

SSL 84.125

SSL 84.025

VENTILATION PATH THROUGH SLAB

VENTILATION CROSS-OVER ZONE TO OFFICE BELOW

SUSPENDED CEILING PANEL WITH AT LEAST 60% TRANSPARENCY

SECTION B-B

SERVICE TRENCH TO CORRIDOR

SSL 80.350

FFL 80.600

SSL 80.450

Conclusion

Left: Wessex Water HQ, Bath.
Architects: Bennetts Associates.

12.10 South facade of The
Environmental Building, BRE, Garston.
Architects: Feilden Clegg Bradley.

Table 12.1 The Environmental Building: main green features

- wave form, double ventilating floors;
- facade ventilation stacks using glass blocks;
- orientation and building planning to reduce solar gain;
- highly-glazed facades to maximize daylight penetration;
- manually openable windows with external motorized louvres;
- combined external shading devices and maintenance decks;
- lighting linked to sensors;
- use of recycled construction materials;
- photovoltaic electrical generation.

Architectural form

The building is undoubtedly unique, a strong architectural statement at the heart of BRE, but is founded on sound, widely applicable principles of environmental design that can be taken on by commercial developers. It optimizes natural ventilation, exploits daylighting, controls glare while still allowing a view out and, very importantly, allows occupants a high degree of control of all aspects of their environment. It incorporates a range of approaches to environmental control, the active south facade being the most evident, which have sufficient flexibility built into them to provide a fertile source of research projects for BRE for a number of years. Once in use it will be extensively monitored by both BRE and the University of Westminster, as part of the EU Thermie grant, which also covers the dissemination of the findings.

Conclusion

The Environmental Building seeks to demonstrate that responsible environmental design is a wider issue than simply hitting lower and lower energy consumption targets. In particular, it starts to illustrate the possibilities and difficulties

of using recycled materials for a reasonable size commercial building and, in doing so, poses some interesting questions for clients, designers and the construction industry as a whole.

Energy consumption is easily measurable and thus the quest for ever lower energy consumption will continue with the probability that buildings may shortly be required to be net energy producers. However, the law of diminishing returns has already started to take effect. Energy is still so cheap that any savings in energy costs, as a proportion of total business turnover, are often so small as to be insignificant. On the other hand, as a result of much publicized research into the negative effects of a poor environment, the commercial world is starting to accept that the working environment has a marked effect on the performance of the people working in it.

We believe that future green buildings will be based on principles that fundamentally address many of the issues that have come to light from this research. They will offer good working environments in which people are able to work to the best of their ability, and have the added bonus of low energy consumption. What better demonstration that green buildings do, indeed, pay?

13

13.1 *Site plan of Barclaycard Headquarters, Northampton. Notice the lake to the north (left) and tree planting for solar shade to the south (right). Architects: Fitzroy Robinson.*

Barclaycard Headquarters, Northampton

Brian Edwards

ECA, Heriot-Watt University

The Barclaycard Headquarters at Northampton designed by Fitzroy Robinson and Partners in 1996 confirms the emergence of a distinctive morphology for 'green' office buildings in the UK.[1] The formal elements consist of long narrow office blocks orientated east–west, shallow floorplates, a central spine of atria or glazed streets which serve as environmental and social spaces, and mixed-mode ventilation supported by air-conditioning in 'hot spots'. The pedigree extends back to the Gateway 2 building at Basingstoke by Arup Associates and embraces among others the PowerGen Headquarters in Coventry by Bennetts Associates and the government's Scottish Office building in Leith by RMJM. All these buildings share common green characteristics at a planning and constructional level.

The Barclaycard building's contribution to the oeuvre is as much architectural as technological. Fitzroy Robinson have explored the aesthetic and spatial opportunities afforded by green offices, concentrating upon traditional architectural elements such as the facade, processional routes, public spaces and the landscape framework. Rather than adopting an overtly high-tech language, the architects have sought a heavier, almost Louis Kahn-like, treatment of weighty constructional elements. Hence to enter the building the visitor passes through a layered facade and into light-filled internal spaces. Solid and transparent materials communicate an effective dialogue between the engineering and aesthetics of the building, creating in the process an attractive and responsive working environment.

Much of the formal language and technological dialogue results from the orientation of the building. The decision to have a long south-facing facade, extending to 260m, with a corresponding facade to the north, has profound implications for solar shading and daylight penetration. The south elevation

13.2 *Plan of Barclaycard Headquarters. Architects: Fitzroy Robinson.*

13.3 *Section through mall, Barclaycard Headquarters. Architects: Fitzroy Robinson.*

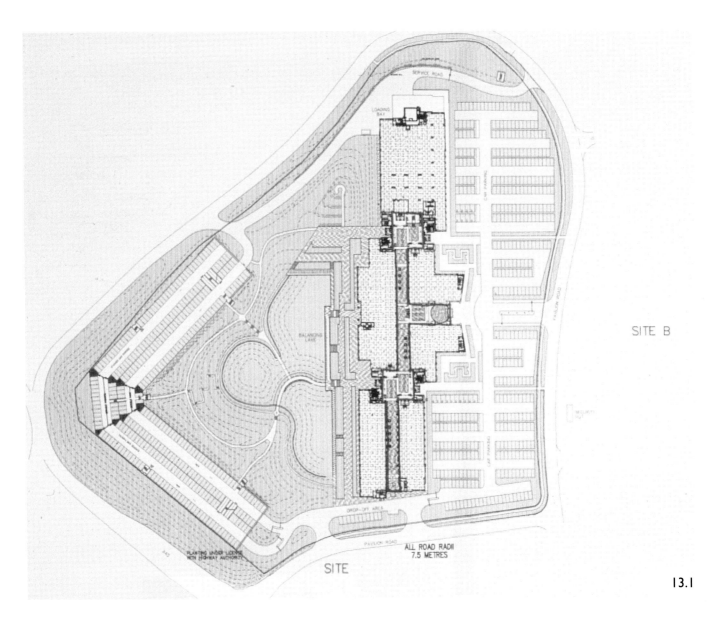

13.1

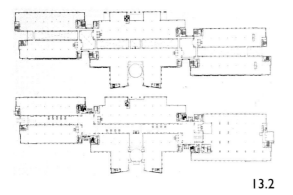

13.2

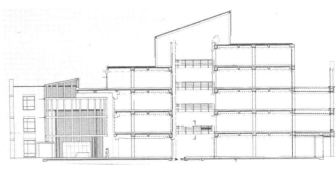

13.3

13.4 *Details of facade*
facing south
a *entrance,* **b** *corner.*
Architect: B. Edwards

a

b

(which is also the main entrance facade) consists of solid veneers of masonry construction and solar protection. Space and light are taken through and between the facade elements in a controlled manner. The solidity of the south elevation is highlighted by the deeply set windows and the separate structural articulation of the two walls. Added to this, sunlight dances off the *brise-soleil*, creating dark shadows across the pre-cast concrete walls in a fashion rarely achieved with lightweight construction.

This building (like Five Brindley Place, Birmingham – see chapter 6) is a counter-point to the well-developed language for the lightweight energy-efficient office. The buildings of Foster, Rogers, Arup Associates and Foggo have refined the glazed perimeter wall to the point where development has practically ceased. The challenge today is

to perfect the responsive solid facade, where solar protection has to be combined with high levels of daylight penetration and external view. The solution adopted at Barclaycard was to look closely at the balance between window and wall area, and to address the technical performance of windows, varying their design according to the needs of daylight, ventilation, user control and solar screening. The result is a series of complex façades, responding as much to the requirements of building physics as to conventional notions of architectural composition and each adjusted according to orientation.

Constructed in 1997, the Barclaycard Headquarters was at the time the largest example in the UK of a mixed-mode building pre-let to a private sector company. The technology is innovative in several areas though the design

13.5 *View along the mall, Barclaycard Headquarters. Architects: Fitzroy Robinson.*

13.6 *View towards the roof of the mall. Notice the animation of the space by sunlight and shadows. Architects: Fitzroy Robinson.*

does not posture its high-tech credentials. Technically much is done without cost or maintenance burdens. The use on the south side, (where solar gain is usually a problem for non-air-conditioned offices) of small windows set deeply into the facade cladding, combined with overhangs and horizontal louvres, reduces the need for more elaborate controls. The windows are aluminium framed with clear double-glazing, large manually operated canopies and fanlights activated by the building management system. Tubes passing through the lintels (5,000mm^2 per metre of facade) provide trickle ventilation.[2]

The soffits of the concrete T-beam floors are left exposed to absorb heat and provide night-time cooling. Attached to alternate rows of these are ceiling-mounted chiller units which provide cooled air via a heat exchanger exploiting greywater extracted from a nearby lake. This is fed by rainwater taken from the roof and surrounding park land. This system of structure, construction and integrated fabric cooling is taken to roof level to avoid the overheating of offices which frequently occurs when such buildings employ lightweight roofs on the upper floor[3]. Internal concrete columns and soffits are also exposed to provide further accessible thermal capacity.

The two parallel banks of offices 15m deep are divided by a glazed mall or internal street which is 9m wide and heated by under-floor coils. Besides the obvious amenity function of the central street, it is an essential element of the energy strategy. Warm air (and smoke in the event of a fire) is taken through this space and vented via angled glazed outlets which have motorized windows. Each wing of offices (there are six in total arranged as three parallel pairs) is treated as a single fire compartment, with sprinklers incorporated into the chilled ceilings.[4]

Because of the extent of accidental heat gains (people, equipment and solar) the designed heat load was only 115KW/m^{2}y, allowing the design to be awarded an excellent BREEAM rating. This was achieved at a construction cost of only £760/m^2 (or £1100/m^2 if the multi-storey car park, lake and landscaping are included). Glare, which is a problem with modern computer-intensive green offices, is carefully controlled by a combination of external blinds, louvres and large internal awnings. Barclaycard is a client which normally occupies fully air-conditioned office space and it placed a requirement on the design team that internal temperatures

13.7 a and b *Fitzroy Robinson's design for the British Energy Building, Gloucester, develops the ideas found at Barclaycard. The lineage of thought allows projects to build upon the experience of predecessors.*

a

should not exceed 25°C (as against 27°C which is more common with green offices). As a consequence there is more mechanical back-up than one would expect, such as a series of concealed ducts in the walls and floors able to achieve three air changes per hour on still hot days.

Lighting is carefully considered. Window design and floorplate depth maximize daylight penetration; blinds and external tree planting further modify conditions to ensure effective light penetration without direct sunlight, glare or reflection on the computer screen. Intelligent luminaries are also employed. The design has led to a significant reduction in electricity usage over comparable offices, although according to a Probe report effective energy and personnel management is required to sustain the improvements.[5]

Modernist orthodoxy destroyed the street as a civilizing urban event: buildings became ends in themselves, sculptural objects in free space. Recently, as buildings have become even larger, the streets and squares have reappeared but now as an

internal element. Big buildings reach the point where they are problems not of architecture alone but of urban design; as Rem Koolhaas has pointed out, really large buildings are primarily exercises in city-making. Here at Barclaycard, with its working population of 2,600, the building is based on an urban typology of streets, blocks and squares – the internal mall taking the place of the urban street, the atrium of the square, and the internal planting the gardens. The advantages are obvious in terms of user navigation through complex spaces, social interaction and the kind of functional-cum-territorial definition which big companies believe helps build team-working. The precedent, of course, is Niels Torp's SAS Building in Stockholm which, with its white lofty sunlit malls, helped give the internal street iconographic status, whilst helping to forge social exchange.

Underpinning the spatial and formal interactions at Barclaycard is a correspondence with energy conservation and its management. The mixed-mode ventilation system depends

upon differences in air pressure which varying degrees of permeability, in both plan and section, create. The office accommodation is provided on a 15m floorplate, enabling air to find its own way around the building. This discipline helps generate the form of the building at both a fundamental and detailed level. The spatial distribution of the office blocks, the layout of the chilled beam ceilings, and the pattern and size of windows all mirror functional and environmental need.

The six main blocks of offices in the building ventilate both to the outside and to the internal street. They are conceived as solid volumes of accommodation surrounded by space and light. Tall, deeply set windows with an urban verticality flank each block. Periodically the long streets are crossed by lightweight bridges which almost float beneath the glazed roof. In the internal street, the unfolding of volumes and spaces bathed in soft sunlight is as good as any external urban experience and clearly helps in the well being and motivation of the call centre staff.

Table 13.1 Barclaycard Building, Northampton: green principles and general characteristics

- office building for 2,600 staff;
- divided into six blocks divided by glazed malls;
- has long solar-protected south facade using louvres and solid panels;
- has long highly glazed north facade for maximum daylight penetration;
- uses exposed concrete construction in offices, steel in glazed malls;
- mixed-mode building incorporating passive solar ventilation and trickle vents in lintels;
- has greywater recycling;
- uses energy strategy to reinforce social objectives;
- company support for public or shared transport;
- densely planted grounds with lake fed by rainwater and greywater.

The justification for the streets and squares is both social and environmental – that they are occupied by cafés and sandwich bars at ground level is as relevant as their role as ventilated spaces. The division of the vertical spaces by horizontal bands of accommodation creates a rhythm which sunlight brings alive. Yellow, blue and grey, the soft colours of the internal walls combined with delicate steelwork evoke an almost Regency calm.

As modern office work is increasingly dictated by the electronic screen, the experience of the working environment grows in importance. It is now increasingly recognized that green office buildings – which give staff some perceptual contact with the natural world of wind, rain and sun – lead to enhanced levels of staff satisfaction and performance. The naturally lit and ventilated office generates less absenteeism through sickness or poor morale – in other words, green offices not only conserve energy, they help reduce company staff costs. In fact, the 2–3% increase in staff productivity recorded by studies of green offices pays for the annual energy costs of a typical building. For companies like Barclaycard, the procurement of green buildings is as much a question of good management and sound investment in people as it is an exercise in saving energy. Certainly when all staffing costs are equated, such as the cost of replacing staff who have voluntarily left, investing in an attractive, healthy, energy-efficient building makes good business sense.

References

1. Abridged from a review by Brian Edwards, *Architecture Today*, No. 80, July 1997, pp. 20-30.
2. Bill Bordass, commentary, 'Barclaycard Headquarters', *Architecture Today*, No. 80, July 1997, p. 25
3. Ibid.
4. Ibid.
5. Ibid.

13.8 a,b, and c *British Energy Building, Gloucester,*
Environmental strategy. Architects: Fitzroy Robinson.

a

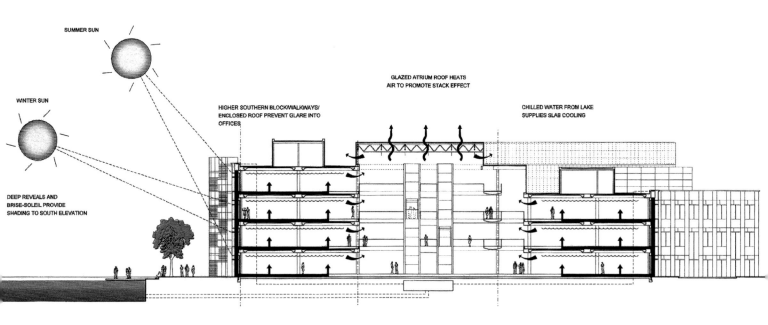

SUMMER SUN

WINTER SUN

DEEP REVEALS AND
BRISE-SOLEIL PROVIDE
SHADING TO SOUTH ELEVATION

HIGHER SOUTHERN BLOCK/WALKWAYS/
ENCLOSED ROOF PREVENT GLARE INTO
OFFICES

GLAZED ATRIUM ROOF HEATS
AIR TO PROMOTE STACK EFFECT

CHILLED WATER FROM LAKE
SUPPLIES SLAB COOLING

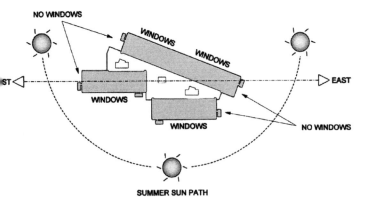

NO WINDOWS

WINDOWS

WINDOWS

WINDOWS

WINDOWS

NO WINDOWS

ST ◁-- --▷ EAST

SUMMER SUN PATH

HADING

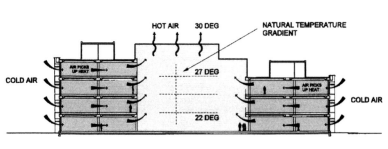

HOT AIR   30 DEG

NATURAL TEMPERATURE
GRADIENT

27 DEG

COLD AIR

AIR PICKS
UP HEAT

AIR PICKS
UP HEAT

COLD AIR

22 DEG

ATRIUM

b

c

121

14

14.1 *Orchard Vale Primary School, Barnstaple, Devon uses natural locally sourced construction materials to blend with the semi-rural location. Notice how the cross section encourages stack-effect ventilation and brings daylight to the centre of the school.*

The importance of the school to learning

Brian Edwards

ECA, Heriot-Watt University

with **Alison Gorf**

University of Huddersfield

The school is, for many children, the first building beyond the home that they experience for a significant length of time. Like the office for adults, the school provides a total environment which forms the physical and social backcloth for the working life of children. It is hardly surprising that many have argued that, through their design, school buildings and playgrounds influence the effectiveness of teaching, learning and social development. However, the specific question as to whether 'green' schools provide further benefit has hitherto remained problematic. It is clear from earlier chapters that 'green' offices have advantages for the companies that occupy them, not only in terms of energy efficiency, but equally importantly in terms of enhanced productivity. The sense of physical and psychological uplift generated by naturally lit and ventilated offices appears to be the key to the improvement in productivity. This chapter asks whether schools designed according to similar principles offer the same benefits to pupils and teachers. Specifically, do 'green' schools lead to:

14.2 *The classroom wing at Orchard Vale School showing study areas outside classrooms on the ground floor.*

— improvement in pupil learning levels;
— improvement in the productivity of teaching staff;
— less antisocial behaviour by pupils?

Unlike offices, schools routinely collect the data necessary to answer these questions. Performance tables published by local education authorities are scrutinized as part of five-yearly Ofsted inspections of schools. The research presented here suggests that 'green' schools may in fact provide a range of wider social benefits and that certain types of green school lead to better performance by pupils in tests conducted at SATs (Standard Assessment Tests) Key Stages 1 and 2. In Hampshire, in particular, 'green' schools out-perform 'ungreen' schools fairly consistently and this is most marked in the schools for young pupils (junior schools as against secondary). The SATs data provide a consistent template of pupil learning attainment at ages 7 (Key Stage 1), 11 (Key Stage 2), 14 (Key Stage 3) and 16 (GCSE Key Stage 4) for all children in all schools in England and Wales. This research compares performance in 42 green schools with that of 42 paired ungreen schools which have similar social,

economic, size and geographical characteristics. The comparison of data allows the performance of schools as a total environment to be assessed, thereby shedding light upon the green aspects of their design.

Earlier work in this area in the UK has concentrated mainly upon the effect of school grounds and the external school environment upon teaching and learning.[1] Here the emphasis is upon the classroom as an environment, looking particularly at lighting, ventilation and spatial characteristics. Since the classroom is where most time is spent (by pupil and teacher) it is clearly central to any assessment of school performance. This is not to deny the importance of the external school environment but to see the school, like the office building, as productive space. Unlike in the UK, fairly extensive research has been undertaken in the USA into classroom design and the effect upon pupil concentration levels. Work by the Heschong Mahone Group[2] and Taylor and Vlastos[3] seems to suggest that daylight levels are the crucial factor and that sunlight offers a further benefit (though it raises problems of glare and over-heating) to keeping the mind active.

14.3 *Hatch Warren School, Basingstoke, Hampshire. Daylight is allowed to penetrate all of the teaching and circulation areas to the benefit of the school environment.*

14.4 *The use of natural materials is usually a sign of sustainable construction as here at Aldershot Park School, Hampshire.*

Table 14.1 *Different perceptions of environmental design in schools*

USA	Daylight is critical
	– helps learning
	– importance of natural light spectrum
	• daylight
	• sunlight
	– teachers enjoy well-lit schools
	– pupils benefit
UK	Ventilation is critical
	– CO_2 levels
	– stimulation of air changes/movement
	– too much light, especially sunlight, is a problem
Hong Kong	Ventilation is critical
	– temperature control
	– air movement
	– air-conditioning units create noise
	– external noise/air quality problems

In the UK the Department for Education and Skills (DfES) has sought to promote better environmental standards in schools via design guides such as *Building Bulletin 87* and more specifically through the Schools Environmental Assessment Method (SEAM). The former, introduced in 1987, prescribed a range of environmental design principles which led to the construction across the UK of a number of innovative green schools (many of which have been monitored by the author's research team). The latter, produced in 1996, is modelled closely on BREEAM and provides a self-assessment toolkit based upon the methodology described earlier for offices. Both guides and the wider interest in sustainable design have led to the construction of at least 52 schools which could be described as 'green'.

For the sake of the analysis the definition of a green school draws upon three widely adopted paradigms – for sustainable development (Brundtland), sustainable design (Foster and Partners) and sustainable construction (BSRIA).

The various scales employed in these definitions allow the 'green' school to address the urban, building and interior dimensions.

In this chapter, a 'green school' is one which in its design and construction gives priority to sustainability. Sustainability embraces:

– *Sustainable development*
'Development that meets the needs of the present without compromising the ability of future generations to meet their own needs.' (Brundtland, 1987)

– *Sustainable design*
'Creating buildings which are energy efficient, healthy, comfortable, flexible in use and designed for long life.' (Foster and Partners, 1999)

– *Sustainable construction*
'The creation and management of healthy buildings based upon resource efficient and ecological principle.' (BSRIA, Centre for Construction Ecology, 1996)

Out of these definitions come four key characteristics of the *green school*:

– resource efficient, particularly in the area of energy;
– healthy, both physically and psychologically;
– comfortable, responsive and flexible;
– ecologically based, particularly as an integrated system of impacts.

Each characteristic is itself subject to sub-division, creating 20 defining factors, e.g:

Resource efficient
– low energy design (in construction and occupation);
– exploits renewable energy;
– puts energy controls in hand of occupants (with appropriate education);
– conserves water;
– local sourcing of materials.

14.3

14.4

Healthy
—   minimum internal pollution;
—   uses natural materials;
—   exploits natural light and ventilation;
—   addresses psychological welfare;
—   accessible for all.

Comfortable
—   attractive and responsive internal environment;
—   sheltered, sunny external environment;
—   noise free;
—   controllable environment;
—   glare free.

Ecological
—   exploits recycling;
—   life-cycle impact;
—   makes nature visible;
—   designed upon ecological principles;
—   uses ecological accounting (eco-footprint).

Not all 'green schools' employ all 20 factors: there is necessarily selection to meet circumstance. For the sake of this analysis, however, a green school is one which takes account of at least 75% of the key factors, i.e. 15 of the 20 listed.

The list is a useful guide in:

—   selecting characteristic green schools for evaluation;
—   analysing DfES, BRE and other assessment methods for schools;
—   discussing key criteria with teachers, pupils, administrators, etc.;
—   identifying likely factors which may influence productivity, behaviour, examination results, Ofsted reports.

From these definitions and factors it is possible to identify 50 'green' schools constructed in England over the past 15 years. The list includes schools of various types (infant, junior, secondary and city technology college) and designed to incorporate a wide range of sustainable design features. Some exploit passive solar design, others maximize natural ventilation by adopting shallow floor depths and angled ceilings, others use thermal flywheel technology, whilst others still maximize the use of locally sourced natural building materials. Some achieve energy efficiency by using mechanical as against natural ventilation, exploiting for example heat pump technology to conserve resources.

Geographically there are two clusters of green schools which meet the above criteria – in Hampshire and Essex. In both counties the local education authority (LEA) has sought to build schools which bring to the fore the design challenge of sustainability. In both cases too innovation has been driven by architects and engineers working within their respective local government offices, although latterly some design work has been put out to tender to private architectural practices. Within the Hampshire and Essex LEAs, however, some schools have been built which do not meet the green criteria listed earlier. These have become the control group schools which allow a comparison of performance with the green schools. Elsewhere in England green schools exist in lower concentrations, but there remain useful examples from across the country.

The research methodology consists of pairing green with ungreen schools which display similar characteristics. The pairing is based upon:

—   geographical proximity;
—   similarity in size;
—   similarity in type;
—   similar social/economic characteristics.

Table 14.2 SEAM environmental assessment summary sheet (from Building Bulletin 87, 2nd edition)

Environmental aspect	New buildings	Maximum no. of points	Existing schools	Maximum no. of points
Site selection	☐	1		
Sources of hardwoods and softwoods	☐	4	☐	2
Low NO_x combustion equipment	☐	1	☐	1
Use of recycled materials	☐	1		
Ozone depleting chemicals	☐	2	☐	2
Volatile organic compounds		3	☐	3
Harmful substances			☐	1
Lead-free paint	☐	1	☐	1
Lead pipework in existing schools			☐	1
School grounds	☐	3	☐	3
Recycling facilities and waste disposal	☐	2	☐	2
Environmental purchasing			☐	1
Ventilation	☐	3	☐	3
Lighting				
— high quality integrated design of daylighting and electric lighting	☐	2	☐	2
— lighting controls or switching arrangements	☐	2	☐	2
Water economy	☐	1	☐	1
Water quality	☐	3	☐	3
Drinking water	☐	1	☐	1
Asbestos in existing buildings			☐	3
Health and safety legislation	☐	2	☐	2
Maintenance				
— complete set of record drawings and maintenance manuals	☐	2	☐	2
— caretaker training	☐	2	☐	2
Energy (carbon dioxide) rating	☐	7	☐	11
Energy management			☐	1
Home to school transport policy	☐	2	☐	2
School environmental policy	☐	1	☐	1
Total number of points	☐	46	☐	53

Environmental classification based on total number of points

Class A	–	35 points and over		
Class B	–	25 – 34 points	**Class**	☐
Class C	–	15 – 24 points		

Table 14.3 Example of pairing of green and ungreen schools for statistical analysis

	Number of pupils on school roll	Free meals %	English as additional language %	Pupils with special educational needs %
Walmley Junior School B76 1JB	360	5	0.3	3
Boldmere Junior B73 5SD	360	7	few	10
Newlands Primary GU46 6EY	290	n/a	0	18
Potley Hill Primary GU46 6AG	320	1	few	26
Stoke Park Infants SO50 8NZ	280	11	0	29
Shakespeare Infants SO50 4EZ	265	12	4	28
Velmead Infant GU13 9LH	270	No data available at present		
Heatherside County GU13 9SB	300	1	0.03	4
Queens Inclosure PO7 8NT	360	5	0	18
Morelands Primary PO7 5QL	335	No data available at present		

The latter is arrived at by using three indicators:
– percentage of pupils for whom English is not their first language;
– percentage of pupils with special needs;
– percentage of pupils with free school meals.

From an initial total 52 green schools, the lack of suitable pairing reduces the research number to 42. Here, particularly in rural schools, the unavailability of a comparable ungreen school nearby results in the green school being removed from the analysis.

14.5 *Schools are important centres for multi-cultural understanding. Social cohesion can benefit from well-designed schools. Hyrstmont School, Batley, West Yorkshire.*

14.6 *Attractive teaching environments reduce teacher stress and add to learning. Hyrstmont School, Batley, West Yorkshire.*

Table 14.4 Database of green schools in England and Wales

School name	LEA	School name	LEA
Deanery First + Second School	Birmingham	Burnham Copse Infants	Hampshire
Walmley Junior School	Birmingham	Hook with Warsash Primary	Hampshire
Green Park Primary	Bucks	Woodlea Primary	Hampshire
Looe Junior and Infant	Cornwall	Bosmere Middle	Hampshire
St Cleer Primary	Cornwall	Frogmore Secondary	Hampshire
Ushaw Moor Primary	Durham	Hulbert Junior	Hampshire
Notley Green Primary	Essex	Farnborough Technical	Hampshire
Tendring Secondary	Essex	Netley Abbey	Hampshire
Cherrytree Primary	Essex	Grange Junior	Hampshire
St Peters Primary	Essex	Woebly Primary	Herefordshire
Great Leighs Primary	Essex	Perronet Thompson Secondary	Humberside
Nabbots Junior	Essex	Ashford Godington Primary	Kent
Ravenscroft Primary	Essex	Hyrstmont School	Kirklees
Thorpe Bay Secondary	Essex	Dickleburgh V.C. Primary	Norfolk
Roach Vale Primary	Essex	Holywell Primary	Nottingham
Barnes Farm Primary	Essex	Perthcelyn Primary	Rhondda Cynon Taf
Mistley Norman Primary	Essex	John Cabot CTC	South Glos
Newlands Primary	Hampshire	Fencedyke Primary	Strathclyde
Stoke Park Infants	Hampshire	Swanlea Secondary	Tower Hamlets
Velmead Infants	Hampshire	Aspull Primary	Wigan
Queens Inclosure Primary	Hampshire	St Thomas, Leigh Primary	Wigan
Whiteley Primary	Hampshire	Poulton Lancelyn Primary	Wirral
Elson Infants	Hampshire	St Mary's Secondary	Wirral

In order to identify the wider social benefits of the schools under investigation, three performance indicators were originally chosen – each representing a major stakeholder interest. The first is pupil examination results, particularly at SATs Key Stages 1, 2, 3 and 4. The second involves pupil and teacher morale as measured by absenteeism rates. The third is the percentage of school funds spent on repairs and utility bills. From these three perspectives (not unlike the triangulation employed in the analysis of green offices where user, client and designer perceptions were employed), it is hoped to gain insight into the school building as an essential component of teaching and learning.

Pupils are major stakeholders in any school, although their voices are not always heard at the level of governance. A successful school environment is one where the children are effectively taught – this being reflected in their performance at the Key Stages of SATs. The availability of national data on a comparable basis for all schools provides a sound platform for the comparative research described here. Similarly, data are available on teacher performance for all schools in the UK. Local education authorities make known to the DfES the percentage of teacher absenteeism days for every school in England and Wales. It is assumed here that the school environment may play a part in sickness, poor morale and rapid staff turnover, just as evidence suggests is the case with the office environment.

Since it costs about £14,000 to replace a teacher, turnover of teaching staff can cost a school more than the annual energy bill. The third data set concerns the physical characteristics of schools and the cost of upkeep as measured by annual heating bills and refurbishment of the fabric. It is assumed that for a green school the energy and water costs will be less than for an ungreen school, and a similar pattern will be found in terms of building fabric repair. The latter assumption is based upon the belief that a green school will be more robust constructionally and less subject to vandalism than a poorly regarded ungreen school. Here a secondary argument emerges: that a green building leads to wider social benefits as well as productivity ones. This in turn influences the level of vandalism and enhances the quality of 'psychological space' as perceived by pupils and teachers. Hence, sustainable design leads to improved life-cycle costing as long as all the costs are accessible and equated.

Table 14.5 Impacts of school on sustainability

Type of sustainability	
Environmental	— energy efficient; — water efficient; — material efficient; — low maintenance; — recycling.
Social	— community asset; — social cohesion; — linked to other community facilities; — retention of teachers; — supports welfare as well as teaching.
Economic	— long-term asset value; — low maintenance; — improves productivity of teachers; — enhances learning of pupils — low utility bills.

Green school design and teacher stress

A school is not only a place of learning for pupils; it is also a place of work for teachers. The investigation undertaken by the authors seeks to establish the perceived relationship between the design of schools and the sense of wellbeing engendered in teachers. Put another way, do green schools with their special characteristics of enhanced level of daylight, natural ventilation, atrium space and organic materials create a working environment that teachers value? Conversely, do poorly designed and maintained schools give a sense of under-investment in education which is not only reflected in poor pupil behaviour and test results, but expressed in low teacher morale? In its report on its 1999 inspection of the green Elson Infants School in Gosport, Hampshire, Ofsted stated that the "high level of staff absences was having a negative impact upon the overall quality of teaching". The inspectors attributed this to, among other factors, a number of limitations in the design of the school, such as the "dark and cramped" undercrofts beneath the loft areas in the classrooms (part of the passive solar ventilation strategy). One could speculate that these lofts, which are the result of angled ceilings, and the need for high-level windows in the classrooms, which were seen as "inaccessible and unsafe", add to stress levels for teachers. Although the school is described in the report as providing a 'bright learning environment' and although it has a central library and drama studio placed within a glazed spine through the school, the report shows the importance of relating design of the classroom to teacher as well as energy need.

The energy strategy and educational need do not always coincide in terms of the design and use of space for teaching and learning. Where a disjuncture occurs (as with the unsafe lofts in an infants school) teachers may be under additional stress which is reflected in high levels of absenteeism. Similar stress may occur when windows are too high to open, or controlled by a complicated computer management system (which teachers cannot override), when there is inadequate solar shading (as in some Essex green schools) or when temperatures are too low in the winter and too high in the summer. These are commonly found problems with green schools, especially those which

14.7 *Solar shading is important where roof lighting is employed.*

14.8 *Controls need to work and be understood by janitorial staff if the environment of the school is to be successfully controlled.*

are inadequately maintained or whose operation is not understood by janitors. As a result there may be pockets of teacher stress within otherwise well-performing schools (as at Elson). Also, the trend towards 'chalk and talk' small group teaching in the classroom results in complex control regimes for the teacher which the shape of the classroom may frustrate because of its green characteristics.

Table 14.6 Comments from Ofsted reports on green schools

Hampshire schools

"Although it is a very attractive and comfortable environment, due to the unusual design, whole class teaching can be very cramped."
Stoke Park School (1998)

"The accommodation is attractive and light and is maintained to a very high standard."
Queens Inclosure School (1999)

"Noise sometimes penetrates into classrooms from adjoining classes . . . which prevents staff and pupils hearing what is being said."
Newlands School (2000)

"The open plan nature of classrooms . . . causes strain and difficulties in concentration for pupils."
Hook with Warsash School (1999)

"The main school building is modern, providing light, bright teaching spaces."
Hulbert Junior School (1997)

"The school's accommodation is good. It allows for the effective teaching of the National Curriculum, but does have a number of limitations. The classrooms provide reasonable sized and bright learning environments, although the "carpet areas" under the "lofts" are dark and cramped (and) . . . although there is ample storage space, a high proportion of it is in the relatively inaccessible and unsafe 'lofts' above the classrooms."
Elson Infants School (1999)

Essex schools

"The open plan nature of the building, whilst supporting team work, results at times in learning being disrupted by sounds from other areas."
Great Leighs School (1999)

"The school is making the best use of the open plan nature of the accommodation . . . however, poor acoustics in some areas and the design of the building creates limitations on the use of space."
Roach Vale Primary School (2000)

"There is inadequate ventilation and the resultant atmosphere can lead to a general weariness."
St Peters School (1999)

"Lessons are sometimes disturbed by the perfectly legitimate activities of neighbouring classes."
Ravenscroft School (1999)

"The accommodation imposes some limitations on the quality of education provided."
Nabbots School (1998)

14.9 *Hedge End School, Berrywood, Hampshire, acts as an important beacon for the local community. It effectively combines sustainability with contemporary design.*

14.10 *Sections, Looe Primary School, Cornwall.*

14.11 *Section, Hayes School, Bromley, Kent, showing the relationship between summer and winter sun and energy flows in the classroom.*

The research seeks to test the hypothesis that 'green' schools bring about wide social and economic benefits just as green offices appear to. The parallel with offices is important since the advantages of green offices occur not so much in reduced utility bills of heating, lighting and ventilation but in terms of enhanced long-term asset value of the building and the improved productivity of those who work in the building. With green schools the potential beneficiaries are the pupils, the teachers and the local education authority. Since most schools are independent budget holders, the fourth beneficiary is the school as part of the community itself. Here reduced energy bills, less spent on building upkeep and less money employed in recruiting staff result in more money being available for teaching aids such as computers and for employing additional teaching staff. There is potentially a virtuous circle of benefits for the school designed to sustainable principles, one which embraces most of those with an interest in teaching and learning – pupils, teachers, administrators and parents. The school then becomes an agent in creating social cohesion, with the architecture of the school achieving civic importance.

In the real world environment of a school it is difficult to be precise about research findings using indicators from different fields. What is needed are patterns which show key inter-relationships. Here the methodology employed is quantitative and qualitative – the search for numerical performance indicators which are then tested on the ground

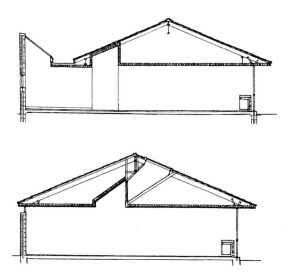

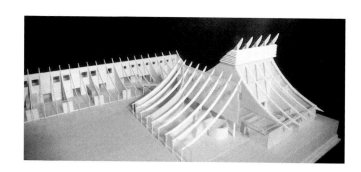

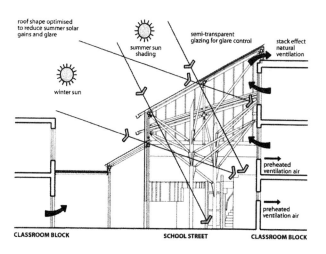

It is evident that in Hampshire Education Authority in particular green schools generally out-perform other schools in their county or education authority, and out-perform national averages as well. This improvement in productivity (by pupil, teacher and school building) exists in both inner-city schools and those in rural areas. However, not all green schools perform well: there are signs that older passive solar schools do not achieve the benefits of 'green' design. This may be attributed to the conflict between energy efficiency and ventilation: many passive solar schools (such as Looe Primary School, Cornwall) suffer from lack of ventilation which leads to stuffy conditions in the classroom for teacher and pupil alike. In the pursuit of energy efficiency windows are kept closed to retain the heat, substantially reducing levels of ventilation. Also many of the passive solar schools examined were open in plan and in cross section, resulting in much noise transfer between classrooms and between classrooms and corridors. Generally speaking, although 75% of green schools out-performed their control group counterparts, this was not generally true of early passive solar schools which often performed less well than the average.

The age of the school is clearly a factor. Most green schools are relatively new buildings and the comparison is often with schools built in the 1960s when system construction (such as CLASP) was commonplace. Frequently too the schools were built in the 1970s and 1980s before *Building Bulletin 87* was published by DfE (now DfES). However, some of the schools date from earlier in the century when design and construction were often of a high standard. Here classrooms constructed of brick and stone with good thermal capacity, high ceilings and large windows begin to approach aspects of sustainable design commonplace today. But age is not as significant as one would expect since many of the control group schools are in fact newer buildings than their green counterparts.

by surveying specific buildings in greater detail or by searching through Ofsted reports for comments on the school or classroom environment. The aim is not only to demonstrate that green schools are beneficial but to identify the key factors of design or construction that play a significant part. The quantitative analysis consists of comparing the selected green schools with their control group school, the LEA average and the national average. From this analysis it is evident that certain green schools out-perform ungreen schools in terms of pupil examination results and that this improvement (up to 5%) is most marked in the younger age groups. In fact in secondary schools there is little or no correlation between green schools and pupil performance as measured by SATs and GCSE results alone

14.13 *The classrooms should be a stimulating environment for teacher and pupil alike. This design for Hallfield School is by Jestico and Whiles. The cost of replacing teachers is on average £14,000 making attention to their working environment particularly important.*

Table 14.7 Design ambitions for Hampshire schools

– to work with landscape and vernacular forms;
– to promote non-institutional character for schools;
– to bring nature into the classroom as inspiration and environmental moderator;
– to create civic landmarks in areas of suburban growth;
– to build a community around the school through holistic green design;
– to achieve comfort and energy efficiency through the design of the cross section;
– to use natural, locally available building materials;
– to use courtyards, atrium spaces and colonnades for energy efficiency and social space;
– to create a continuity with school design in the nineteenth and early twentieth centuries.

Based upon an interview conducted with Sir Colin Stansfield Smith on 18 June 2002.

The research has highlighted the benefits of adopting a broad plural strategy for achieving sustainable design. The definition of a green school cited earlier brings into the framework resources beyond energy (such as water), the preference for local material sourcing, and for respecting vernacular building traditions. Within these parameters the Hampshire schools designed by Colin Stansfield Smith and his team of local authority architects led by Ian Templeton are admirable examples. By way of contrast the other cluster of green schools in the UK, in Essex, has adopted a largely low-energy approach, most of them applying passive solar principles. In Hampshire about 80% of the green primary schools out-perform the control group whilst in Essex there is no obvious benefit. The answer for this anomaly (already mentioned) is the failure of older passive schools to deal with summertime overheating and wintertime under-ventilation. A conclusion which should be drawn is the need for holistic design strategies (as in Hampshire) rather than concentrating upon a single (i.e. low-energy) aspect of green design (as in Essex). The wider approach is supported by the concept of 'Eco-schools' (see later) where design, construction and the curriculum are brought together.

The qualitative research seeks to establish the key factors that are active in the enhanced performance of the green schools. Mention was made earlier of the importance of levels of daylight in creating a stimulating environment for pupil and teacher alike. Since many of the green schools analysed employed passive solar gain, daylight (and sunlight) levels were higher than average. This was true not only of classrooms but also of common areas such as halls, corridors, malls and atria which are a frequent feature of such schools. The changing pattern of sunlight and cloud keeps the mind active although there is the risk of classrooms overheating. A growing body of research supports the view that ventilation rates are also important and, although this can be high in schools designed to maximize solar-assisted ventilation, some argue that ventilation is more crucial than natural light.[4] Here supporters of ventilation advocate mechanical ventilation of schools (action which is not condoned by DfES on the grounds of cost and noise disturbance), arguing that with modern heat recovery technology the school can be highly energy efficient (see Greenwich Millennium School, chapter 17). Unfortunately, only one school amongst the study group of 42 employed mechanical ventilation. What is

14.14 *The school and its playground prepare pupils for the future. They should project values such as environmental care and social interaction. Design sketch for Burnham Copse Infant School, Tadley, Hampshire.*

14.15 *Typical sections through Burnham Copse Infant School, Tadley, Hampshire. This school won a variety of design and education awards.*

14.16 *Site plan (a) and plan (b) of Burnham Copse Infant School, Tadley, Hampshire.*

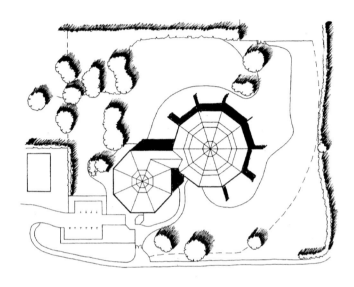

a

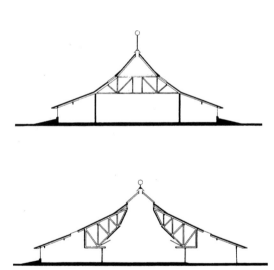

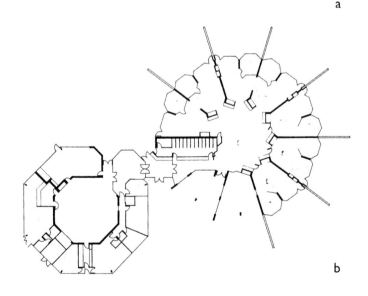

b

evident from this study is that certain types of green schools which employ fan and solar-assisted flywheel ventilation (thereby achieving high levels of light and ventilation) out-performed other green schools which in the pursuit of energy efficiency were sometimes too highly sealed against unwanted air movement. Lack of ventilation subjects children to higher levels of carbon dioxide pollution which makes them feel drowsy. This was a problem particularly with Looe School in Cornwall (noted for its passive solar design) where ventilation rates were significantly below the recommended minimum.[5]

14.17 *Effective shading of south-facing classrooms is essential if solar gain and glare are to be adequately addressed.*

14.18 *Trees provide effective shade in summer and in winter permit good levels of daylight penetration. They can also help with delivering aspects of the National Curriculum through classes in biology or natural science.*

The particular problem with early passive solar schools

It is evident that several passive solar schools designed in the 1970s and 1980s are not performing well in terms of energy efficiency or from the point of view of creating an enhanced learning environment. Excessive expectation was attached to the power of the sun to provide heat throughout the year, with over-ambitious or ill-understood ventilation systems compounding the problem. Many early green schools have suffered from excess summer-time temperatures, under-heating in the winter, noise disturbance, glare at the classroom edge, and generally inadequate levels of ventilation. As a result the schools have suffered seasonal stress in temperature levels and both seasonal and universal under-performance of mechanical and natural ventilation systems.

Table 14.8
Common problems with passive solar open-plan schools

— too hot in summer;
— too cold in winter;
— under-ventilated in both summer and winter;
— too noisy;
— glare at classroom edge;
— environmental systems (blinds, window opening and heating valves/controls) do not operate as intended or are not understood by janitors.

The problems cannot be attributed solely to poor design. Sometimes budgets did not allow for the external shading specified on drawings or the installation of internal blinds. Sometimes too the double glazing or intelligent glass systems planned at the outset were subsequently abandoned without adjustment in design elsewhere. However, those are minor problems compared with failures in the operation of buildings. Frequently the high-level vents are kept closed either because they cannot be reached or because the winding gear is broken. In some instances once the window has been opened it cannot be fully shut again. Janitors also may be inadequately trained or do not

14.19 *The section through the school has to consider air flows throughout the year and on sunny and sunless days. (a) Abbey Infant School, Netley, Hampshire. (b) Swanlea Secondary School, Whitechapel, London.*

14.20 *Greenwich Millennium Village School includes a large community hall, crèche and adjoining health centre. It provides a school with added social and community facilities, thereby allowing the school to support social inclusion in an inner-city area. Architects: Edward Cullinan Architects.*

understand the workings of a responsive solar-heated school. Sometimes too the computer building management system does not operate satisfactorily or the sensors in the school have been vandalized. Mechanical failure of window systems, difficulty of access to high-level windows (a problem exacerbated by growing health and safety legislation), computer failure, poor janitorial training and vandalism have conspired to undermine the performance of several passive solar schools. Coupled with these problems have been a decline in school budgets and growing pressure under the impact of external performance measures to invest in books, computers and auxiliary teachers rather than address building maintenance problems. The key to a successful green design rests in support for its design ideals by school managers, teachers and janitors.

Where windows can be reached there is often a further problem. Low-level windows are frequently kept closed because of external noise levels. Teachers do not encourage the opening of windows during class because it is seen as distracting. The growth in traffic, with consequent noise and air pollution, has been a major deterrent to the exploitation of natural ventilation, especially in urban schools. In schools where theft and truancy are a problem, windows are often left locked to deter pupils from slipping away, and to prevent theft of equipment.

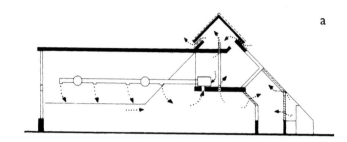

a

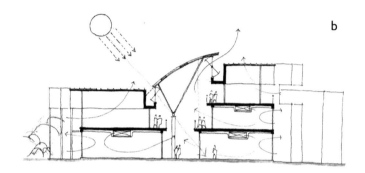

b

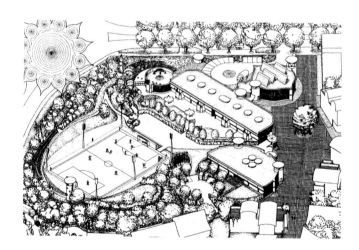

Table 14.9
Action to remedy failures of passive solar schools

— review condition of high-level vents and windows;
— install additional mechanical or natural ventilation systems;
— provide package of training for teachers and janitors;
— install external shading and internal blinds to reduce summertime overheating;
— supplement heating system to avoid under-heating in winter;
— install double- or triple-glazing with 'intelligent' glass where necessary.

A qualitative survey embracing the school as a total environment using techniques similar to those employed by Alice Coleman is planned. Surveys are to be undertaken of litter, vandalism and the state of school repair. Coleman[6] had surveyed council housing estates (though not all academics were happy with her techniques), mapping correlations between tenant satisfaction and built form.

14.21 *The spirit and ethos of green schools help with the development of a caring attitude to the environment. Hedge End Primary School, Berrywood, Hampshire.*

With regards to schools a selection of green and ungreen schools (two from Hampshire and two from Essex) are planned to be surveyed in detail. Interviews are to be conducted with teachers and parent–teacher groups. The findings will test the perception of green schools as responsive buildings – able to respond to the dynamics of the external climate and to changing teaching practices. Earlier work suggests that where teachers have used the school as a resource, green buildings have allowed the curriculum to be developed around the school building. The large glazed malls, such as at Swanlea School, Whitechapel, also offer the opportunity of housing exhibitions of pupil work and performing drama in a space which, according to

an Ofsted report on Swanlea, promoted social discourse in conditions that were environmentally stimulating.[7] Visual surveys and comments made in Ofsted reports (especially since 1998 when 'staffing and accommodation' was added to the survey template) provide much of the qualitative basis for the arguments presented.

The results from the work described in this chapter reinforce the findings of Probe Studies on offices and provide some insight into the role green school buildings play in teaching and learning and in cementing social cohesion. Schools are widely viewed as community centres, creating social and cultural relationships which complement educational ones. It is the wider benefit of the green schools to the community which appears to be as important as the resource efficiencies of their design. This is particularly true of primary schools in rural areas, which are often used as an important point of contact for young mothers and are used also outside the curriculum for other purposes (e.g. scout groups, meeting hall). It appears also to be true of larger secondary schools in inner-city areas where there are qualitative social or community benefits beyond those measurable by SATs or GCSE results.

The work undertaken to date is by no means conclusive. The school building offers both productive and psychological space. There are meanings in green schools which are part of the symbolic landscape of the mind of children (and to a degree of teachers and parents). It is clear that a well-designed school supports the curriculum by providing a pattern of space which complements the pattern of learning. How children interpret school space is as important as how effectively teachers exploit it at a volumetric, technological and environmental level. The research conducted into green schools is necessarily problematic – as an environment to be surveyed, measured and interpreted the school displays the same methodological limitations as the office. However, certain conclusions can be drawn:

– evidence suggests that schools which link sustainable design to the educational ethos offer potential learning advantages;
– this advantage appears most marked in younger age groups;
– green schools appear to provide an environment that

14.22 *Average of SATs scores 1998–2000 for selection of Essex green and un-green schools at Key Stage 2. Notice how there is little evidence of improvement in pupil performance in Essex green schools, many of which display passive solar principles.*

14.23 *Average of SATs scores 1997–2000 for selection of Hampshire green and un-green schools at Key Stage 2. Notice how the green schools (first in each group of four) out-perform the control school in all but one example.*

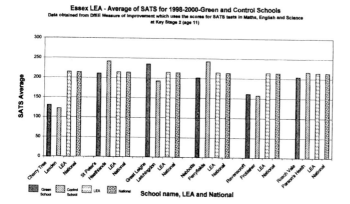

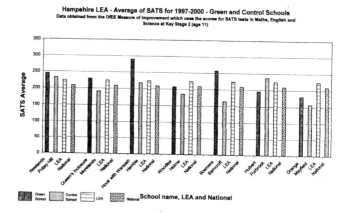

teachers also value and enjoy; this in turn reduces stress and absenteeism which in turn improves productivity;

— older passive solar schools do not appear to perform well and should be subject to retrofit action;

— further work is needed on the relationship between daylight levels, ventilation rates and noise disturbance.

These conclusions suggest that whilst further work is required to support some of the preliminary conclusions, green schools (like green offices and green university buildings) offer investment advantages over ungreen counterparts. The enhanced image of a school designed to environmental principles may help in the recruitment of staff, in the drawing to the school of gifted children, in cementing a relationship between the school and its community. A school which is cherished will be used out of hours, reducing the level of vandalism and hence money spent on repairs. In a full life-cycle costing assessment, a green school will be a reduced investment risk if all the social, educational, productivity and community costs are equated. Too often the building costs ignore the wider social benefits with, as a consequence, too little investment in green schools which, although sometimes more expensive to construct, appear to be a better long-term investment.

The research described here suggests that a relationship may exist between school design, energy conservation and environmental understanding in a broad sense. This confirms the National Curriculum Council's claim that the "spirit and ethos of the school contributes

significantly towards the development of a caring attitude towards the environment"[8]. In the Hampshire schools in particular the general sense of environmental harmony between school, playground and hinterland is captured well in their design and commented upon favourably by teachers and parent groups and in Ofsted reports. It is no coincidence that eight out of ten green schools surveyed in Hampshire out-performed their control group schools in terms of performance and league table results.

A lesson from Hampshire schools

The green schools designed by Hampshire County Council between 1984 and 1996 provide clear evidence that green buildings do provide a wide range of social as well as environmental benefits. The green schools surveyed out-perform their control group schools by a factor of 8–10%. Designed under the leadership of the Hampshire County Council Chief Architect, Sir Colin Stansfield Smith, and later Ian Templeton, they adopt many sustainable design strategies from vernacular-inspired building forms to local sourcing of materials, to intelligent glazing systems. What they demonstrate is that sustainability and good modern design are not inconsistent but mutually beneficial, and that green design does achieve the wider social and educational benefits that many claim. They offer these advantages by striking a balance between temperature, air movement and humidity, using interior volume, orientation and the choice

14.24 *Plans of two primary schools in Hampshire. (a) Velmead Infant School, Fleet, designed by Michael Hopkins and Partners. (b) Queen's Inclosure First School, Cowplain, designed by Hampshire County Council, Architects' Department.*

14.25 *Sections through typical Hampshire primary schools, showing the importance of maximizing daylight through different green design strategies. (a) Velmead Infant School, Fleet. (b) Queens Inclosure First School, Cowplain. (c) Newlands Primary School, Yateley. (d) Elson Infant School, Gosport.*

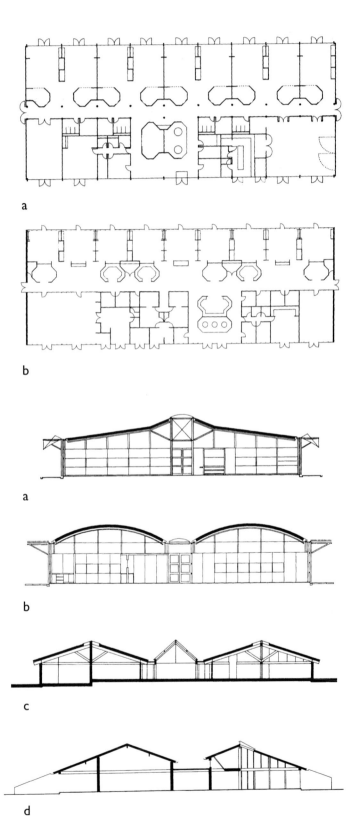

a

b

a

b

c

d

of construction to moderate the school environment.

In achieving these benefits it has to be admitted that green schools on the whole cost more to construct than DfES guidelines advocate. Some of the Hampshire green schools cost up to 12% more than typical schools constructed by other education authorities but they demonstrably achieve good value for money. For example, Stoke Park School was constructed at a cost of around £840/m² whilst the DfES grant to local education authorities of £7,000 per primary school place works out at about £750/m². By way of contrast, the Essex green schools surveyed were only marginally more expensive than other schools of their type. What the evidence suggests is that full life-cycle costing benefits occur when the initial capital investment is above that of minimum government guidelines. However, not all Hampshire schools are expensive: the education authority does not accept a uniform cost for schools, believing that adjustment is needed to address local circumstances.[9]

The argument used by the education authorities in Hampshire to justify the additional expenditure is threefold. First, the schools are often in conservation areas or other sensitive environmental neighbourhoods and this requires a higher investment to reduce environmental or amenity damage. Second, the local authority is relatively wealthy and can afford to pay the additional expenditure out of the rates (local taxes). Third, the council is committed to investing in high-quality public services (schools, libraries, etc.) as a statement of enlightened patronage by an authority conscious of quality of life issues. As a result the schools have benefited, as have the communities they serve. Not all the schools described here have been designed by in-house council architects. For example, Velmead Infant School, Fleet, was designed by Michael Hopkins and Partners. But all the schools share a common green purpose which is to be energy efficient, to conserve other scarce resources such as water, to be sensitive to the local urban or rural context (especially in the choice of materials or built forms), and to create a learning environment which brings environmentalism into the classroom. Hence, the teacher can use the school as part of the curriculum, children are helped to respect and understand nature, the school encourages socializing via the communal green spaces that are created, and the school buildings are cherished rather than vandalized. In the process, fossil fuel energy and other resources are conserved, but the impetus is not low-energy design as such but a holistic view of the agenda of sustainability – environmentally, economically and socially. This is an important lesson of Hampshire schools and one which other education authorities have yet to heed: low-energy design is a factor in the big picture of performance, productivity and life-cycle costing.

The statistical analysis undertaken of the performance of Hampshire schools as measured by SATs results begs the question as to whether it is pupils who are directly benefiting from the building environments created, or whether the improved performance is a result of the fact that the green schools attract and retain better teachers. If green schools do lead to the recruitment of better quality teachers and reduced 'sick' days (and hence reduction in the need to recruit supply teachers), pupils will receive a better education and hence SATs results will improve. Of the green schools in Hampshire, 80% do appear to offer better performance and productivity than the control group schools, and teaching staff and parents value these schools as well, according to Ofsted inspections. So the case for wider social and educational benefits appears to be made by the schools designed to green principles. However, it could be argued that the improved productivity (of teachers) and performance (of pupils) are attributable to good design, not to good green design. This is an argument made by the Commission on Architecture and the Built Environment (CABE) in support of the value of design indicators. Certainly, CABE's research and that described here share common ground but the statistical analysis does support the case for the benefits of designing to sustainable principles. In Hampshire many of the control group schools are, in fact, examples of good design but they do not give priority to the green dimension. There is less natural light and ventilation and less use made of locally sourced materials and organic plans, although in other regards they are well-designed schools. So it does appear that green design offers advantages over merely good design.

The important consequence of the analysis of Hampshire schools is determining the critical factors involved in the apparent productivity and added value improvement. Is there a particular type of green environment which is benefiting education? To what extent is

maximising daylight a contributory factor, as research in the USA suggests? Is it the design as such or the relationship between the building and the school grounds? To what degree can the improvement in SATs results be assigned to well-motivated and contented teachers? If the teachers and parents like the school as an environment, will this not have an effect upon the pupils? These are questions which further research needs to address.

Eco-schools in the UK

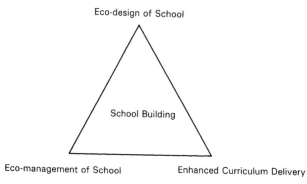

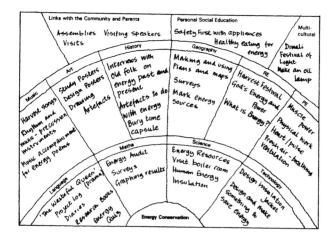

Although much of this chapter explores the relationship, real and perceived, between green design and school performance, it is clear also that the eco-management of

14.28 *The whole School Approach Action Plan for integrating energy awareness with school management and the curriculum of a typical secondary school.*

14.29 *Swanlea School, Whitechapel, London, makes an important civic statement about the role of design. Architects: Percy Thomas Partnership.*

The Whole School Approach Action Plan

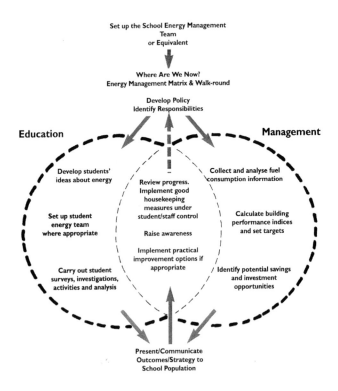

subject requires action under various sub-headings, with conformity across a broad front of 75% to achieve successful designation. Although Eco-schools are a recent initiative, the question arises as to whether good practice here reinforces the evidence that good green design enhances teaching and learning. Can, in fact, the green management of schools collectively enhance the performance of pupils and the productivity of teachers in a way which complements the benefits of green school design?

The authors wish to acknowledge the assistance of Professor Cedric Cullingford of the University of Huddersfield in the research for this chapter.

the school is equally important. It is assumed that sustainable design will lead to school management practices which also focus upon sustainability. The decision to build a green school is likely to be the result of green enthusiasms expressed via the school governors or local education authority in the design brief issued to the architect. Equally likely is that this interest will be articulated in the running of the school and in the maintenance of the building and its grounds.

To help reinforce the connection between sustainable design, sustainable management and the curriculum, an interest group known as 'Eco-schools' was established in 2000. This is an organization, partly funded by the Department for Education and Skills (DfES) – formerly DfESE – aimed at ensuring that schools become the forum for promoting an interest in nature, energy efficiency and healthy living. To become registered as an Eco-school, a school needs to demonstrate a commitment to environmental action across a broad front (Table 14.10). Each

Table 14.10
Criteria for designation of Eco-schools in the UK

–	litter policy;	
–	waste minimization and recycling;	
–	energy efficiency;	
–	water conservation;	
–	transport to school;	
–	healthy living;	
–	school grounds	– art;
		– comfort;
		– welcoming;
		– signage;
		– wildlife.

Source: www.eco.schools.org.uk

14.30 *Victorian vision of school design showing how far ideas have developed. This view is of Poplar Primary School, London in 1950.*

References

1. See for instance Building Bulletin 71, *The Outdoor Classroom*, HMSO, 1990 and *Wildlife and the School Environment*, RSPB and LTL, 1991.

2. 'Students shine in daylit classrooms', *The Washington Post*, 5 September 1996.

3. Anne Taylor and George Vlastos, *School Zone, Learning Environments for Children*, 2nd edition. Albuquerque: Horizon, 1984.

4. 'Lessons in Ventilation', *Building Services Journal*, February 2001, pp. 24 – 25.

5. *Building Services Journal*, September 1989, p. 25.

6. Alice Coleman, *Utopia on Trial*, Harmondsworth, Penguin, 1985.

7. Ofsted Report 704646, March 1999.

8. National Curriculum Council, Annual Report, 1990, preamble.

9. Personal communication with Sir Colin Stansfield Smith, 23 May 2002.

15 Design guidance for green schools

15.1 *Typical school plan types. (a) Compact plan: Great Notley Primary School, Essex. (b) Courtyard plan: St Aloysius Junior School, Glasgow. (c) Finger plan: Looe Primary School, Cornwall. (d) Linear plan: Hatch Warren Junior School, Hampshire.*

Brian Edwards
ECA, Heriot-Watt University

A number of design guides are available to help architects and engineers develop school designs which are both effective as learning environments and help exploit low-energy solutions. Most architects aspire to create a "stimulating, light, spacious and airy"[1] interior whilst utilizing solar gains and introducing a degree of water conservation. The most useful guides (in the UK) are *Building Bulletin 87* (revised 1997), published by the Department for Education and Employment (DfEE), and *Energy Efficient Design of New Buildings and Extensions – for Schools and Colleges* (BRECSU Good Practice Guide 173). Both provide valuable guidance on topics such as orientation, materials, finishes, daylight, ventilation, acoustics and thermal performance. Some guidance is also offered on plan type and to a degree on the sectional profile of school buildings. As a consequence school design is relatively well prescribed (certainly more so than offices described elsewhere in this book), leading to recognizable plan types.

Four main plan typologies[2] are commonly adopted for schools:

— compact plan;
— courtyard plan;
— finger plan;
— linear plan.

And three common sectional profiles:

— flat roof with central atrium or glazed mall;
— pitched roof with glazed perimeter buffer or solar spaces;
— wave or stepped shaped roof to provide cross-ventilation.

a

b

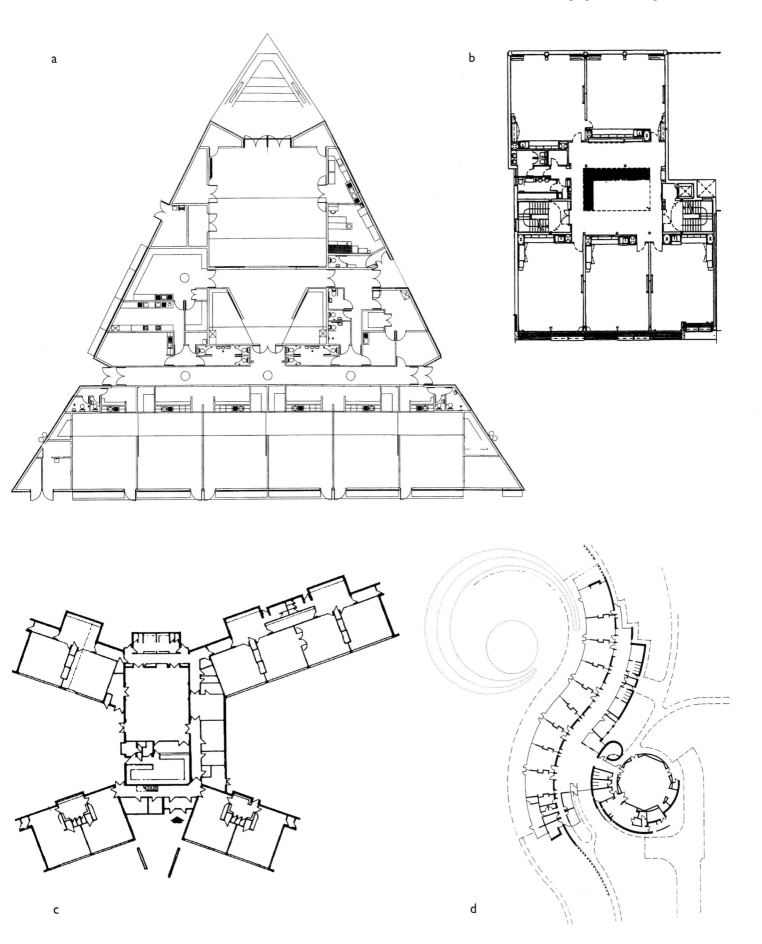

c

d

15.2 *Typical school section profiles.* **a** *Angled roof with central atrium: Perthcelyn Primary School, Rhondda.* **b** *Pitched roof with glazed perimeter solar spaces: Stoke Park Infant School, Bishopstoke, Hampshire.* **c** *Wave or stepped roof to provide ventilation: Chafford Hundred School, Essex.*

a

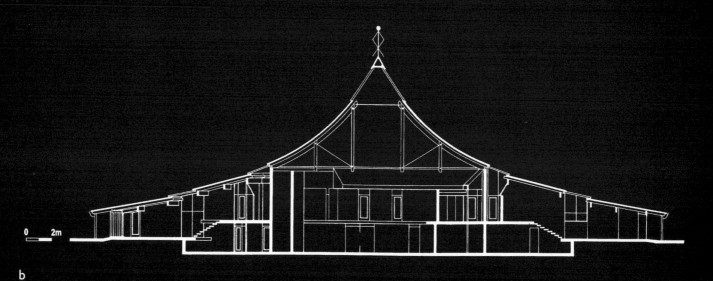

b

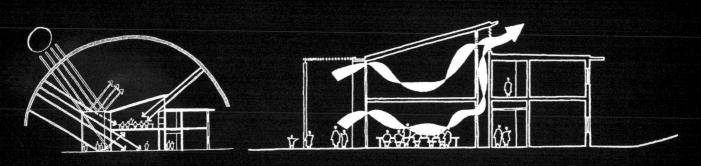

c

15.3 Organic school plan inspired by vernacular buildings. Stoke Park Infant School, Bishopstoke, Hampshire.

15.4 Energy costs of heating and lighting in a typical school. Notice how lighting energy costs are about half those of heating, and the longer the school day the greater the impact of lighting on energy bills.

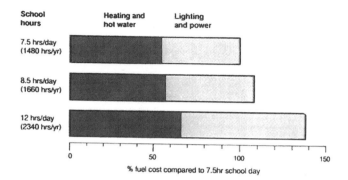

These plan and sectional typologies are used in simple or hybrid form according to site, design brief, orientation or school characteristics. Of the green schools analysed in chapter 14, all subscribe to these general design characteristics. However, most of the early passive design schools are single storey with extensive south-facing glazing, and they often utilize conservatories and high-level ventilation. Many of the later green schools adopt a more pluralistic approach: some employ wind-scoop ventilation systems, others have organic shapes inspired by vernacular buildings, others utilize central glazed malls which provide inform teaching-cum-social space. In all configurations, the objective is that of meeting educational need at reduced energy and resource cost.

Whatever plan form is adopted, it is vital that there is ample and well-distributed daylight and sufficient ventilation to exhaust internal pollutants including carbon dioxide whose levels can be high. It is also important to consider the acoustic needs of classrooms, especially in school designs which seek to maximize natural cross-ventilation. Here the use of carpet finishes employed often by head teachers for comfort and sound insulation may run counter to the need for exposed thermal mass (to moderate peaks in temperature, especially with passive solar schools) and the reflectivity of floor finishes (needed for daylight penetration into deep classrooms). Also since electricity has a high carbon dioxide content per unit of power, there needs to be particular attention paid to artificial lighting and fan-assisted mechanical ventilation.

Atria, glazed malls and externally attached conservatories are increasingly common features of school design. They provide a valuable unheated amenity space which can be employed for socializing, for the display of pupil work, for casual drama and informal teaching. A central roof-glazed street, which is employed, for example, at Swanlea School in Whitechapel, London, provides a chance for pupils to socialize under a degree of teacher surveillance. Unlike playgrounds, where socializing is not commonly supervised (and hence where bullying tends to occur), these amenity spaces justified on low-energy grounds provide useful support for the life of the school. However, such spaces often prove so attractive that teachers are tempted to heat them using mobile fan heaters. This practice negates their environmental benefit and can undermine the heating and ventilation strategy of the remainder of the school.

It is important that glazed malls, conservatories and atria are isolated from the teaching areas by having opening windows and doors between classrooms and sun-spaces. The flow of warmed air from the sun-space should be encouraged on sunny days and discouraged on grey

15.5 *The use of a central atrium.* **a** *In a large city school: Hampden Gurney School, London, designed by BDP.* **b** *Plans.*

15.6 *Glazed mall through Hatch Warren Primary School, Basingstoke, Hampshire, used for occasional teaching purposes.*

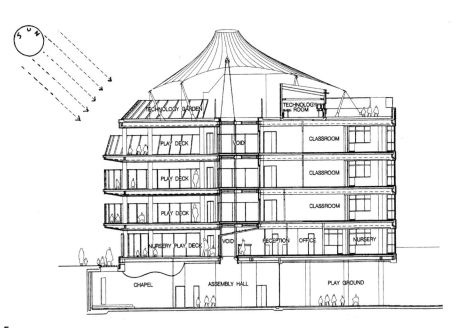

5a

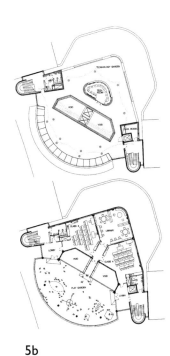

5b

6

cold days. The obvious benefit of glazed malls is that of environmental modification of the internal climate of the school but to be effective there needs to be:

- adequate window and door control between teaching areas and sun-spaces;
- adequate acoustic protection of the classroom;
- recognition that sun-spaces reduce the daylight and ventilation of the teaching areas to which they are attached;
- a responsive system of blinds and solar shading to prevent overheating.

The advantages of different plan types[3]

The *compact plan* is commonly adopted in school design, especially for primary schools (ages 5–11). It consists roughly of a square of accommodation with classrooms on two or three sides and the school hall, offices and library on the fourth. Between the two types of accommodation (classrooms and shared facilities) there is normally a roof-lit corridor or internal street. As a compact plan, it is relatively

15.7 *Courtyard plan with a central hall: Hazlewood First School, Totton, Hampshire.*

15.7 *Courtyard plan with a central hall: Hazlewood First School, Totton, Hampshire.*

energy efficient as long as the classrooms face mainly to the south and advantage is taken of the roof for lighting and ventilation purposes.

In the compact plan particular attention needs to be paid to the profile of the roofs. Classrooms should have monopitch roofs tilted downwards to the south and ending in generous eaves overhangs (to prevent summertime overheating). At the higher north side clerestory lighting should be provided plus high-level vents or opening windows. Lighting the classroom from both sides gives an even distribution of daylight and facilitates cross-ventilation. Assuming a 300 lux threshold for classroom lighting, the compact plan with angled section achieves an annual primary energy use of 93kWh/m²/y. The disadvantage is that mechanical ventilation and cooling are often necessary and demand is likely to increase as schools expand their use of IT and as mean average temperatures rise under the impact of global warming.

A good example of the compact plan type is Great Notley Primary School in Essex designed in 1998 by Allford Hall Monaghan Morris (Fig 15.1a). It adopts a triangular plan and places six classrooms on the southern side and an entrance hall at the northern apex. There is a central covered internal court-*cum*-library with large roof lights. Offices and ancillary spaces are arranged in the north-west and north-east wings.[4]

The *courtyard plan* shares similarities with the compact plan except that there is an open square in the centre. Normally the entrance and school hall are placed to the north and the classrooms wrap around on the southern sides. Since the number of classrooms does not normally fill three sides of the courtyard it is more common for the classrooms to occupy two wings (orientated south-east and south-west) with offices, library, etc. placed on the third side.

With the courtyard plan the profile of classrooms is similar to that in compact layouts (southerly roof overhangs and high-level north-facing windows). One advantage of the courtyard plan is that the linking corridor provides views into both the courtyard and classrooms, thereby providing good

surveillance for teachers. One disadvantage is the extent of perimeter wall area which can add to construction and heating costs. However, the courtyard form readily adapts to irregularly shaped sites, providing an organic architecture which suits the character of many semi-rural locations, and in more formal guise, many inner-city locations.

A good example of the courtyard plan is St Aloysius Junior School in Glasgow, designed by Elder and Cannon.[5] Built in a dense tenemental area of Glasgow not far from the School of Art, it is an unusual three-storey school of ten classrooms built around a central courtyard (Fig 15.1b). The courtyard is glazed at the top making it akin to an atrium. However, as a means of organizing the school spatially the central courtyard offers environmental and social benefits. Routes through the school are placed around the courtyard, making it the heart of the institution. From the balconies on each side it is possible to view almost every aspect of the school – offices, library, IT area and hall on the ground floor, classrooms on the two floors above. The south facade is protected by adjustable louvres held about a metre forward of the glazing line and a massive cornice which oversails the street elevation. Constructed at a cost of £1,043/m² in 1998, the building is marginally more expensive than more orthodox schools; however, the compact form and central courtyard help achieve commendable levels of energy efficiency.

The *finger plan* is arranged so that the classrooms occupy linear projections from a central communal area. There is an obvious analogy with the hand, with the classrooms spread as fingers from a palm which houses the school hall, library, offices and toilet areas. The plan allows the fingers to radiate out or to be placed as parallel blocks. It is important that the classrooms face generally to the south but action must be taken to avoid summertime overheating (by reduced window areas, external sun-shading, internal blinds or special glass). Ideally south-east orientation should be sought for classrooms rather than south-west since winter solar gain can be beneficial in reducing heating loads. The remainder of the school (hall, offices, etc.) can also benefit from sunshine since there is a space between the classroom wings. This allows the larger or more specialist spaces in the school to benefit from both southern and northern light. As a general rule in schools, south-facing glazing should be around 60% of the wall area

Design guidance for green schools

15.8 *Infant school, Sevenoaks, Kent designed by Architects Design Partnership showing the impact of sustainability on school design.*

15.9 *School design is important in encouraging socializing among children and in introducing them to the concept of environmental custodianship. Swanlea School, Whitechapel, London. Architects: Percy Thomas Architects.*

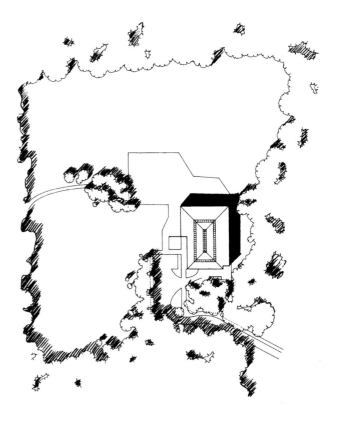

and northern glazing about 30%. This allows for an optimum balance to be struck between winter solar gain, daylight penetration, the avoidance of excessive fabric heat loss and summer overheating.[6]

A good example of the finger plan is Looe Junior and Infant School in Cornwall,[7] designed by Cornwall County Architects' Department in 1983. It is an early example of a passive solar school and has proved to be both energy efficient in operation and popular with staff in spite of having higher than anticipated levels of internal carbon dioxide. The plan is relatively simple: a central block has four fingers of classrooms – six for juniors and four for infants, arranged as opposite pairs (see figure 15.1(c)). All classrooms face either south-east or south-west, giving a space heating saving of 40% (due to passive solar gains).[8] The classrooms are designed to maximize renewable energy, utilizing a 'Trombe' wall to the south and narrow

high-level windows to the north. South-facing roof lights also allows sunlight to penetrate to the rear of the classrooms.

The *linear plan* is arguably the most common plan type for schools. It offers many organizational, social and environmental benefits. Normally the classrooms face south with the other accommodation to the north and separated by a street or glazed mall. The building section is manipulated so that the classrooms benefit from northlights alongside the spine corridor. The accommodation to the north also benefits from roof lights facing the south. The section not only allows light to penetrate deep into the plan (normally such schools are 20–25m deep) but facilitates cross-ventilation without mechanical support.

The linear form requires particular attention to be paid to the shape of roofs and height of walls. Daylight, sunlight and ventilation are encouraged by employing wave-shaped

15.10 *This compact infant school sits in a sheltered clearing in a forest. It is a metaphor justified partly by climatic considerations. Four Lanes Infant School, Waterlooville, Hampshire.*

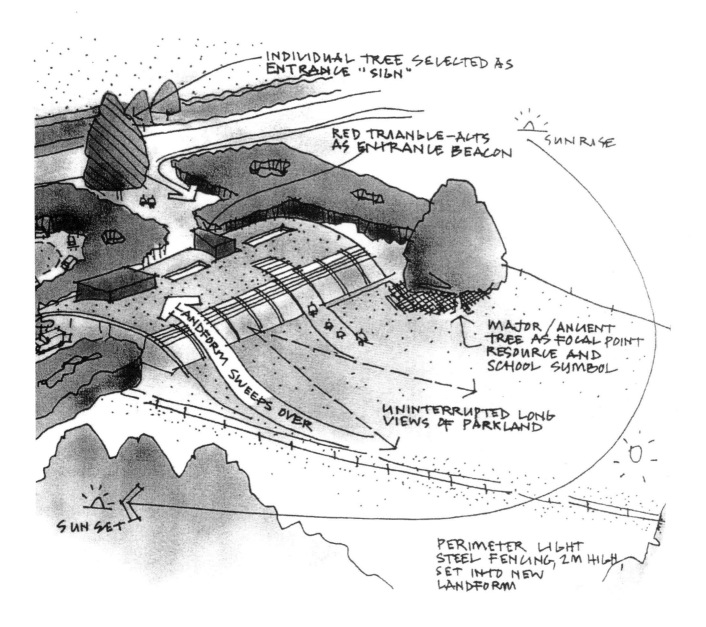

roofs and different room heights. Some light is direct and other light borrowed by shafting through the ceiling space of other rooms. As with other green school plan types the area of glazing needs to be adjusted according to orientation. To the south the glazing area should be around 50–60%, to the east and west around 40%, and to the north about 30%. Above the central mall extensive roof glazing can be employed, if unheated, and reduced to about 10% if heated.[9]

A typical example of this plan type is a design for a 270-pupil infant school in Sevenoaks, Kent by the Architects Design Partnership[10]. The deep plan is divided by a central roof-lit corridor which runs between nine classrooms to the south and halls and offices to the north. Unusually, two internal tree-planted squares occur equally spaced along the corridor, providing green relief within a rational rectilinear plan. The design has other features which depart from the norm, such as a turf roof, angled glazing and outdoor classrooms beneath a pergola.

15.11 *Planting adjacent to a school brings nature into the classroom, benefiting the school spiritually and climatically. Swanlea School, Whitechapel, London. Architects: Percy Thomas Architects.*

15.12 *Pitched roofs allow designers to optimize interior volume and create ventilation through the eaves. Swanlea School, Whitechapel, London. Architects: Percy Thomas Architects.*

Table 15.1 Comparison of energy use for different plan type of schools based on the LT method

Plan type	Energy use: light kWh/m²/yr	Energy use: heat kWh/m²/yr	Energy use: total kWh/m²/yr	% floor area passively heated
Compact	13	78	91	94
Courtyard	12	75	87	100
Finger	9	74	83	100
Linear	19	73	92	100

Source: The Architects' Journal, 26 February 1998, p. 54.

15.13 *Plan and section of Druk White Lotus School, Ladakh, India, using the courtyard design by Arup Associates. The school uses no imported energy and recycles its water and wastes.*

Key

1 Entrance to courtyard
2 External teaching spaces
3 Water point and play
4 Nursery
5 Lower kindergarten
6 Upper kindergarten
7 Year 1
8 Teachers/admin spaces
9 Solar assisted VIP latrines
10 Air lock and lockers
11 Warm/quiet corner

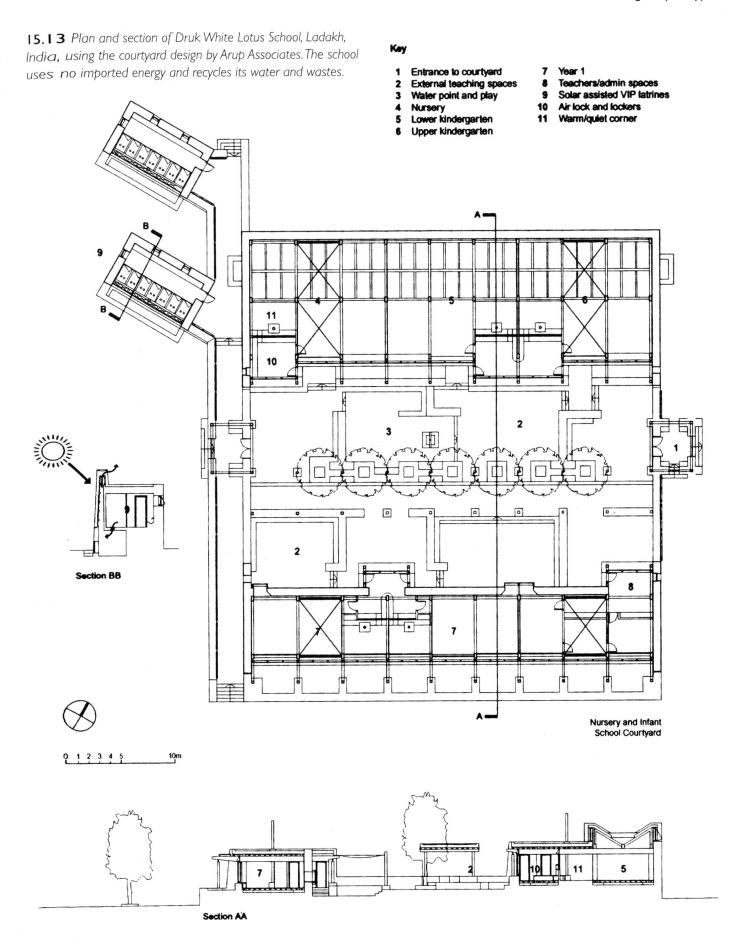

Section BB

Section A'A

Nursery and Infant
School Courtyard

0 1 2 3 4 5   10m

a

b

15.14 *View of* **a** *central courtyard and* **b** *classrooms at Druk White Lotus School, Ladakh, India. Architects: Arup Associates.*

Selecting the plan type

All four configurations of plan offer advantages for different types of site or different type or size of school. They are also remarkably similar in terms of energy efficiency. However, the compact form does require an element of mechanical ventilation, adding to construction, maintenance and operating costs. The choice of plan type is more likely to be the result of site characteristics and the preferences of the local education authority rather than the search for sustainable design per se. In fact several notable green schools have adopted the compact form (e.g. Great Notley Primary School, Essex) and achieved remarkable energy efficiency through the use of renewable sources (wind and solar) and by addressing embodied energy in construction.[11]

The choice of plan type needs to address other factors besides sustainable construction. For example, the school is an important part of the social development of children and different plan types offer quite distinctive spaces for socializing. The courtyard form, for instance, provides an inner world which is easily supervised; the linear form offers a long central space whose characteristics are street-like; and the finger plan provides spaces which address the external world of playgrounds and adjoining town. Different plan types also take advantage of differing degrees of solar access and different levels of climatic exposure. The linear form is well suited to an open southerly aspect, the courtyard form to where shelter is required (from wind, driving rain and noise) and the compact plan to where land is at a premium. In choosing the best planning strategy it is necessary to relate the preferred building footprint to environmental, social and economic sustainability.

References

1. Sebastian Macmillan, Nick Baker and Michael Buckley, "Educational environments", *The Architects' Journal*, 26 February 1998, p. 53.
2. Ibid.
3. The author is indebted to Macmillan et al., op. cit., for the analysis of plan types.
4. For further information on Great Notley School, see *The Architects' Journal*, 5 February 1998, p. 44–45 and 23 July 1998, pp. 46–47.
5. For more details, see *RIBA Journal*, February 1999, pp. 28–35.
6. Macmillan, Baker and Buckley. op. cit., p 54.
7. ETSU 1163/5BS/1.
8. "Passive solar design: Looe Primary School", *The Architects' Journal*, 13 December 1989, pp. 55–61. See also "Building dossier – Looe School", *Building*, Vol. 250, No. 19, 9 May 1986, pp. 43–50.
9. *The Architects' Journal*, 26 February 1998, p. 54.
10. For details, see *The Architects' Journal*, 25 February 2001, pp. 6–7.
11. Ruth Slavid, "Keener to be greener", *The Architects' Journal*, 23 July 1998, pp. 46–47.

16

Brian Edwards

ECA, Heriot-Watt University

16.1 *Site plan, John Cabot City Technology College, Bristol. Architects: Feilden Clegg Bradley.*

16.2 *Ground-floor plan, John Cabot City Technology College, Bristol. Architects: Feilden Clegg Bradley.*

John Cabot City Technology College, Bristol

Designed by Feilden Clegg (now Feilden Clegg Bradley) in 1990, the John Cabot City Technology College in the Kingswood area of Bristol is one of 15 City Technology Colleges (CTCs) established under the Thatcher administration. The objective of CTCs was to provide a mathematics-, science- and technology-based education for young people drawn predominantly from the inner cities. Each CTC had an industrial sponsor and the design of this new breed of colleges was intended to signal the use of technology as a means of regenerating Britain's industrial base.

The John Cabot CTC was sponsored by the tele-communications company Cable & Wireless and the Wolfson Foundation. Feilden Clegg Bradley's design, developed in partnership with consulting engineers Buro Happold, consists of a finger plan arrangement of three wings of classrooms and workshops projecting from a double-height central street. The basic form is two storeys and extends eastwards from an existing building which has been converted to a sixth form centre. The assembly hall and dining room anchor the design to the east with a sports hall to the west.[1] A linking crescent of offices, staff rooms, library and IT facilities on the north side joins the assembly hall block to the sports hall. The building footprint offers several advantages. It takes advantage of the site slope to improve the microclimate; it allows sunlight into the central street and classroom blocks; it provides via the street a valuable social and orientating space; and it separates the noisy and quiet areas effectively. The need for orientation is important in a school of 1,000 pupils when movement between lessons has to be efficiently conducted. The main school entrance is strategically located at the eastern end of the street and is marked by being a double-height fully glazed volume.

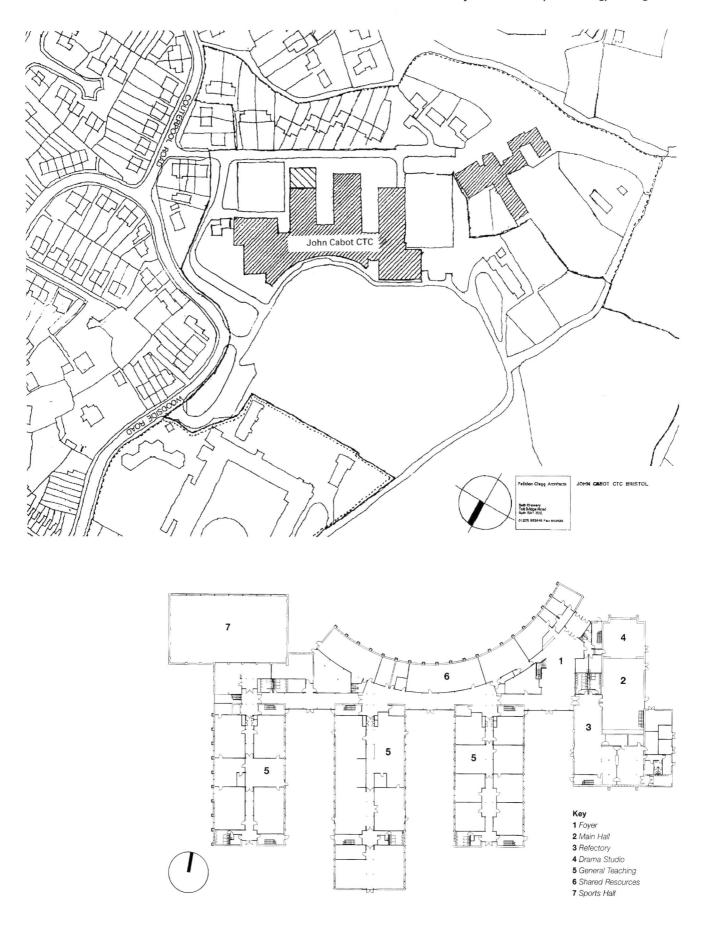

Key
1 Foyer
2 Main Hall
3 Refectory
4 Drama Studio
5 General Teaching
6 Shared Resources
7 Sports Hall

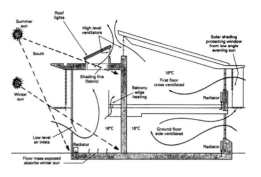

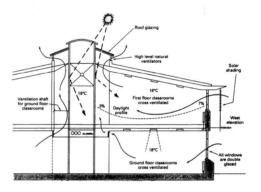

16.3 *Section, John Cabot City Technology College, Bristol. Notice the solar shading and glazed mall. (a) Crescent (b) Teaching block. Architects: Feilden Clegg Bradley.*

As the teaching day is from 08.30 h to 16.00 h the school is able to take advantage of daylight as the main means of providing the 300 lux necessary in the teaching spaces. Maximizing daylight is important as electricity consumption is met from the school's operating budget and can seriously eat into scarce teaching resources. Also electricity carries a high load compared with gas or oil in terms of carbon dioxide per unit of power. The school has a floor area of about 900m² of which about two-thirds are standard well-lit classrooms. Typically classrooms have cill to ceiling glazing to the outside and enjoy borrowed light from light wells at the rear of classrooms where they adjoin the corridor space. West-facing glazing is protected by motorized external roller blinds operated by teachers rather than via the building management system. Classrooms wings are on average 12m wide to maximize daylight penetration. Daylight is also effectively employed to light the main hall and dining area, employing a mixture of perimeter glazing and roof lights. The sports hall exploits its northerly orientation with a fully glazed hall, supplemented by high-level clerestories to the south.[2]

Table 16.1

John Cabot City Technology College: main design features

— finger plan which maximizes daylight penetration;
— shallow classroom depth (6-7m) to achieve effective cross-ventilation;
— double-height 'street' to act as daylight and ventilation zone;
— extensive use of perimeter glazing (65% to classroom);
— elaborate solar shading on south and west sides;
— roof-level windows and ventilation chimneys to encourage natural ventilation.

Buro Happold was determined to maximize the use of natural light and ventilation in order to produce an energy-efficient building which was also a joy to work and study in. Good levels of daylight are evident throughout the school, not just in classrooms but in the hall and offices. Although daylight factors of 1–2% are the minimum target for schools, the John Cabot CTC attains generally twice that

level without heat loss penalties. This is achieved by striking a balance between good daylighting and heat loss which tends to side towards daylight and a degree of direct sunlight penetration. Buro Happold's analysis of a typical teaching module found that a glazing area of 65% was the optimum ratio for the window to wall area.[3] However, because of glare problems, particularly reflected light on VDU screens, elaborate measures had to be taken to screen sunlight at the classroom perimeter.

Daylight, natural ventilation and passive solar design are treated as an integral package. Rather than plan the classrooms with single-sided ventilation, the strategy was one of cross-ventilation using the cross section of classrooms to encourage the necessary air movement for reducing heat and toxicity build-up from computers and other equipment. Most classrooms have an angled ceiling with top ventilation directly to the outside. Ground-floor classrooms ventilate to a duct in the double-height street as well as to the outside. The use of ventilating "chimneys" with relatively narrow classrooms (7m), profiled ceilings and manually opened ventilating ducts achieves about 6 ac/h which was considered acceptable.[4]

16.4 *External shading of a typical classroom. Architects: Feilden Clegg Bradley.*

16.5 *Gable end of classroom block showing the glazed mall which brings daylight and sunlight to the interior. Good levels of daylight, animated by controlled sunlight, add to energy efficiency and create a stimulating environment for learning. Architects: Feilden Clegg Bradley.*

The building services technology is simple, unobtrusive and contributes to the architectural character of the building. This is a City Technology College which does not hide its engineering; here building science is made visible, providing a potential learning resource which could be integrated with the curriculum.

There are three categories of classroom, each with its own operational and use demands. Most classrooms are what the architects classify as Class A. These are normal teaching rooms where the natural ventilation design will provide "effective cooling and fresh air ... throughout the year". Class B classrooms, where higher levels of equipment load are envisaged, contain in addition small fans placed in the classroom ducting. This category also embraces classrooms facing directly south where, with global warming, summertime overheating could become a problem. Class C classrooms are workshops where fume removal requires the installation of extract ducting within the classroom volume itself. The classification of classrooms into types allows each category to develop energy-efficient solutions, but it does limit operational flexibility – a problem especially evident when considering the growing use of IT equipment in schools.

Architecturally, the ventilating chimneys, the ridge of roof-top glazing, and the highly transparent facades with their finely engineered daylight shelves and solar shading make for a distinctive school. As a working environment, the central street and crescent of offices provide an attractive sequence of spaces for pupils and teachers alike. The use of single- and double-height volumes, the expression of the building services element architecturally, plus the employment of bright colours in the fabric blinds, create a lively and stimulating school committed to science, technology and business studies. The school acts as a beacon of regeneration in a relatively deprived area of Bristol, using the architectural language of low-energy design to signal optimism. The combination of the natural ventilation and maximization of daylight measures, plus good levels of insulation in walls ($0.32kWh/m^2$) and roofs ($0.3kWh/m^2$) produces an efficient building to operate. The John Cabot CTC has an energy consumption of about $187kWh/m^2y$, compared with a design prediction of around $173kWh/m^2y$ and a norm set in DfEE Design Note 17 of $240kWh/m^2y$.[5] However, electricity consumption is higher than predicted mainly due to manually operated lights.

16.6 *Double-height mall with pools of sunlight. Architects: Feilden Clegg Bradley.*

16.7 *Co-ordination of student lockers and seating at John Cabot CTC. Architects: Feilden Clegg Bradley.*

The design of the school allows building users (mainly teachers) to influence their immediate environment. Teachers can change the temperature and lighting levels in the classroom by operating the manual blinds and by opening windows or other vents. As a result "comfort, quality of space and appropriateness for its educational purposes"[6] are in the hands of teachers. This results in a responsive building but one with, in this case, problems with the energy control system (both manual and automated). Giving teachers and janitorial staff the ability to adjust the environmental controls locally leads to good psychological conditions but in terms of energy efficiency it can reduce performance. It is not uncommon in energy-efficient school buildings to find the blinds down (to reduce solar gain or glare) and the lights on. As Linton Ross, an architect with Feilden Clegg Bradley, states, "the system's interface needs to be easily understood and simple to adapt" to allow the building and the user to have confidence in the environmental engineering of the school.[7]

It is clear from monitoring the school's performance in terms of educational achievement that there is evidence to suggest that John Cabot out-performs other City Technology Colleges. There are signs of improvement in teacher performance and this is borne out by pupils taking their GCSE examinations. John Cabot CTC is in the top half of City Technology Colleges in the UK with 74% of pupils achieving above average results. Just as in smaller schools, especially for younger age groups and in rural areas, there was a correlation between performance in SATs test and green design, this is also borne out by evidence at John Cabot CTC. This may be due to aspects of the environmental design of the school, especially the emphasis upon daylight. Certainly, the students at John Cabot achieve 60% above intake expectations, with an average improvement of 90% on SATs outcomes.[8]

The match between the aspirations in the design of the school, the operating of the building management systems and the priority given to energy-efficiency measures (especially daylight and sunlight) may account for the correlation between green design and enhanced productivity. At an institutional level, the energy savings help to pay for extra computers and the employment of auxiliary teaching staff, which enhance teaching and learning. Less easily measured is the role the John Cabot CTC is

Table 16.2
John Cabot City Technology College: main user responses

- teachers perceive 6% improvement in productivity;
- school attractive to parents and pupils;
- image of school good for recruitment;
- summertime overheating problems (since rectified);
- difficulty in opening and shutting some windows (since rectified);
- noise transmission problems (solved by management changes);
- congestion due to lockers placed in central street (since rectified).

---

playing in revitalizing an inner-city neighbourhood of Bristol. There are signs, however, that this interesting design which gives maximum visibility to the sustainability agenda is leading to wider social and community benefits such as reduced community crime. In terms of life-cycle costing the initial stages of building management and maintenance have proved expensive, but there is evidence of enhanced value as a result of good green design. As with many innovative buildings, this college teaches that the true value of design becomes evident over time.

In the Probe survey (an independent evaluation of building performance; see p.204-7) conducted into the response to the building by staff and pupils, favourable reactions were received to "overall comfort, noise, lighting,

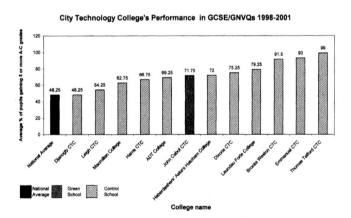

City Technology College's Performance in GCSE/GNVQs 1998-2001

winter temperature and winter air quality".[9] There were, however, problems encountered by users who expressed concerns over excessive summertime temperatures. Probe found that, as perceived by teachers, productivity was good with a gain of 6% attributable to the building. This perception of improvement is reflected in student examination results. Staff commented favourably upon the good working environment and overall image of the John Cabot CTC, and pupils and parents mention the popularity of the school, which is proving too small compared with the demand for places made by the local community: in 2001 there were 858 applications for 160 places. Also pupils are more likely to stay on into the sixth form than is the norm, confirming the added value attached to the school. So whereas performance indicators provide evidence of educational benefit for pupils, this school is also achieving wider social benefit in terms of community perceptions and teacher morale.

John Cabot CTC applied many of the educational and environmental standards outlined for City Technology Colleges in *Building Bulletin 72*.[10] In particular the design sought to create a 'place of learning' rather than just a

16.8 *Roofscape at John Cabot CTC showing the integration of energy and IT systems. Architects: Feilden Clegg Bradley.*

16.9 *Comparison of performance between City Technology Colleges. John Cabot CTC is highlighted. Architects: Feilden Clegg Bradley.*

school or college. The environmental approach led to spaces in the school (such as the central double-height street) which gave character and dignity to education. The crescent of offices on the north side and the fingers of classrooms to the south created a building which sits well in the landscape. Added to this the vertical articulation of columns and sub-frames, counter-balanced by the solar shading louvres and external blinds, provides animation of the facade whose logic derives from low-energy design. Built at a cost of £720/m² in 1992 the building provides good value for money. It is not only energy efficient but economical in the use of water. Consumption of delivered water is less than half that in similar colleges.[11]

The Probe report on John Cabot CTC encountered several problems with the school in operation. The main areas of design where performance initially was fully satisfactory were:

— the ridge ventilation above the first-floor corridors had been closed off due to poor winter performance; as a result the intended summertime cooling by stack effect did not occur;
— the high-level fanlights in classrooms and above the central street proved difficult to open and close; this affected the efficiency of ventilation and hence energy use;
— the installation of student lockers in the central street has caused congestion and noise in this important central space; however, recent changes in the management of the area have reduced adverse impacts;
— the building energy management system had failed to work properly, acting as a deterrent to effective building operation from an energy efficiency point of view.

In conclusion John Cabot CTC provides facilities which teachers, pupils and parents value. Although aspects of the design and management of the building have not performed as well as anticipated, remedial action has subsequently corrected the failings. The main finding in the Probe study of the building is the improvement in productivity (6%) perceived by teachers.[12] This is attributable to the attractive, responsive design and the favourable image created by the building. This suggests that the aesthetics of green design are important at a psychological level – the building is delightful and attractive to use. As found in earlier case studies the physical, psychological and physiological world of school buildings is important to successful teaching and learning.

The author wishes to acknowledge the help of James Wynn, Principal, and Peter Newland, Facilities Manager at John Cabot CTC, in preparing this chapter.

References

1. *Probe II: John Cabot City Technology College*, CIBSE members CD-Rom 2000, p. 1; see also A. Brister, "A lesson in school building", *Building Services Journal*, May 1994, pp. 17–20.
2. A. Brister, op.cit., p. 5.
3. Ibid., p.18.
4. Ibid.
5. *Probe II, op.cit.*, p. 8.
6. Ibid., p. 10.
7. Ibid.
8. Personal communications from James Wynn, Principal, John Cabot CTC.
9. *Probe II, op.cit.*, p. 13.
10. *Building Bulletin 72: Educational Design Initiatives in City Technology Colleges*, DfEE, 1991.
11. *Managing School Facilities Guide 1: Saving Water*, Norwich, HMSO, 1993. The typical figure is 12m³/pupil/yr. John Cabot CTC achieves 5.3m³/pupil/yr.
12. *Probe II, op. cit.*, p. 15.

17

Brian Edwards

ECA, Heriot-Watt University

17.1 *Location plan, Greenwich Millennium Village Primary School. Architects: Edward Cullinan Architects.*

Greenwich Millennium Village Primary School

The Greenwich Millennium Village School is part of a wider community of housing and public buildings designed to test the application of sustainable development. Built on the Greenwich peninsula, there is medium- and high-density housing designed by Ralph Erskine with Hunt Thompson Architects, a green Sainsbury's supermarket by Chetwood Associates, the Dome itself by the Richard Rogers Partnership and now a school and health centre designed by Edward Cullinan Architects with service engineers Fulcrum. These buildings and an ecology park along the River Thames form an integrated package of low-energy projects constructed to demonstrate the technical and aesthetic possibilities of sustainability.

The new school provides accommodation also for a community hall and crèche and has a health centre built alongside. Unlike most schools the Greenwich Millennium Village School will have over 300 operational days compared with the usual 200 days for a typical primary school. This is the result partly of the wider facilities provided as annexes to the school but also the ambition to use the school facilities (such as the sports hall) to help cement together the new community being built at Greenwich on this large brownfield site. As such the school and its grounds will be used in the evenings and at the weekends for a variety of social and community purposes. This has resulted in the school employing a 'centre manager' to ensure that the use of space is managed effectively to generate income for the school without impeding the core educational functions.

Not only is the school unusual in the wider facilities provided, it is designed and engineered to use mechanical ventilation and heat recovery rather than rely upon natural ventilation.[1] The system adopted is the Swedish hollow-

17.2 *Site plan, Greenwich Millennium Village Primary School, designed by Edward Cullinan Architects. Architects: Edward Cullinan Architects.*

17.3 *Plan, Greenwich Millennium Village Primary School. Architects: Edward Cullinan Architects.*

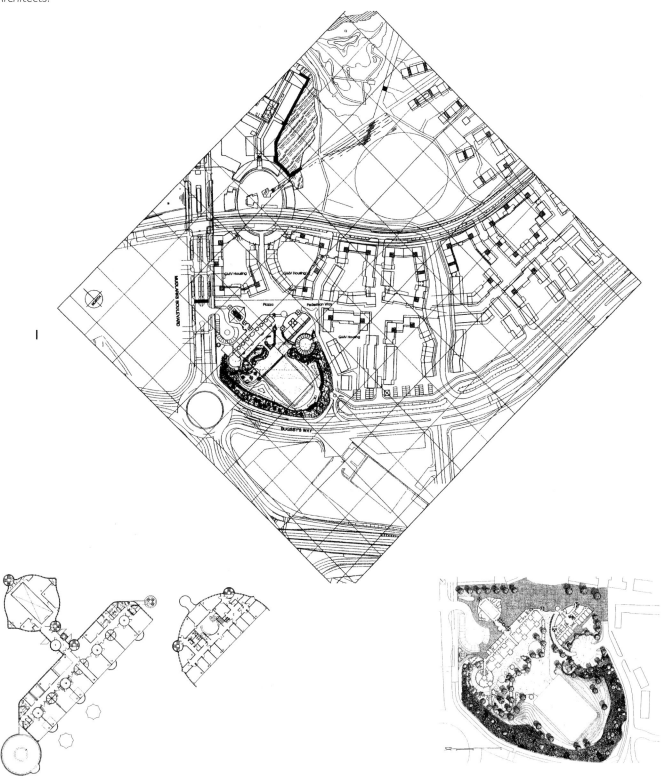

1

2

3

17.4 *Section, Greenwich Millennium Village Primary School.*
Architects: Edward Cullinan Architects.

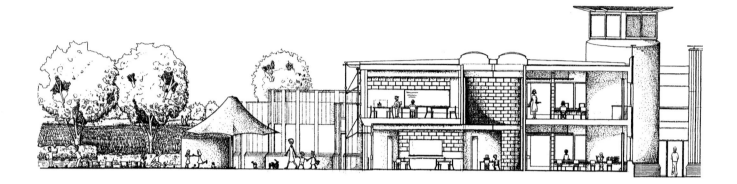

core system known as 'Termodeck', which the service engineers Fulcrum also used at the Elizabeth Fry Building at the University of East Anglia (see chapter 19). In adopting mechanical ventilation the Greenwich school departs from the guidance on design offered by DfEE *Building Bulletin 87* – especially the reliance on cross-ventilation to achieve the 8litres/second of fresh air per person required.[2] As mentioned previously, the difficulties with opening windows, the degree of external noise, the risk of truancy associated with low-level windows and the inaccessibility of high-level ones make this target difficult to reach in the reality of a typical school. This school tests the possibility of an alternative mechanical strategy and one where carbon dioxide levels of 1,000 ppm are practically guaranteed as against the reality of 4,000 ppm which occurs in winter in many existing schools, especially those designed to passive solar principles. Levels of carbon dioxide of 4,000 ppm are known to cause drowsiness, leading to a loss of performance and concentration in children.[3]

As is commonly the case the classrooms face south in a two-storey block. Each of the eight classrooms has a glazing area of about 70% and is 8m deep. The classrooms are divided by small circular drums which provide shared group rooms and WCs and act as light shafts within the depth of the classroom, allowing daylight to penetrate to the back of classrooms. The drums also provide service links between the Termodeck floors. The long length of the classroom wing is anchored architecturally to the east by a semi-circular health centre and to the west by a small circular crèche.

The south facade is necessarily finely engineered to strike a balance between daylight maximization, solar control and reduction in winter of heat loss and in summer of heat gain. The glazing is designed to a U-value of 1.6kWh/m², achieved by using double-glazing with external automatic blinds to control excessive heat. The west-facing windows have triple-glazing incorporating double panes of low-E units with integral blinds. The cost was kept down by standardizing sizes and bulk buying from the Scandinavian market. Classrooms use motorized awning blinds activated by a computerized system triggered by room temperature and sun altitude (with a high wind speed cut-off). Generally the school, health centre and crèche are highly glazed to the south and solidly constructed on other facades. Here walls are highly insulated and finished with a rainscreen of vertical English larch panelling, giving a U-value of 0.2kWh/m².[4]

The floor slabs of the school are constructed of standard concrete planks of Termodeck flooring at 1200mm centres. Each plank has a 150mm hollow core through which filtered and temperature-adjusted fresh air is ducted to the various rooms. Generally fan noise is controlled by using attenuated extract grilles able to achieve a 6bB reduction.

Termodeck offers advantages but the noise of fans can be a problem in spaces like classrooms where the teacher's voice is critical, and where exposed concrete plank construction provides little absorption of background noise. In the classroom, the hard ceiling surfaces are advantageous for projecting the voice of the teacher to the back of the classroom, but here a 0.8m strip of absorbent panelling has

17.5 *Section through school hall. Architects: Edward Cullinan Architects.*

17.6 *Sections through health centre. Architects: Edward Cullinan Architects.*

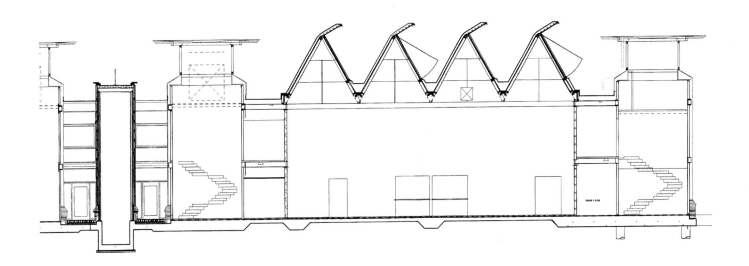

5

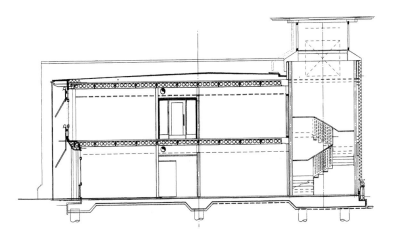

6

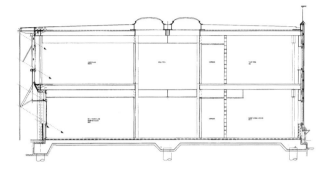

been constructed beneath the ceiling above the teacher's desk to combat specular sound reflection.[5] The amount of acoustic treatment to the walls and ceiling was dictated by DfES guidelines for reverberation times. The choice of surfaces in the classroom (carpet, plaster and concrete) had to be carefully considered to strike the correct balance between light penetration, sound quality and heat transfer.

Termodeck allows heat recovery to be exploited, thereby aiding energy conservation. Here two air-handling units incorporating heat exchangers achieve a 92% efficiency in heat recovery.[6] Although some cross-contamination occurs, the level of 1–2% is within guidelines and is less than with a passive solar flywheel.

Lighting levels are crucial to effective operation of the classroom. Research from the USA suggests that children learn quicker in well-lit classrooms and perform better in daylit examination halls than in those lit by artificial means. Here at this new Greenwich school a daylight factor of 4–5% has been achieved by full-height glazing on the south side and by providing 4m diameter daylight drums to pull light to the back of the 8m deep classrooms on the ground floor. Two classrooms share each drum – the light illuminating the corner opposite the circular study drums.

By way of contrast the school hall is lit by north lights set steeply pitched within the ceiling (Figure 17.7). The avoidance of direct sunlight is critical for sport and the design does allows for the incorporation of fluorescent lighting into the base of the north lights. Offices and a small library are generally to the north of a linking corridor which joins together the classrooms and gives access to the lift and stairs. Here light is controlled and more subdued for general IT areas.

The Greenwich Millennium Village School departs from orthodoxy in the UK and challenges many assumptions in *Building Bulletin 87*. In taking a fresh look at primary school design, and in integrating the school with other social facilities (such as a health centre), the building effectively bridges environmental and social sustainability. In adopting mechanical ventilation it also overcomes an increasing problem with highly insulated air-tight schools – that of inadequate levels of natural ventilation. Cullinan and Fulcrum have designed a school which deserves to be carefully monitored to measure not only the energy efficiency of the building but the effect upon teacher productivity and pupil performance.

Table 17.1
Greenwich Millennium Village Primary School: main features of design

- uses mechanical ventilation (Termodeck) with heat recovery;
- maximizes daylight with 70% south-facing glazing area to achieve solar gain;
- incorporates daylight drums to improve daylight penetration;
- uses triple-glazing and extensive blinds and awnings on west side;
- has English larch rainshield cladding;
- incorporates a crèche, community hall and nearby health centre, thereby supporting social sustainability.

Table 17.2
Energy features at Greenwich Millennium Village Primary School

- high levels of insulation to reduce running costs;
- high levels of air-tightness;
- double- and triple- glazing incorporating low-E glazing;
- south-facing classrooms for passive solar gain;
- high levels of daylight penetration using light wells;
- automatic sensors for lighting.

8

Table 17.3
Special educational features at Greenwich Millennium
Village Primary School

— links to health centre;
— after school club and crèche;
— drama and music studio available for community use;
— open learning centre for adult learning;
— food area designed for socializing before and after
  school;
— large class areas for special numeracy and literacy
  teaching.

9

Table 17.4
General environment features

— limited parking to discourage car use;
— integrated with bus, river bus and Tube facilities;
— encouragement of walking and cycling;
— sustainable construction with avoidance of PVC;
— indigenous species planted;
— area for children's planting;
— re-use of brownfield site.

References

1. John Field, 'Top of the class', *Building Sciences Journal*,
    February 2001, p. 26.
2. Ibid., p. 27.
3. Ibid.
4. Edward Cullinan Architects, Press Pack: Greenwich
    Millennium School, 2000.
5. Field, op. cit., p. 28.
6. Ibid., p. 29.

18

18.1 *Section and plan of Queen's Building, Anglia Polytechnic University. Architects: ECD Architects.*

Queen's Building, Anglia Polytechnic University, Chelmsford

David Turrent

ECD Architects

and **Mel Barlex**

Anglia Polytechnic University

The Learning Resource Centre (Queen's Building) at Anglia Polytechnic University in Chelmsford, Essex, is one of the first generation of interactive libraries to be built in Britain. Since the university already had an environmental policy when the design team was appointed it was natural that the building should be a model of best practice in energy efficiency. The site, a derelict former ball-bearing factory, signified the university's commitment to renewing the fabric of its home town.

The design stage

The building comprises 6000m² of library accommodation providing traditional bookshelf facilities, 700 reader spaces, a television studio and media production area, and seminar and catering facilities. The brief had three key features:

— to create a green building which would not cost more than other learning resource centres;
— to design a building which the university could use to enhance its reputation for good environmental practice and sympathetic urban renewal;
— to create a building from which lessons could be learned.

After some discussion the cost limit was set at £680/m² and in March 1993 the design team was assembled. It consisted of energy experts ECD as architects, and Ove Arup and Partners to provide structural and engineering design services. The technical team was assisted by the university's own project director Tim Mathews and Bucknall Austin, who provided cost advice.

The bones of the design evolved during a week-long workshop held at the beginning of the project. The design

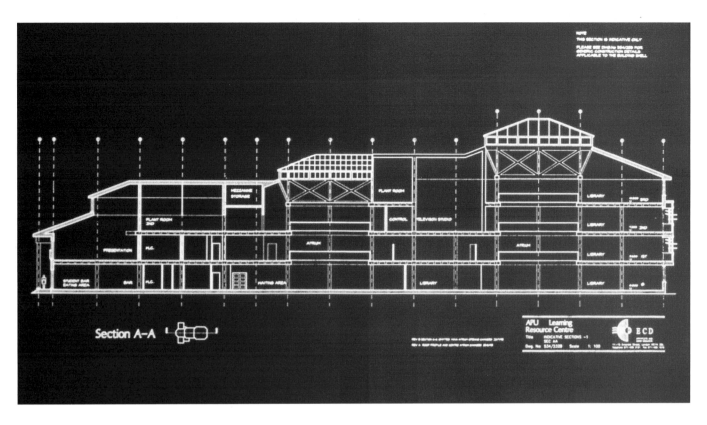

Section A-A

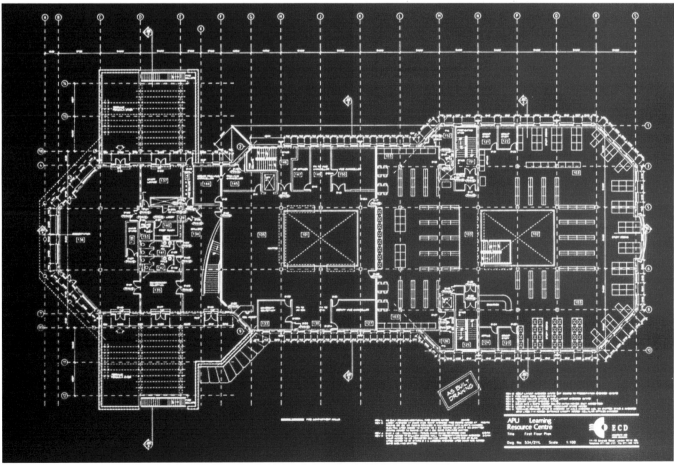

Table 18.1 Queen's Building, Anglia Polytechnic University: annual energy conservation kWh/m²

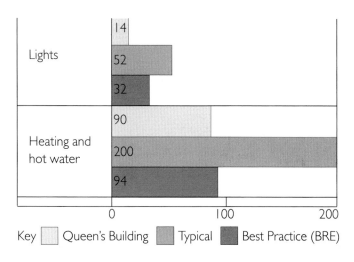

Lights	14
	52
	32
Heating and hot water	90
	200
	94

Key ▢ Queen's Building ▢ Typical ▢ Best Practice (BRE)

Source: Building Performance Research Unit, 1996.

team spent the week with the client, evolving on the first day the energy strategy and producing by the end of the week the building footprint. As this took shape and was modified, it influenced other factors from lighting design to plan shape and external planting layout. The team sought a holistic approach that integrated the design input of the architect, engineer and landscape designer. By assembling the design team at the start of the project and by working closely with client representatives, the cross-fertilization essential in green design emerged without difficulty.

Finding an energy-efficient solution

Aware that electricity was the greatest slice of bought-in energy, the design team evolved a layout which maximized natural light and ventilation. By integrating the thermal and lighting analysis, and by relating the results of the synthesis to fundamental architectural and planning questions such as plan depth, building height, orientation and landscape design, we achieved what proved to be a remarkably energy-efficient solution.

Our strategy was based upon the principles of natural lighting, natural ventilation, use of thermal mass in the building for radiant cooling, and high-efficiency condensing

gas boilers. These decisions added nothing to the cost of the library over funding council norms, but allowed the building to achieve a 74% saving in energy use in the first year. Since it opened in 1995 the Queen's Building has been monitored under an EU Thermie Programme (Chapter 11, pp.99-100) and results so far indicate an annual energy performance of 113 kW/m² as against the predicted 116 kW/m². Equated as a reduction in CO_2 emissions (the main greenhouse gas) the building achieves an 82% saving compared to an air-conditioned library. The Queen's Building uses about half the fossil fuel of a typical building, which is slightly better than the Best Practice guidelines of the Building Research Establishment (BRE). Remarkably these savings have been achieved at no additional capital cost.

Using the atria to maximum effect

The concept for the building is simple: two central atria, one at the north and one at the south, with library book stacks grouped around them (and hence contributing towards structural thermal capacity) and study spaces at the perimeter of the building to maximize daylight penetration. In cross section the building steps down from four to two storeys adding to the stack effect where the building is at its highest. The two atria are enclosed within the angled roof slope of the building, an arrangement which avoids turbulence and improves the look of the library.

The sectional profile of the atria was designed to deflect as much daylight into the building as possible. The angle of the balustrade and atrium walls at the top is splayed to bounce light into the lower areas and into adjoining library spaces. We also used fabric blinds in the atrium to diffuse daylight and screen glare.

The width, profile and height of the atria was chosen to maximize the stack effect in what is not a high building. Fresh air is drawn in around the perimeter of the building through window openings and low level vents, and exhausted through the atrium roofs. The currents of air are fan-assisted within the enclosed library study rooms. Floor to ceiling heights are fairly lofty (3.3m) in order to encourage thermal stratification. Since electric lighting is the main source of heat (about 60% of total gains) task lighting operated by the students at desk level is used rather than high levels of blanket ceiling lighting. Background lighting levels are 300 lux.

18.2 *Queen's Building, Anglia Polytechnic University. Architects: ECD Architects.*

Table 18.2 Queen's Building, Anglia Polytechnic University: main green features

— two atria to promote natural ventilation;
— triple-glazed windows with twin light shelves;
— lofty floor to ceiling heights;
— natural materials and low toxicity in construction;
— high structural thermal capacity;
— use of tree planting to provide solar shade and enhance micro-climate;
— energy performance better than BRE Best Practice, but at no extra cost.

Window operation

The design of windows is crucial to green buildings of any type. Working with Samson Windows, we evolved a triple-glazed window with a horizontal pivot-opening top section and associated twin light shelves. As is normal these days, the light shelves double up as solar shading on the south, west and east elevations. Their main function is to prevent glare on the VDUs around the perimeter, but they also reflect light onto the ceiling. The opening of windows is operated automatically since in a library there is little long-term investment by students in the quality of the working environment (unlike in offices). The Building Energy Management System (BEMS) controls not only the opening of windows but also the heating system and fan speeds. Beneath each window there is an air brick which brings fresh air into the building via the perimeter heating system, giving a constant half an air change per hour.

Innovation within a budget

The Queen's Building is in many ways a prototype, and a variety of design principles were married in its construction. We had to evolve a relatively new type of building while also subjecting it to recent thinking on environmental and energy strategy. Though energy conservation was a prime objective, we were also keen to look more broadly at the environmental performance of the building. We sought a design which would have a small ecological footprint while positively enhancing both the health and comfort of the building's users and the university's reputation. Materials were selected for their low toxicity; the finishes are mainly organic — stone, timber natural fibre carpeting. It seemed to us that the strategy of a low-energy, naturally ventilated building required a complementary palette of natural materials left in their untreated state wherever possible.

Anglia Polytechnic University was keen that while being innovatory the Queen's Building was delivered on time and on budget, both of which were achieved. The new Learning Resources Centre has produced the energy savings predicted, and provides a pleasant and healthy environment in which to study and work. Of course, it is not perfect, but considering the scale of design risk entered into by the professional team and client alike, monitoring in the first two years confirms the appropriateness of the concepts.

Monitoring performance

Since the university was testing many new ideas in the Queen's Building it was decided to seek the reaction of users. The university's own Building Performance Research Unit (BPRU) conducted a user survey in the form of a questionnaire issued on ECD's behalf. The results of the 100 detailed responses confirmed that in the eyes of both students and staff the Queen's Building is a qualified success. Generally speaking the heating, cooling and daylight strategy work well in terms of user perceptions, although there is an acoustic problem of noise transfer from the open atria areas to the study spaces. It is clear that the thermal benefits of atria in buildings such as this can be negated by the transmission of noise.

Table 12.3 Queen's Building, Anglia Polytechnic University: perception of thermal comfort

Season	hot	warm	slightly warm	neutral	slightly cool	cool
Summer	6%	17%	37%	33%	5%	2%
Winter	6%	7%	49%	28%	7%	3%

Source: Building Performance Research Unit, 1996.

Table 12.4 Queen's Building, Anglia Polytechnic University: comfort symptoms

	Sleepiness	Stuffy Nose	Headaches	Dry nose	Dry eyes
Summer	30%	10%	25%	9%	15%
Winter	40%	1%	15%	58%	12%

Source: Building Performance Research Unit, 1996.

18.6 Sketch by Ove Arup and Partners of window design, lighting and air currents, Anglia Polytechnic University. Architects: ECD Architects.

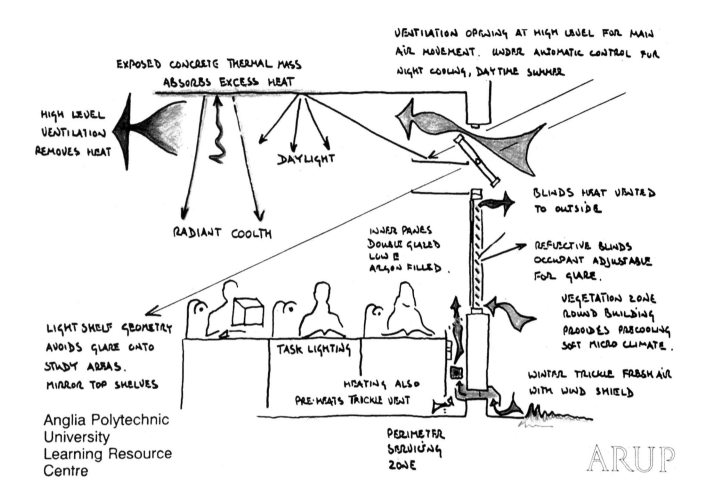

VENTILATION OPENING AT HIGH LEVEL FOR MAIN AIR MOVEMENT. UNDER AUTOMATIC CONTROL FOR NIGHT COOLING, DAYTIME SUMMER

EXPOSED CONCRETE THERMAL MASS ABSORBS EXCESS HEAT

HIGH LEVEL VENTILATION REMOVES HEAT

DAYLIGHT

RADIANT COOLTH

INNER PANES DOUBLE GLAZED LOW E ARGON FILLED.

BLINDS HEAT VENTED TO OUTSIDE

REFLECTIVE BLINDS OCCUPANT ADJUSTABLE FOR GLARE.

VEGETATION ZONE ROUND BUILDING PROVIDES PRECOOLING SOFT MICRO CLIMATE.

LIGHT SHELF GEOMETRY AVOIDS GLARE ONTO STUDY AREAS. MIRROR TOP SHELVES

TASK LIGHTING

HEATING ALSO PRE-HEATS TRICKLE VENT

WINTER TRICKLE FRESH AIR WITH WIND SHIELD

Anglia Polytechnic University Learning Resource Centre

PERIMETER SERVICING ZONE

ARUP

In the summer the building was perceived as being consistently too warm and in the winter too dry; 33% of people found the library slightly too warm in summer and 29% in the winter the remainder were happy except for experiencing headaches and drowsiness. The over-heating was largely the result of a sub-contractor who had over-ridden the routine for cooling to begin at 5.30am and forgotten to reset it, although even after this fault was rectified temperatures were still slightly too high. Evidence suggested that users were adapting their own clothes to suit the thermal environment. The problems of headaches and sleepiness could have been related to the air vents at the north gable not being opened in the early stages of the building's operation due to a short circuit resulting in the stack-effect air flows not occurring.

The following performance indicators are being monitored:

– monthly thermal electrical energy consumption;
– annual passive solar gain;
– measured overall building heat and loss coefficient;
– energy saving from the daylighting strategy;
– incidents of over and under heating;
– occupant responses;
– maintenance and implementation problems.

This data is being fed into the BEMS, which has dedicated software (developed by BPRU) to analyse the information and take appropriate action. The process has already highlighted weakness in the system and allowed fine tuning to occur. One effect of the data was to show that night-time purging of the structure was not working as planned,

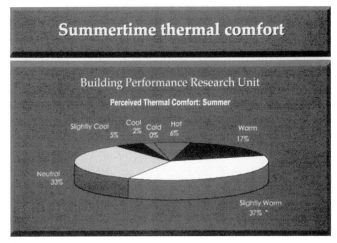

18.7 a, b *Pie chart by BPRU showing thermal comfort in summer and winter, Anglia Polytechnic University. Architects: ECD Architects.*

resulting in a higher ambient temperature than expected.

There is a great deal to learn from the Queen's Building – from its conception, construction and now from its users. One problem that did occur is that as a result of the design-and-build contract, a fair amount of contractor variation was permitted. The BEMS is useful, but did not provide the whole answer to the effective operation of the building from a user, energy and environmental impact point of view. We had a great deal of information, but did not have the integrated intelligence to allow us to interpret it and take the necessary action. The building controls are sophisticated, the performance information gathered under the Thermie Programme comprehensive, but without a proper framework we could not refine the building management system to resolve some of the initial difficulties; however, the problem has subsequently been overcome.

It is clear that there is a mismatch between the assumptions in the BEMS and how the building was actually constructed, rather than designed. The principles upon which we decided to operate the building have proved robust enough, but the fine tuning essential in all prototypes has yet to occur. We are confident that when a few small changes have been made the slightly stuffy conditions and higher than expected temperatures will be rectified. The points currently being reviewed are:

– daylight redistribution from atria;
– reduction of energy use from lighting and catering;
– introduction of passive humidification;
– refinement of night-time cooling controls.

Conclusion

The Queen's Building is a challenge to many people's perception of a library. The sense of openness and energy efficiency depart from normal practice. In our view it is one of the roles of higher education to set an environmental example by developing new approaches to sustainable construction. Naturally, the building suffers from the teething problems of any prototype, but we needed to address both the physics of the building and the cultural understanding of environmental issues for everybody involved from client to contractor and student.

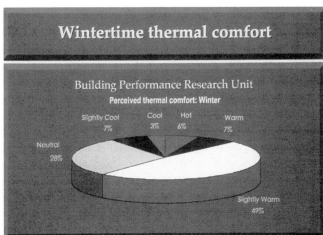

19

Elizabeth Fry Building, University of East Anglia, Norwich

Peter Yorke

formerly University of East Anglia

and **Richard Brearley**

John Miller and Partners

The University of East Anglia (UEA), founded in 1962, has a fine pedigree of Modern Movement buildings. The master-plan and many of the original buildings were designed by Sir Denys Lasdun. Sir Norman Foster designed the Sainsbury Centre for the Visual Arts in 1977, and more recently Rick Mather has added significantly to the ensemble. Other than Mather's contribution, however, most of the university's estate is marked by architectural rather than low-energy ambition. The most recent development, the Elizabeth Fry Building, is different: it seeks a marriage between high architectural art and low-impact environmental design.

Projecting an image

In the early 1990s the University of East Anglia learned through Mather's innovative approach to low-energy design that green architecture made sense financially and projected the right kind of image for a modern university. At Nelson Court and Constable Terrace, both designed by Mather to a brief that considered sustainable principles, the resulting buildings proved to be cost effective and, in their unusual design philosophy, attracted favourable publicity. Mather claimed, and monitoring subsequently confirmed, that the highly insulated residences would be heated mainly by the students' own body heat. The publicity was good for a university seeking to attract bright young students and helped to legitimise energy conservation and give it cachet on the campus.

Low-energy design principles

The brief for the Elizabeth Fry Building was written in 1992. It required the new building to be extremely good value for money both in capital and running costs. Although the

19.1 *Site plan of the Elizabeth Fry Building at the University of East Anglia in the context of the adjacent Nelson Court and at right angles the curving wing of Constable Terrace. Architects: John Miller and Partners.*

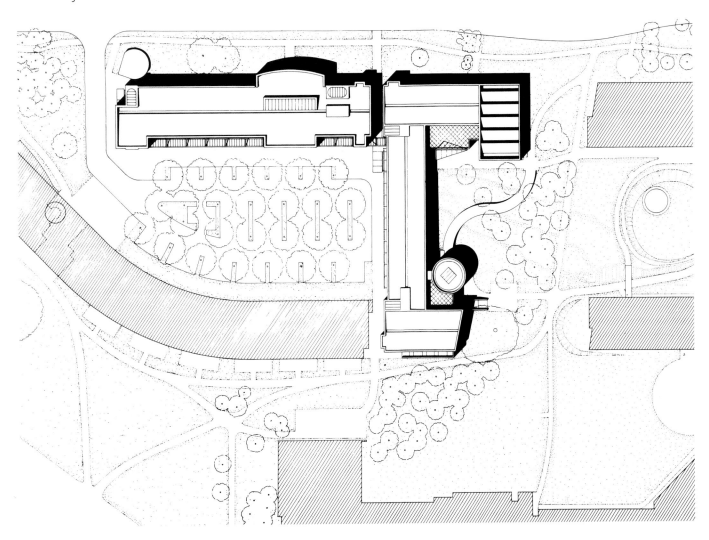

building was to demonstrate low-energy design principles, it was not to cost more than more orthodox approaches. This was the challenge for architects John Miller and Partners, who were appointed to prepare the design and competitive tender under the JCT 80 Contract.

The site for the Elizabeth Fry Building forms a courtyard with the wing of Constable Terrace residences and an earlier teaching building by John Miller and Partners. It is situated near the Sainsbury Centre in an area of the campus sheltered by trees to the west and Lasdun's megastructure of teaching areas and laboratories to the south and east.

Unlike the residences, which are occupied for 24 hours a day, the Elizabeth Fry Building was to be a conven-

tional university teaching building inhabited during normal office hours. It was not, therefore, possible to exploit process' heat from students and equipment to the same degree. Calculations showed that the Elizabeth Fry Building needed two 241KW gas boilers (with a third as back-up), but not the full central heating systems normally encountered. Our target outlined in the leaflet Energy Efficiency in Buildings for Further and Higher Education (1992) was to get well below 190kWh/m^2, which is considered 'good practice', and approach the 'best practice' figure of 100Wh/m^2. In the event we achieved 119kWh/m^2, including not only heating, but also hot water, power and lighting.

19.2 *Detail of 'Termodeck' construction, Elizabeth Fry Building, University of East Anglia. Architects: John Miller and Partners.*

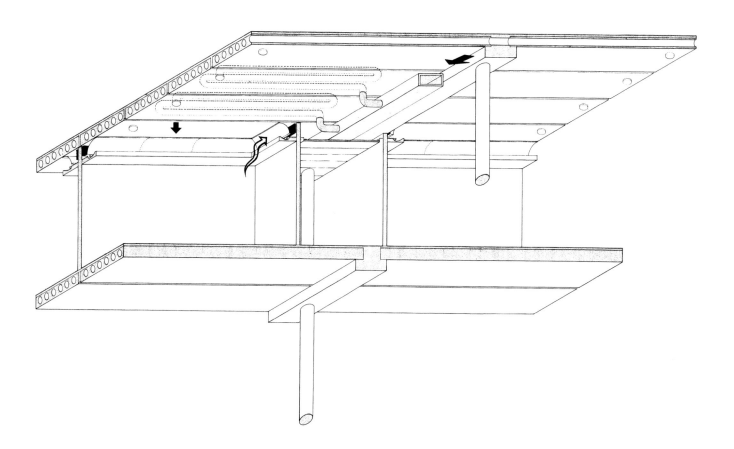

Finding an alternative to air-conditioning

The key to energy efficiency lies in the brief and the presence of an enlightened client willing to take risks. The university was particularly keen to avoid air-conditioning. Taking a long-term view of energy and building maintenance costs, and with concern for the health and wellbeing of those on campus, its policy was only to employ full air-conditioning in special areas such as the conservation room in the Sainsbury Centre and in certain laboratories. In the Elizabeth Fry Building even the enclosed lecture theatres avoid its use.

With the assistance of the energy consultants Fulcrum Engineering Partnership and Energy Advisory Associates, John Miller and Partners employed a novel form of construction known as 'Termodeck', which utilizes standard precast hollow core planks. These hollow structural members allow circulating air moved by pumps to moderate temperatures (see Chapter 12 on BRE building).

In winter warm air, heated by three domestic-sized boilers, is circulated through the building fabric: in summer night-time purging of the structure takes place using cool night air in contact with the ground. In both seasons the thermal capacity of the concrete structure has a moderating effect upon interior temperatures, assisted by air circulating through the hollow construction.

Maintaining high design standards

With a tradition on campus of providing high standards of architectural design, the new building had to achieve energy efficiency without compromise to the design expectations of the university. This double challenge led to many of the design decisions. It encouraged us to look to thermal mass as a means of giving thickness and architectural weight to the walls and contrasting this with deep cut expressive windows. It informed the organization of functions, with the

19.3 *Sectional isometric view, Elizabeth Fry Building, University of East Anglia. Architects: John Miller and Partners.*

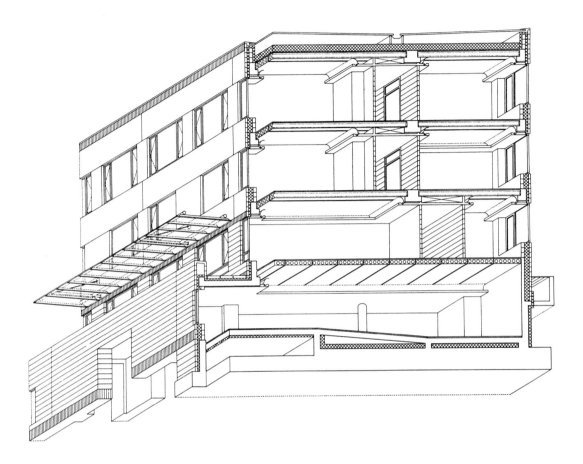

largest occupancy rooms at the base. It led also to the simple rectangular and linear form. The choice of colour and texture of the materials helps to give meaning, in both a green and an architectural sense, to the parts of the building, which become visually lighter as they rise from the ground.

We sought an engineered solution to architectural design, but not a high-tech one. By sourcing materials locally and referring to conventional building techniques we were able to combine a form of contexturalism with more universal architectural aims. It was evident that with no additional capital cost available, the architecture, building services and structure would each have to contribute positively to energy performance. David Olivier, an energy adviser, helped to identify the critical requirements and evolve a simple sustainable energy strategy to suit.

When we analyzed the brief it became evident that the building could house at any one time a population of around 800 people in an internal floor area of about 3000m². With these numbers heat gains and adequate ventilation in the summer were identified as critical items which had to be addressed. Summer temperatures are particularly important to universities since this is the time of the year when students sit their examinations and precedent has established that poor environmental conditions are legitimate grounds for appeal for poor examination results.

Planning the building

The site for the Elizabeth Fry Building was a narrow sloping strip edged to the north by trees, to the south by Mather's curving Constable Terrace and parking courtyard, and to the east by our earlier occupational and physiotherapy building. Orientation of the land suggested an east/west axis with the main student entrance to the south. The linear form of the building allows it to define a square with its neighbours and the choice of common materials and heights encourages

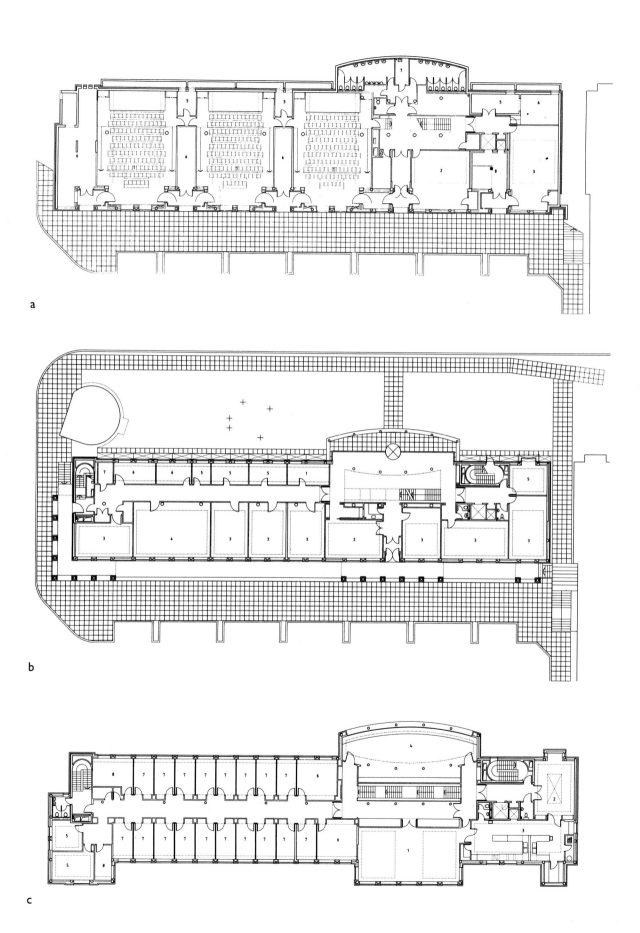

a

b

c

19.4 a, b, c *Lower ground, ground and second floor plans, Elizabeth Fry Building, University of East Anglia. Architects: John Miller and Partners.*

19.5 *South elevation with open arcade above ground-floor lecture theatres, Elizabeth Fry Building, University of East Anglia. Architects: John Miller and Partners.*

a sense of integrated and cohesive development in contrast with the openness of earlier parts of the UEA campus.

The planning of the building places the lecture theatres in a lower ground floor with single side access directly from a pedestrian walkway on the south side. Seminar and conference rooms for outside courses are situated on the upper ground floor with access from the north side, and a further two floors above are provided for more discrete departmental use. The arrangement of open arcade and solid concrete encased lecture theatres and conference seminar rooms on the south side allowed us to take advantage of the thermal capacity of the structure in contact with the ground while also providing solar shading. The heavy thermal load of 800 students, however, exceeded the ability of thermal mass alone to cool the building in the summer.

Energy-saving solutions

The employment of Termodeck in the construction assisted the cooling process. Widely used in Sweden, Termodeck is a proprietary system whereby the ventilation supply air is passed through precast hollow core concrete to adjust internal temperatures.[1] The system uses displacement ventilation with an air supply which brings air into direct contact with the ground via pipes placed under the ground floor slab. The result is a 'fresh-air feeling' and remarkably constant temperatures even under extreme external conditions.[2]

Two other factors led to low-energy consumption: a heavily insulated building envelope (U value 0.2W/m²°C) with the avoidance of thermal bridging and highly airtight construction. The involvement of David Olivier and Fulcrum Engineering Partnership, the appointed building services engineers, at the detailed design stage, and co-operation with the contractor on site, helped to ensure air-tightness of one air-change per hour at 50Pa under the BRE fan pressurisation test.[3]

Cost margins did not permit raised floors and the exploitation of the thermal capacity of the structure prohibited suspended ceilings. As a result service ducts are limited in extent to the main central corridors. Also with no distributed radiator-based heating system, pipework is limited to vertically stacked wc cores. While the use of Termodeck added to cost, there was a considerable balance of benefit elsewhere.

Lighting and air extraction are combined in a system developed by Fulcrum Engineering Partnership. Air is extracted over the light fittings to minimize heat build-up in cellular offices with corridors providing low pressure drop-return air paths.[4] Artificial lighting is confined to the perimeter of the rooms to expose the soffits, which act as light reflecting surfaces. Behind the light fittings are removable coved reflectors which provide cable ways for small power and data distribution.

The placement of lecture theatres and the use of exposed concrete structure meant that we had to maximize the surface contact between structure and air. The main structural frame of *in-situ* concrete with closely spaced perimeter columns supports a system of hollow pre-cast concrete floor and roof units. Below the raking ground-floor slab concrete chambers are constructed for the circulating ground cooled air. The integration of structural and services design is a notable feature of the building, especially the way fresh-air ventilation incorporates recycled energy from the

19.6 *Entrance hall at Elizabeth Fry Building, University of East Anglia. Note heavyweight construction and recessed windows. Architects: John Miller and Partners.*

19.7 *Translucent solar protection screens on south side of Elizabeth Fry Building, University of East Anglia. Architects: John Miller and Partners.*

heat exchanges. Since energy saving was our priority each step in the heat exchange route was checked for its efficiency.

Table 19.1 Elizabeth Fry Building, University of East Anglia: main green features

- orientation and building planning to reduce solar gain and maximize passive cooling;
- use of thermal capacity of concrete structure for cooling;
- use of Termodeck system of hollow construction for ventilation;
- use of ground temperature for cooling linked to Termodeck construction;
- shallow floor plan to maximize use of daylight;
- very high levels of insulation;
- high levels of structural air-tightness;
- integral lighting and ventilation design;
- triple glazing and integral solar shading on south elevation.

It is widely recognized that high thermal mass requires high insulation levels in the building envelope. At the Elizabeth Fry Building we employed 200mm full fill mineral fibre baths cavity insulation with plastic wall-ties to avoid thermal bridging, and 300mm mineral quilt at roof level. Windows are triple glazed with anti-sun coating and integral venetian blinds to control solar gain.

External solar protection is provided to windows on the south elevation where trees have also been planted close to the building for the same purpose. Rainwater from the building is collected into a holding tank, to irrigate the trees in summer. To comply with the client's need for low-energy and healthy design we employed high-efficiency fluorescent lights with anti-flicker ballasts and generally placed the control of the working environment directly in the hands of the user.

Conclusion

The Elizabeth Fry Building continues the UEA's well-publicized policy of procuring environmentally responsible, low-energy buildings. Like the slightly earlier buildings, the emphasis is upon a passive environmental response, good air-tightness, high levels of insulation, and active use of the thermal capacity of the structure. Built at a cost of £812/m^2, the building provides considerable benefits in terms of energy bills at no great increase over university norms.

The solution is novel in some respects (especially the use of the Termodeck system) and is currently being monitored by the Building Research Establishment. Early results suggest that the predicted savings in energy costs are being met, and equally important, that the building is providing a satisfactory environment for learning while adding to the UEAs legacy of fine modern architecture.[5]

References

1. 'Sensitive addition to a campus', *The Architects' Journal*, 15 June 1995, p. 35. The building services account was prepared by Andy Ford of Fulcrum Engineering Partnership.
2. Ibid.
3. Ibid.
4. Ibid.
5. Personal communication with Professor John Tarrant, former Pro Vice Chancellor, University of East Anglia, at a meeting on 24 October 1996.

20

Cable and Wireless College, Coventry

David Prichard

MacCormac Jamieson Prichard
Architects
and **John Beatson**
Cable and Wireless Plc

The Cable and Wireless College outside Coventry is a special kind of building with unusual environmental needs. Because of the large amount of telecommunications equipment used in training, the building has high heat loads and, since a plan depth of more than 40m was required in the teaching wings, the environmental and energy constraints on design were considerable.

The brief

The brief in 1993 from Cable and Wireless was for a green building, reflecting the company's demanding environmental policy as well as a tradition of naturally conditioned buildings as expressed in the Fiji branch headquarters building constructed about 100 years ago in Suva. This has big balconies, large open windows and a roof profile that encourages air flow. The new college was also to be environmentally friendly though for a vastly different climate and for an age when IT equipment represents a significant source of unwanted heat gains.

The site chosen for the new college is centrally located in England close to the University of Warwick and has good access for both public and private transport. The college operates as an autonomous business, providing short courses and residential training for Cable and Wireless and other telecommunication companies.

The client, architect (MacCormac Jamieson Prichard) and engineer (Ove Arup and Partners) collaborated at the outset to generate building forms that achieved the required environmental and energy standards. Building procurement from a green perspective meant that the environmental strategy for the new college had to dovetail into other areas of green operation, such as waste management, paper use, and employing suppliers with sound environmental credentials. This perspective influenced all aspects of the procurement

20.1 *View of model showing teaching rooms in foreground, Cable and Wireless College, Coventry. Architects: MacCormac Jamieson Prichard.*

20.2 *Plan of Cable and Wireless College, Coventry. showing relationship between teaching wings (bottom), residences (top) and leisure pavilion (right). Architects: MacCormac Jamieson Prichard.*

1

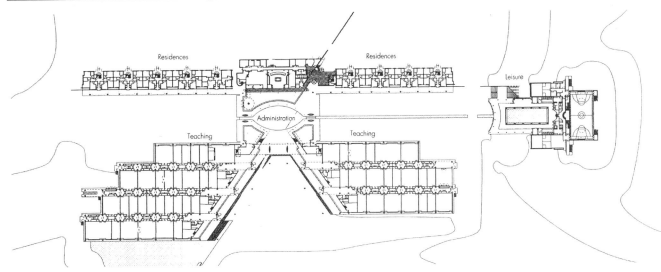

2

of the building from the choice of site to the selection of consultants and contractor. When you have a company committed to good environmental practice, the carrying out of building development provides an ideal opportunity to project a green image to clients and employees.

Commitment to biodiversity

The Cable and Wireless green building strategy does not stop at energy efficiency or waste disposal. It seeks to help to sustain biodiversity in both remote and urban situations

by simple schemes such as building nesting boxes for the Bermudan Blue Bird into the walls of a new Earth Station on that island, and a development in Richmond providing roosting space for bats within the roof of the building. The need to develop new sustainable energy sources has not been neglected and pilot schemes for powering telephone switches by wind and solar power have been implemented in St Vincent and the Falklands.

The college at Coventry was not the only green building under development by Cable and Wireless at the time. The John Cabot City Technology College in Bristol, designed by

20.3 *Detail of facade, Cable and Wireless College, Coventry. The wave-shaped roof is based upon the optional profile far natural ventilation. Architects: MacCormac Jamieson Prichard.*

20.4 *The rationale for the classroom profile, Cable and Wireless College, Coventry. Architects: MacCormac Jamieson Prichard.*

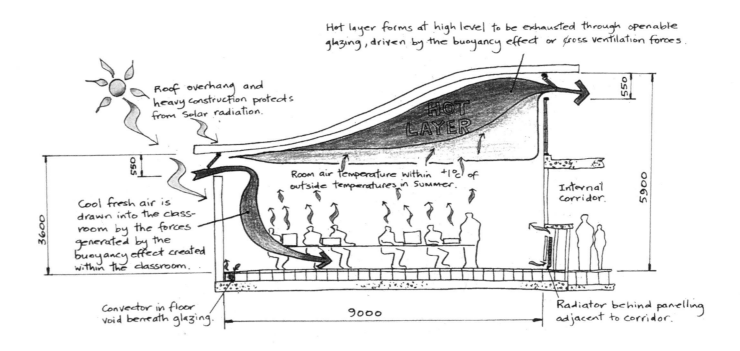

Hot layer forms at high level to be exhausted through openable glazing, driven by the buoyancy effect or cross ventilation forces.

Roof overhang and heavy construction protects from solar radiation.

HOT LAYER

550

Room air temperature within ±1°C of outside temperatures in Summer.

Internal corridor.

5900

550

3600

Cool fresh air is drawn into the class-room by the forces generated by the buoyancy effect created within the classroom.

Convector in floor void beneath glazing.

9000

Radiator behind panelling adjacent to corridor.

Feilden Clegg Bradley and engineered by Buro Happold, emphasized the use of natural daylight, natural ventilation and control of solar gain by user-operated external blinds and the integration of security with energy efficiency in the design of the facade. The green aspects of the Bristol College for 1000-plus pupils have been warmly welcomed by its users and were one of the reasons for the adoption by the college of a pilot 'global action plan' environmental scheme.

At the Cable and Wireless College at Coventry we sought a design solution which enhanced the company image, maximized the quality of the learning environment, and was energy efficient. The college consists of four building types, residential, teaching, administration and a leisure pavilion. The teaching wings (the subject of this case study) are arrays of 9m x 4.5m modules, which were derived from furniture layout studies for the different room uses. We had to be able to configure the space into a variety of sizes for lecture, seminar and laboratory rooms, and so for flexibility the dividing walls between the modules were non-load bearing and lightweight. For reasons of adaptability the

teaching wings are on one level and in the west wing there are four rows of modules creating a 43m-deep plan.

Environmental control

Going back to first principles, the design team sought to minimize heat loss in the winter and heat gain in the summer and to reduce the use of mechanical plant and electric lighting. We also sought a solution that is simple in concept and operation. Implicit in the approach was the view that people learn better in an attractive, natural environment and that low-energy consumption is best achieved by straightforward measures such as orientation, built form, layout and understandable controls. Desk-top analysis suggested that a naturally ventilated college would use 50% less energy than a fully air-conditioned one. The precedent for the concept behind the teaching wings is the typical Victorian classroom with its height, large opening windows, perimeter radiators and high-level ventilation.

20.5 *The wave-form roof profile and deeply set windows at the Cable and Wireless College, Coventry, reduce both glare and solar gain. Architects: MacCormac Jamieson Prichard.*

Table 20.1 Cable and Wireless College, Coventry: main green features

— high ceiling, wave-form roof profile based upon modelled air movement;
— natural ventilation for internal heat gains of up to 50kW/m²;
— chilled water recirculating fan coils in laboratories;
— natural and mechanical cooling systems used in complementary manner;
— high level of occupant control of working environment through blind and light switches;
— natural buoyancy ventilation using high-level windows and low-level air intake;
— differentiation of window area between south and north to prevent over-heating;
— extensive eaves oversail to provide solar shading.

Our preference for simple low-tech solutions led us to analyze the three levels of environmental control:

— the building fabric is the primary climate moderator;
— the building services provide the basic stability;
— the personal 'trim' devices (e.g. opening windows) are the psychological safety valve.

The interaction between these levels leads to the building section which is the basis of the low-energy component of the design.

Wave-form roof

Architecturally, the most distinctive element of the college buildings is the wave-form of the roof, the precise profile of which evolved as we modelled air movement. The profile of the roof allows the building to achieve natural (i.e. non-mechanical) ventilation for internal heat gains of up to 50kW/m². In some technical laboratories where gains are likely to exceed 50kW/m² there are recirculating fan coil units served with chilled water from a 47kW chiller unit. Cooled air is supplied through the raised floor void to outlets below the heat-emitting equipment, thus neutralizing heat spill at source. This results in the natural and mechanical cooling systems

complementing each other. We reduced cooling to 47kW, which is very low for a 5000m² building. In the teaching wings heating is provided by perimeter convector heaters served by a central plantroom, and within each classroom there is a pair of thermostatically controlled radiators which can be operated by the occupants.

Ventilation

The section of the roof allows independent ventilation for each room of the deep-plan building and there are controls within each room. Heat accumulates at high level and is convected out of the space and replaced by cooler air, which enters at low level. The section reflects the fact that natural buoyancy takes the heated stale air out through high-level windows and thus draws fresh air in at low level. The solution is elegant, reasonably cheap in capital cost, and efficient in terms of energy use.

A typical classroom has 2m² of double-glazed window to the south and 8m² facing north. Two-thirds of the north face is translucent to reduce glare. The roof eaves oversail the perimeter wall to provide solar screening for the exposed elevations. Additional glare control is provided by motorized diffusing roller blinds. A single row of switches by

20.6 *Cable and Wireless College, Coventry, with PowerGen Building in background. Architects: MacCormac Jamieson Prichard and Bennetts Associates respectively.*

the door to each room activates blinds, two gangs of lights and opening windows, thus enabling independent control by the occupants. Corridors are lit by a combination of domed rooflights, wall glazing and halogen lamps.

By testing different classroom height and roof section profiles in the Department of Applied Mathematics and Theoretical Physics at the University of Cambridge (using the saline modelling technique) we were able to confirm the near linear relationship between air-change rates and internal heat gains. The models helped us to arrive at the optimum configuration for opening windows.

Conclusion

Major companies normally spend far more on personnel than buildings or energy. This means that staff comfort and satisfaction with the working environment is more important than energy savings, assuming that satisfaction leads to improved productivity Simple, easily understood buildings such as this make sound assets if you take a medium to long-term view. Energy costs are currently low (though they may not remain so) so benefit to a company

lies in having a building in which staff are happy, productive and encouraged to engage in creative intercourse. The simplicity of the Cable and Wireless building is important too – a typical college spends 32% of the building budget on mechanical and electrical services, but here the figure was half that in the teaching wings.

A Probe study has revealed that the building has not performed quite as well as was hoped. Probe is a post-occupancy research project managed by *Building Services Journal* and Halcrow Gilbert. It provides feedback on the actual performance of the building after a period of use. Perhaps in this case too many controls have been placed in the hands of untrained users, resulting in overheating, underheating and high energy consumption for lighting. Like all innovative buildings there is a learning curve for occupants who are used to either air-conditioned space or the simple controls of a home. When staff and delegates have adjusted to the unusual design and its controls, and with a little education on blinds and lights, the building should perform much as predicted.

For Cable and Wireless the building emphasizes its commitment to innovation and sustainable business operations. After a period at the college delegates will return to often distant regions of the world with a greater understanding of the energy environment. That is another way in which 'green buildings pay' – they are part of the education needed for a more sustainable age.

Further reading

1. Probe 5: Cable and Wireless College, *Building Services Journal*, June 1996.
2. Where delegates go to have fun, *The Architects' Journal*, 11 August 1994, pp. 31–39.
3. Cable Talk, *Building Services Journal*, November 1993.
4. Facilities Economics, Bernard Williams Associates.
5. 'The Green Wave', *Arup Journal*, 1.1995.
6. 'Only Connect', *Architectural Review*, May 1994, pp. 24–31.
7. 'Wave Power', *Building*, 25 March 1994.
8. 'Hidden Assets', *The Times*, 22 March 1997.

21

Sustainability for the longer term: new technologies and building design

Peter F. Smith

Sheffield Hallam University

and **Brian Edwards**

ECA, Heriot-Watt University

Since the first edition of this book, two events have changed the balance of the account further in favour of green buildings. The first is the *Third Assessment Report* (*TAR*) published at the end of 2000 by the Scientific Committee of the International Panel on Climate Change (IPCC). The second is the cataclysmic events in New York and Washington of September 11th 2001.

Global warming

The report from the IPCC Working Group 2 has up-rated most of its predictions regarding global warming. It states that

> regional changes in climate, particularly temperature, have already affected a diverse set of physical and biological systems in many parts of the world. Examples include shrinking of glaciers, thawing of permafrost, later freezing and earlier break-up of ice on rivers and lakes, lengthening of mid- to high-latitude growing seasons (now put at 18 days), poleward and altitudinal shifts of plant and animal ranges, decline in some plant and animal populations, and earlier flowering of trees, emergence of insects, and egg-laying birds.[1]

Atmospheric concentrations of carbon dioxide are at their highest for at least 420,000 years and probably 20 million years. The same can be said for methane (another greenhouse gas) which has increased 151% since 1750 as a result of human activity. Yet there are still those who affirm that the climate changes that are clearly in evidence are merely part of the Earth's normal cyclic activity. The *TAR* states that 'There is new and stronger evidence that most of the warming observed over the last 50 years is attributable to human activities.'[2] This evidence is the result of new detection techniques which are able to identify anthropogenic greenhouse gases and distinguish them from agents of natural warming. The *TAR* has expanded on its original scenarios with its Special Report on Emission Scenarios (SRES). This is not the place to consider them in detail. What they amount to is the prediction that, by 2100, the level of atmospheric carbon dioxide will be between 540 and 970 ppm against the pre-industrial level of 270 ppm. The absolute range is between 450 ppm and 1260 ppm, that is 350% higher than in 1750.[3]

If we are already seeing significant climate changes, as indicated by the report, at 350 ppm concentration, the effect of 970 ppm is unimaginable, yet that is where we are heading at present. At a RIBA conference in October 2001 Sir John Houghton, the co-chairman of the IPCC Working Group 2, confirmed that the world has not departed one iota from the 'business as usual' scenario presented by the first IPCC report in 1991. The report of 2000 slightly raises temperature rise predictions over the 1995 *Second Assessment Report*. Now it is expected to peak at 5.8° C by 2100. But what really should set alarm bells ringing is the statement that "all land areas will warm more rapidly than the global average, particularly those in the northern high latitudes in the cold season". The report adds that in certain parts the overland warming could be more than 40% higher than the global mean. We may be talking of around 8.5° C probably in central southern Europe.

The report adds a further note of uncertainty sounded by the fact that the models indicate that current carbon dioxide emission levels should be producing double the atmospheric concentration that is evident from measurement. Somewhere it is being sequestered. The probable answer is the Amazon rainforest. It was thought to be in carbon balance, but in fact it is soaking up substantial extra carbon dioxide by expanding rapidly. The palaeo-climatic record shows that this happened in the distant past and during that period there came a point at which warming and drought caused rapid die-back and enormous releases of carbon back to the atmosphere. Fifty-five million years ago all the ice caps had disappeared; the sea level was 21m higher than today and the temperature was about 6°

C above today's average. Then suddenly there was a rapid rise of a further 8° C, probably triggered by the warming oceans releasing methane hydrates trapped on the ocean bed. The results were catastrophic at 14° C above today. No one is sure what this threshold is, but a 6 degree rise would seem to be the danger point and 2050 the trigger date for a rapid acceleration in temperature.

The latest suggestion from Antarctic scientists is that sea levels could rise by 6m within 25 years. Many millions of people live below 1m above sea level. In the UK the government acknowledges that the 5m contour is the high-risk threshold. The Thames barrage is already deemed to be inadequate. By 2050 we could be seeing a remarkable change to the character of London.

September 11th 2001

The events of September 11th 2001 have added enormous weight to the importance of green buildings. They now have a heightened security dimension as alternative and benign platforms for renewable energy generation. Green buildings are often relatively low-rise and hence do not provide a conspicuous target and can be readily evacuated.

The government is rightly concerned about the future of energy in the UK since the current nuclear capacity will have been decommissioned at the latest by 2025. In addition we will be faced with:

– obsolescence of large conventional power stations like Drax;
– increasing uncertainties regarding oil in terms of reserves, access and price; as the Princeton professor and petroleum geologist Kenneth Deffeyes put it recently: "We have ten years to get over our dependency on crude oil";
– diminishing gas reserves with increasing reliance on unstable countries.

Now, as a result of September 11th, we are faced with recalibrating our scales of vulnerability, especially in terms of the reliability of supplies of energy. Large power plants, especially nuclear, are potential prime targets now that

21.1 *Nuclear power stations face an uncertain future after September 11 2001.*

21.2 *Key interactions in future electricity generation.*

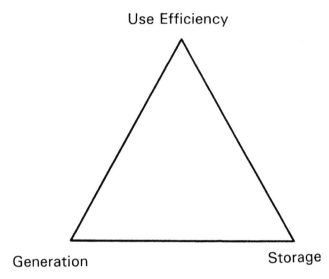

terrorism has been ratcheted up to a hitherto inconceivable level. As buildings are the largest single sectoral users of energy, this has particular concern for all involved in the construction industry.

Even before these events the Royal Commission on Pollution report on energy recommended: "a shift from very large, all-electricity plant towards smaller and more numerous combined heat and power plants. The electricity system will have to undergo major changes to cope with this development and with the expansion of smaller scale, intermittent renewable energy sources."[4] This accords with the view of the Washington Worldwatch Institute which states "An electricity grid with many small generators is inherently more stable than a grid serviced by only a few large plants."[5] Now there are even more compelling reasons why the government should act on the advice of the Royal Commission, because for the World Trade Center you could easily substitute Sellafield or Sizewell B. Many nuclear plants are sited along the coast so are vulnerable to attack from either the air or the sea. A 179-tonne Boeing 767 or an Exocet missile from a rusty freighter which is then abandoned will do untold radiation damage.

Table 21.1
Comparison of energy strategies between twentieth and twenty-first centuries

Twentieth century	Twenty-first century
— large fossil fuel power stations;	— community-based 'waste' power stations;
— nuclear power;	— renewable energy;
— buildings as major consumers of energy;	— buildings as generators of energy;
— transport via fossil fuels;	— transport via hydrogen fuel;
— dispersed physical development.	— concentrated physical development.

21.3 *Key integrations necessary for sustainable solutions.*

21.4 *Over-cladding of a university building from the 1960s with photovoltaic panels. Southampton University.*

Renewable energy

In the situation that now prevails there is an opportunity to adopt an energy policy covering the next 50 years that makes the UK self-sufficient in energy, and energy which causes minimum carbon dioxide emissions and is risk free. That rules out nuclear and fossil-based power. Such a policy would, on the one hand, make a major contribution to reducing carbon dioxide emissions and, on the other, safeguard the country from being paralysed by a few well-placed terrorist assaults. A fragmented and highly dispersed energy system is virtually bomb-proof.

This is not an impossible dream. The UK has probably the best range of natural resources in Europe from which to extract enough renewable energy to meet all its needs.

Buildings also have the potential to play a major role in a future energy scenario. They can be daytime power stations through photovoltaic cells (PVs) on roofs and elevations. At the moment PVs are not cost effective set against conventional fossil fuel generation. But things are changing. We should factor-in not only the climate change benefit but also the security gain. Quantify these and offset them against cost and PVs even today become affordable. However, things are set to change across a range of low-energy technologies, not least in the sphere of PVs.

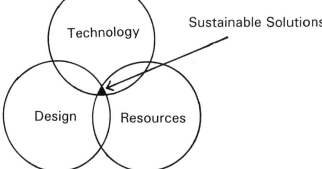

Photovoltaics

It seems inevitable that we shall move away from crystalline silicon-based PVs, which have relied heavily on waste from the computer industry, to dye-sensitized nanocrystalline solar cells. Rather than using silicon to absorb the light, this type of cell relies on molecules of a dye containing ruthenium ions that absorb light. Nanocrystals of the semiconductor titanium dioxode (titania) are coated with ruthenium dye. Effectively the titania nanocrystals are white paint since the white pigment is a fine suspension of titania particles. It turns out that titania has just the right properties to pull electrons out of the ruthenium dye and propel them into an electrical circuit.

21.5 *Office building at Doxford Business Park, Sunderland, incorporating passive solar principles and areas of photovoltaic energy production. Notice the orientation of the building to maximize renewable energy efficiency. Studio E Architects.*

The good thing about titania is that it is cheap, especially since a huge deposit of the ore has recently been discovered in Australia. It is reckoned that the peak efficiency of these cells will be 10–12% but they will be about one-quarter the cost of crystalline silicon. Obviously these titania cells are opaque, so the next task is to replace the ruthenium dye with dyes that absorb light from the infra-red part of the sun's spectrum. This would make them transparent and therefore suitable for inclusion in windows. Titania cells are ready for the market and a firm in Australia is the first to produce them commercially. The development of different light-sensitive dyes will provide the option of a variety of coloured PVs.

Shell is in partnership with Akzo Nobel to develop a low-cost PV cell based on the application of a sensitized coating to rolls of a flexible substrate. The process lends itself to mass production and will have a wide variety of building and other applications. This research is being conducted in parallel by a number of academic and technical bodies in the Netherlands. A solar cell developed by Spectrolab could also revolutionize the cost effectiveness of PVs. It consists of a three-layered structure with each layer designed to capture and convert a different portion of the solar spectrum. It embodies a solar concentrator which maximizes solar gain, thus reducing the number of cells needed to generate a given amount of power. In the laboratory it is achieving a 34% conversion efficiency rate which is twice the peak efficiency of crystalline silicon cells.

Within 5–10 years we can expect to see solid state PV cells in which an organic solid replaces the liquid electrolyte. On the horizon are cells which exploit the principle of photosynthesis, capturing solar energy using biological instead of electrochemical cells. Rather than generating electro-motive force like the normal PV, these cells create electrical *potential* capable of driving the microscopic motors and other devices of living cells. So, one possibility is that such cells could generate clean fuel by splitting water into hydrogen and oxygen, or by degrading organic industrial waster into harmless molecules.[6] PVs will really come into their own when there is a suitable technology for storing electricity, and this may be just round the corner.

Electricity storage

It was reported in the October 2001 issue of *Scientific American* that some thousands of homes are to receive their electricity via superconducting cables. Superconductivity has been the holy grail of electricity supply and storage, and the problem has been that it has only been possible at extremely low temperatures. In the American case the superconducting cables are cooled at their core by liquid nitrogen, thereby offering no transmission resistance. Normal cables suffer around 10% line loss, sometimes much more. This technology offers the prospect of the ideal storage technology since coils of superconducting cable can store electricity without any degrading of the power. Energy can be drawn off as needed. This, at a stroke, removes the problem of fluctuating generation from PVs, wind, wave, etc.

Fuel cells

Fuel cells are another evolving technology, driven in this case by the automotive industry. The cells run on hydrogen which reacts with oxygen in the air in such a way that a voltage is generated between two electrodes. The reactions occur in a chemical mediator called an electrolyte. Fuel cells are almost endlessly rechargeable; they are quiet, efficient and clean. Using hydrogen directly they produce virtually no emissions; using reformed natural gas they produce carbon dioxide but 40% less than if the gas were burnt directly. The downside is the expense. One kilowatt costs around $5,000 compared with $400 from a combined cycle gas turbine. The main reason is the cost of the platinum catalyst and this is where savings will be found. In the past five years the quantity of platinum needed has been cut by a factor of 20 and experts think they can make a further cut by a factor of 5. But the biggest reduction will come from economies of mass market production.

One scenario for the future is that cars will be powered by a fuel cell and fed by direct hydrogen stored in safe nanofibre carbon packs. When the vehicle is parked, either at home or at the office, which, on average, is 96% of its time, it would be plugged in to a hydrogen grid, the

21.6 *Proton Exchange Membrane Fuel Cell.*

21.7 *The Schubert Photon Recycling Semiconductor (PRS-LED).*

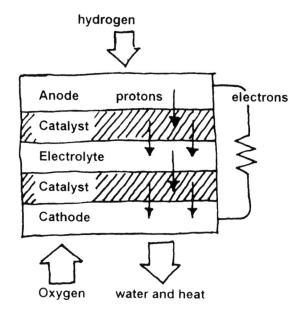

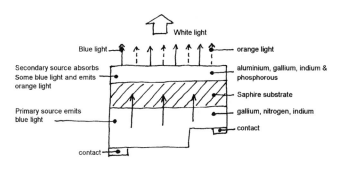

The Schubert Photon Recycling Semiconductor (PRS-LED)

electricity grid and the hot water system (Figure 21.11). The hydrogen would produce about 50-80kW of electricity per vehicle which would be fed to the grid via the host plug. The hot water would supply a domestic hot water or central heating system. At the same time, the water is of drinking quality. The vehicle owner would be credited with the electricity and hot water and charged for the gas. One option would be for local utilities to own the fuel cell and charge the owner on a per mile basis.

Another application that is now viable is for a community of houses to own a fuel cell fed by hydrogen reformed from natural gas which would supply both heat and power to the homes. With exhaust heat running a turbine the overall efficiency could be up to 80%. One problem is that a fuel cell operates continually at peak capacity. So, peak demand may be around 4kW per house in the evening but only 300W during the day. The obvious solution is for the excess electricity to be sold to the grid where daytime demand is quite high. For this to be viable, the buy-in rate would have to be in line with market prices.

The ideal will be a closed loop system with PVs on roofs and elevations dedicated to producing hydrogen through electrolysis. This would charge the storage system during the

day to meet demand overnight. With adequate storage capacity the system could ensure that seasonal peaks and troughs are catered for. Natural gas would be available as a fall-back resource. This will be the ultimate zero carbon system and it will be building, not power station, based.

Wind

Wind energy is not generally regarded as applicable to buildings. A system developed by Altechnica could change that perception. Known as the Aeolian system it is designed to be accommodated on the apex of roofs.[7] It consists of an aerofoil wing concentrator a small distance above the ridge or peak of a curved roof. Cross or axial flow wind turbines are located in the gap. The aerofoil is also a suitable site for PVs. The system can be turned on its side as in the case of Bill Dunster's Skyzed project. Turbines are placed vertically between the aerofoil shaped lobes of a tower block. Micro-generators of more conventional nature can also be positioned on roofs to supplement the energy generated by PV means.

21.8 *Community-based horizontal axis wind generator at Findhorn, Scotland.*

21.9 *Demonstration vertical axis wind generator at The Earth Centre, Doncaster, Yorkshire.*

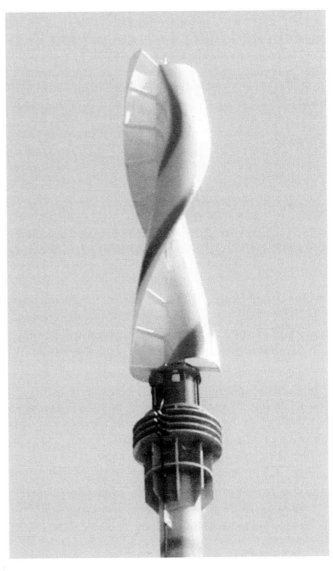

Lighting

Another technical step change will occur in the sphere of lighting. Already the days of the compact fluorescent light are numbered. It will be made redundant by developments in light-emitting 'photonic' materials. Solid state light-emitting diodes (LEDs) are based on the quantum principle that an atom's electrons emit energy when they jump from a high energy level to a lower one. By adjusting the 'band gap' between the two levels, light of different colours can be emitted. LEDs are a by-product of semiconductor technology and produce light at much lower watts per lumen than conventional systems. They also have a size advantage. For example, an LED of less than one square centimetre would, using only 3 watts, emit as much light as a 60-watt bulb. Whereas an incandescent lamp achieves an efficiency of 10–20 lumens per watt, LEDs are predicted to realize 300 lumens per watt. They are almost unbreakable and have a life expectancy of 100,000 hours. It is estimated that, if existing light sources in the USA were converted to LEDs,

21.10 *Solar cooling employed by Foster and Partners at Duisburg, Germany. (a) Detail. (b) Plan and section.*

there would be no need for new power stations for 20 years, assuming the present annual rate of increase of consumption of 2.7%. As lighting accounts for most electricity used in offices and shops, LEDs will offer signifi-cant savings in annual cost and carbon dioxide production.

Air-conditioning

Air-conditioning is the *bête noire* of the green lobby. Alternatives to the conventional compressor refrigeration system are appearing. Nottingham University is one of the UK's centres for research into emerging cooling alternatives. Two systems are particularly interesting. The first uses a chemical heat sink to soak up warm air and then to pump cool air into a building. It uses only a fraction of the energy of conventional air-conditioning and is based on phase change materials (PCMs) which are capable of storing vast quantities of latent heat. Warm air from the atmosphere is drawn over an array of fluid-filled pipes which convey the heat to storage tanks containing a solid PCM such as sodium sulphate. The PCM absorbs the heat and melts in the process. The resulting cool air is then circulated round the building. At night the process is reversed. Cool night air is drawn over the heat pipes which in turn solidify the PCM. The consequent warmth is dumped outside the building. Additives can change the melting point of the PCM, enabling the system to be fine tuned to the local climate.

The second system is based on solar cooling. Solar collectors heat water to around above 90° C after which it

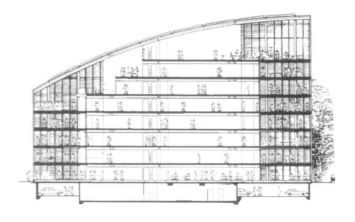

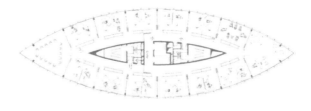

b

is fed to a heat exchanger. The water boils rapidly and is expelled at around MACH 2, passing through an ejector like a Venturi which causes the pressure to drop and adiabatic cooling to occur down to -1° C. Steam is condensed and the water recirculated. In the Nottingham project the evacuated heat pipe array collects 13kW of heat and converts it to 6kW of refrigeration. The system is backed up by natural gas when the temperature is high but cloudy conditions prevent the solar gain.

Future technologies

The technology of energy generation and storage is changing rapidly in response to long-term security concerns over available fossil fuels. The events of September 11th 2001 have also had a profound impact on the safety policy of large-scale energy-generating facilities, such as nuclear power stations. As we have seen technological advances are

a

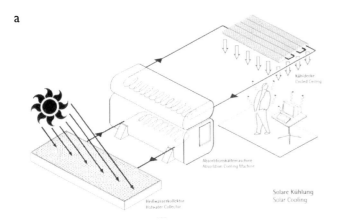

21.11 *Hydrogen gas system for use in the home and car.*

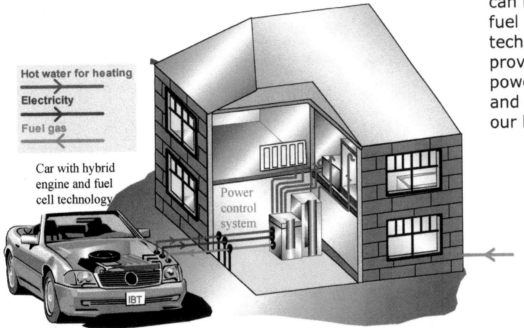

Hydrogen gas supplied safely through the main gas network can be used in fuel cell technology to provide efficient power, heating and cooling for our homes.

Hot water for heating

Electricity

Fuel gas

Car with hybrid engine and fuel cell technology

Power control system

Courtesy of School of the Built Environment - Nottingham University

being made in conductors, cell storage and lighting. The trend is towards smaller, smarter energy technologies. As these become more widely available and cheaper, the building itself has the opportunity not just to consume energy but to generate it. Buildings which have access to sun and wind have obvious advantages over those which are shaded and sheltered, in terms of local energy generation. Over the next few years there could be a convergence of smart energy technologies and the engineering of buildings. Then 'Green Buildings will Pay' not just in terms of performance, productivity and aesthetics, but in terms of reduced carbon dioxide emissions and lower running costs. In fact, such buildings may become so efficient that they are net exporters of energy over a 12-month period.

Green offices, libraries and schools clearly bring about wide social, economic and environmental benefits. This book has established via the many case studies that green design pays. There are benefits to be had in the improved image for

the company, school or university in enhanced worker productivity, in lower exposure to health and environmental legislation, and in reduced utility bills. There are risks in adopting innovative technologies and new sustainable design practices but they, as this book explains, are outweighed by the direct and indirect benefits of green design. It is clear also that the line between good green design and merely good design is a fine one. Many of the buildings examined in the book have been the recipients of a host of design awards, not just awards for energy efficiency. CABE and the RIBA increasingly recognize the wide social, economic and cultural benefits of good architecture. That green buildings play their part in this is no coincidence.

What innovative green design displays is a willingness to adopt new technology. Sustainable construction is frequently based upon research – learning from best practice and pushing the frontiers of design, material use and detail to their limits. Green buildings are the result of a partnership between client, designer, engineer, contractor and often user. The complex set of considerations has at its centre the adoption of change – in design method, in design goal and in the technology and spatial consequences. Sustainable offices and schools draw upon research and in their turn add to the body of example from which we can all learn.

Table 21.2
Construction waste in the UK

78 million tonnes a year:
–   waste of resources;
–   waste of energy;
–   waste of land (for landfill);
–   waste of time and effort.

Table 21.3
Drivers for change in UK construction industry 1992–2000

Year	Subject	Main Theme
1992	UN Earth Summit	– global warming and energy; – biodiversity; – environmental action.
1994	Latham Report	– communicate better; – improve management; – team building.
1998	Egan Report	– re-thinking construction; – greater standardization; – faster construction.
1998	DETR : Sustainable Development	– integrate sustainable development into design;
2000	DETR : Sustainable Construction	– indicators for sustainable construction; – greater use of renewable energy.

Lessons from Probe studies

Too few green buildings are, however, adequately monitored to test their environmental performance against predictions made at the design stage. As a result not only does the building fail to respond to the realities of use but the lessons learnt from the performance of one building too rarely influence the design of another. These shortcomings have been addressed by the Department of the Environment, Transport and the Regions (DETR) and *Building Sciences Journal* sponsorship since 1995 of Probe studies which "focus on occupant and management satisfaction as well as

environmental and energy performance".[8] Over the past six years there have been nearly 20 Probe studies covering offices, university buildings and schools. Most of these have been of green buildings, allowing new design approaches and innovative technologies to be tested. This book draws upon the result of Probe studies, setting findings against client and designer expectations and user reactions. Since Probe studies address management issues, there is an inevitable reinforcement of key findings in the actual operation of the building. The main conclusions of the Probe studies to date are:[9]

21.12 *Green design draws upon research into building performance. The innovative buildings created should then be monitored with the results disseminated to the construction industry. This example from Hong Kong uses shaped roofs to promote air flow through the building, thereby reducing air-conditioning loads.*

21.13 *Key interactions in a successful green building.*

Design issues

Air-tightness

Buildings are not as air-tight as architects and engineers predict, resulting in extra plant size to overcome risks at the design stage and sometimes extensive remedial action once the building is occupied. Poor air-tightness is the result of leakage at eaves, around and through windows (especially motorized ones), and at junctions between heavyweight and lightweight cladding.

Blind design

Internal blinds are often left in one position irrespective of external conditions and external blinds suffer from wind turbulence (especially near corners of the building), requiring them to be retracted. Also lack of occupant control leads to general dissatisfaction within the workplace.

Management issues

Lack of responsiveness

Users complain of the inability to override controls, and the difficulty when they fail of correcting them. Management is often too slow in responding to necessary system adjustment.

Noise

Green offices and green libraries (e.g. Queen's Building, Anglia Polytechnic University) have suffered from unexpectedly high levels of noise. This is the result of open planning (necessary for natural cross-ventilation), exposure of hard fabric surfaces (for night-time fabric cooling), greater intensification of space, more use of equipment (computers, etc.) and the trend towards a greater mix of internal functions.

Access

Building plant, light fittings, fire detectors, external sensors, blinds and motorized window equipment are increasingly inaccessible, making maintenance and safety checks difficult. As health and safety regulations become more stringent, access becomes more problematic.

In drawing attention to these design and management problems, the Probe studies have provided a useful service

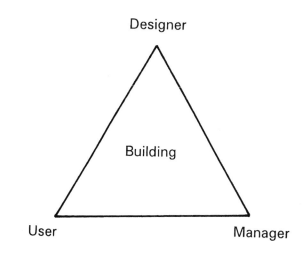

to the UK construction industry. Most of the buildings described in this book suffer to a greater or lesser extent from one or more of these problems, yet in bringing them to public notice, there is the possibility of improving the design of the next generation of green buildings. In fact, it is clear that in the new case studies added to this book since the last edition (e.g. Barclaycard Headquarters, chapter 13), there is evidence of feedback from these studies. However, one weakness of the Probe studies is the uneven distribution of building types studied. Only two schools have been the subject of a detailed examination in

21.14 *Wessex Water Offices near Bath provides a good model for others to follow. Architects: Bennetts Associates.*

21.15 *View of Wessex Water Offices showing the simplicity and elegance of sustainable design. (a) Sunscreen. (b) Interior. (c) Detail. Architects: Bennetts Associates*

b

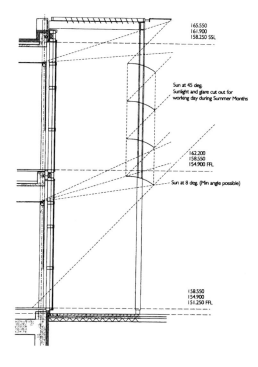

c

spite of Hampshire County Council's pioneering work in applying cutting-edge green technologies to this building type (see chapter 14). However, John Cabot City Technology College has been assessed by Probe and the results provide an important input into chapter 16.

The Probe team under the engineer Bill Bordass working with Building Use Studies has drawn to the industry's attention those features of green buildings which occupants most value. Users of offices prefer:

- shallow plans;
- thermal mass (as against lightweight construction);
- openable windows;
- clearly defined occupancy zones (cellular offices rather than open plan);
- personal interface between VDU usage and environmental controls;
- management which responds quickly to internal environmental problems.

a

21.16 *Newlands Primary School, Yateley, Hampshire orientates the classrooms to the south-east to achieve maximum solar gain benefit. Notice how the conservatory acts as a bridge between parts of the school.*

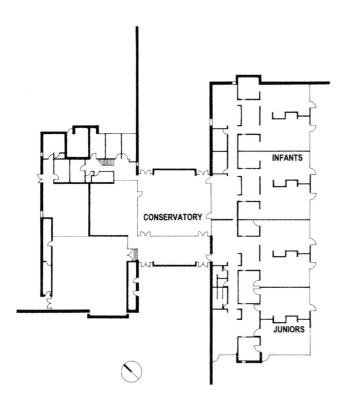

Not all are within the realm of design but the list highlights not only the necessary overlap between design and management but the importance of placing the user to the fore at the briefing stage. Probe has also drawn attention to the gap which often exists between concept and execution, at both the technical and the management level. Poor workmanship and specification are responsible for the bulk of air-tightness problems whilst management is often indifferent or under-informed about the technical operation of the building (such as blinds and heater controls). The more innovative the building, the greater the need for information, access to controls and understanding of key concepts by those who own, lease, manage and use the building.

It is clear that good performance normally stems from "relatively simple, thoughtful solutions, implemented and thought through with attention to detail".[10] Major technological innovation requires good communication via the building design between architect and end user. If the meanings and methods of environmental control are unclear there is the risk that the solution to one problem (e.g. energy) becomes a problem for another (e.g. noise or overheating). Unless the user is taken on board and management acts as an effective bridge between concept and reality, the benefits of a sustainable design can be undermined by a revengeful workforce. The Probe findings suggest that the most successful first generation of green buildings (those constructed mainly in the early 1990s) kept the environmental engineering relatively simple and paid close attention to detail.

As with all evaluations, it is essential to adopt benchmarks against which performance can be measured. The routine collection of data on both technical performance and user satisfaction allows for adjustment to be made. A responsive building is one which learns from its mistakes, which is periodically upgraded environmentally, and which can readily adjust to new resource imperatives (the exploitation of renewable energy or the recycling of water). This requires a robust initial building concept; a shared vision between designer, client and user; and a shared language of technological terms. Probe has been right to advocate a culture of continuous upgrading (using its own studies to benchmark this) and the importance of a commonality of values across the design development and construction industry.

Table 21.4

Environmental design objectives at Wessex Water Headquarters Building, Bath

— improve operating efficiency;
— create an excellent working environment that encourages team work and informality;
— demonstrate leading edge sustainable development that minimizes energy use, maximizes recycling and encourages sustainable transport solutions;
— use new technology to improve communications and reduce paper and storage;
— provide facilities that can be used by the local community.

21.17 *A model of healthy sustainable living for the future. Architects: Richard Rogers Partnership.*

In an important sense this book continues with the dialogue of continuous evaluation which Probe and others advocate. Measuring the value of design is by no means easy, especially when key stakeholders (user, designer, client) have differing expectations. The case studies discussed here raise an important new basis for such evaluation – that of performance as measured not just in energy-efficiency terms but with regard to wider social and economic benefits. The contextual relationship between designers and users varies according to building type but the value systems inherent in green approaches to design cross frontiers. In bringing about a cultural change in favour of more sustainable solutions to design and construction, research into performance plays an important part. It is clear that green buildings are beginning to be recognized for their user benefits, not just in the context of office buildings, but in a range of building types. Ultimately, it is those who use buildings who are the real clients and their needs will increasingly drive design towards sustainable practice. The potential synergy between global warming and personal health holds the key to the next generation of green buildings.

21.18 *The sun provides all the energy we need. The problem is how to design buildings which capture, store and distribute it. Hampden Gurney School, London. Architects: Building Design Partnership.*

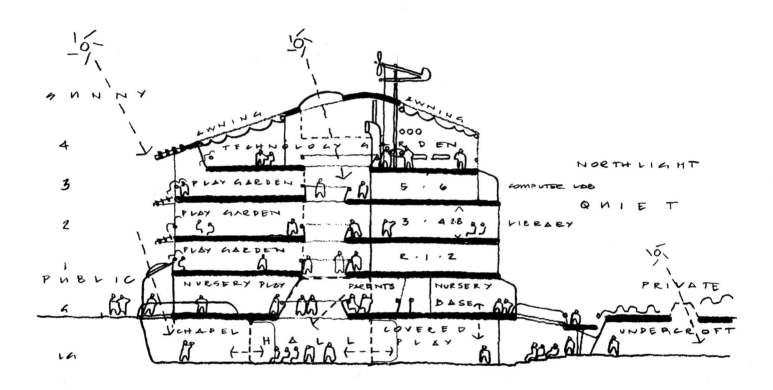

References

1. Scientific Committee of the International Panel on Climate Change, *Third Assessment Report (TAR)*, Geneva, United Nations, 2000, p. 3.
2. Ibid., p. 4.
3. Ibid.
4. Royal Commission on Pollution, 22nd Report, *Energy and the Changing Climate*, 2000.
5. Washington Worldwatch Institute, http://www.worldwatch.org.
6. *New Scientist*, 23 January 1999, pp. 40–42.
7. Brian Edwards and David Turrent, *Sustainable Housing: Principles and Practice*, London, Spon Press, 2000, pp. 55-56.
8. Bill Bordass, "Lessons from post-occupancy surveys", *EcoTech* 1, March 2000, p. 30.
9. Ibid., pp. 30–31.
10. Ibid., p. 31.

Index

Guildford College
Learning Resource Centre
Please return on or before the last date shown.
No further issues or renewals if any items are overdue.
"7 Day" loans are **NOT** renewable.

Class: 720.47 EDW

Title: Green Buildings Pay

Author: EDWARDS, Brian